5. Ea
   dra
   the s

THE IDEOLOGIES
OF RELIGION

THE IDEOLOGIES
OF RELIGION

BY

GEORGE PERRIGO CONGER

Essay Index Reprint Series

BOOKS FOR LIBRARIES PRESS
FREEPORT, NEW YORK

First Published 1940
Reprinted 1969

STANDARD BOOK NUMBER:
8369-1283-7

LIBRARY OF CONGRESS CATALOG CARD NUMBER:
70-93329

PRINTED IN THE UNITED STATES OF AMERICA

PREFACE

In these tumultuous days religion is assailed more openly and defended more uncompromisingly than at any time for centuries. Whole nations move virtually to abolish older faiths in the name of science or patriotism; they are met by groups new and old which profess to rescue religion either by rationalizing it almost beyond recognition or by placing it altogether outside the range of any human criticism or achievement. The philosophies of idealism and pragmatism, which for three generations provided a set of fairly satisfactory answers, have begun to show serious weaknesses. To many men now the older orthodoxies are stifling, the newer liberalisms superficial, and the newer supernaturalisms unreasonable.

The conviction deepens that sooner or later the problems of religion will have to be faced in a new way, however bold and untried it may be. In this book an attempt is made to understand the situation and to suggest how to deal constructively with it.

GEORGE PERRIGO CONGER

CONTENTS

vii

CONTENTS

CHAPTER I

A SPECTRUM OF RELIGIOUS IDEOLOGIES[1]

The philosophies, like a dome of many-colored glass, stain the white radiance of religion. With surprising aptness, the principal ideologies of religion can be exhibited as a kind of spectrum, as if the light from some Object had been refracted through the prism composed of various historic cultures and schools of thought, each with its atomic individual minds thrown into vibration, and had cast upon a screen a rainbow image, extending through a range of different wave-lengths. This is of course only a series of analogies, the kind of analogies which show serious defects if they are carried too far, but they can be developed far enough to be of considerable service in studying the ideologies and outlining the present situation in religious thought.

Without longer preface, and without here considering many possible alternative arrangements, let us put down as our "spectrum" the following list of ideologies. Most of the entries might well be in the plural, to indicate differences within the various systems which we shall later analyze, but for introductory purposes the singular terms will suffice. We have

(Occultism)
Mysticism
Supernaturalism
Idealism
Pragmatism
Evolutionism
Naturalism
Humanism
(Economic Nationalism)

The scheme has a number of suggestive features. First, we find that over most of its range it conforms rather well to the chronological order of the appearance of these ideologies in the Western world, or the order of their rise to prominence there. Rudolf Otto, with his insistence on the "numinous," or sense of a Great Impending Something as the matrix of religion, might trace the historical continuity from the second entry of the list. Be this as it may, the list from "Supernaturalism" on could easily serve as chapter headings for a history covering major developments in Western mediaeval and modern philosophy. Of course the schools do not succeed one another chronologically in any such cut and dried fashion; they overlap and interpenetrate, and there are many cases of new names for old ways of thinking. But some serial order is necessary, and the order of our spectrum, as we shall hope to show in succeeding chapters, serves as well as any other. This is a point of some importance, because the attempt of Wieman and Meland to classify a number of contemporary philosophies of religion in a classification independent of the history of general philosophy [2] appears to be not merely confusing in its result, but wrong in its principle. The closer the philosophy of religion can be kept to the developments of general philosophy, the better will be the result for all concerned. It should be added that the spectrum is not well adapted to show the chronological development of Eastern philosophies, although this is not so strange when one remembers that sometimes in these cases the chronology is not accurately known, and sometimes the development, except for some modern importations, has been virtually arrested at one stage or another, without running the whole gamut as in the West.

As another feature of the arrangement, it appears that the principal world religions can be allocated among various regions of the spectrum with some definiteness, although again without much regard for chronological sequence. Thus, while it is true that somewhere within the generous range of Hinduism, practically every ideology is, at least in rudimentary fashion, represented, Hinduism has in the main confined itself to the first four of our entries, and particularly, in the Vedanta system, to the fourth. If Taoism is interpreted along Vedantist lines as a philosophy of the universe expressed, albeit vaguely, in terms of mind, it belongs here too; if it is interpreted as more like our naturalism, it belongs with those naturalist schools which hold that religion is adjustment to the universe. Primitive Buddhism was in a way an anticipation of Western subjective idealism and pragmatism. Confucianism, with all its archaic setting, has a humanistic strain, which gives some of its present day adherents hope that it will be useful in the modernizing of China. Judaism belongs chiefly in the region of supernaturalism, but shows affiliations on both sides of that entry—shall we place on the one side, or on the other, the light that was in Spinoza? Islam, true to its genius, belongs in the same region, predominantly supernaturalist, although its sufi mystics are famous, and recently, in the work of Muhammad Iqbal in India, it shows a single idealistic line.[3] Christianity, which, sometimes at the cost of inner conflict, has tried to be all things to all men, now stretches all the way from mysticism (if not from occultism) into or through naturalism and at least to the borders of humanism. Sometimes there is a spread so broad that something which at least approximates the economic nationalism or internationalism of communism is, over the protest of economic conservatives, included in its range and stoutly asserted to be Christian.

Once more, there are analogies here for the "warm" and "cold" colors, as one passes from one end of the scale to the other. In the list, as in the world of to-day, the glowing personalism of some ancient faiths stands

3

in sharp contrast to the newer mechanisms. The belief in life after death, as it has been regarded in the philosophies indicated, affords an almost uncanny determinant of "temperature" as one passes along the scale and compares the reactions.

Noticeable also are the analogies for infra-red and ultra-violet radiations: the end-terms of our series are printed in parentheses to indicate that for many interpretations of religion, occultism at one extreme and economic nationalism at the other do not belong in the "visible spectrum." Many of our friends "can not see them at all," and sometimes can not see a book which says anything about them. It does, forsooth, need some breadth of view to include them, but the conviction deepens that one does not really understand the religious situation of the past or the present, and perhaps of the future, unless one gives these eccentric and extreme views their places in the scale. Occultism is under serious question from the sciences which have been developed in the West (or would be under serious question if it were taken seriously), but increasing acquaintance with the East and sharper understanding of the limitations which some sciences have traditionally set for themselves in the West allow the inclusion of occultism, with the proviso that it may be kept in the infra-red, safely off the record. At the other extreme, economic nationalism is meant to include Shintoism, communism and Nazism in so far as these economic-political systems take on religious or quasi-religious character. Of these, communism is often represented as the very antithesis of religion, but, in the opinion of many observers who have seen it at first hand and have talked with its adherents in its home land, it amounts to a kind of religion. The same is true to some extent of Nazism. We have no other word for such flaming emotion, such glowing faith and such fulness of devotion, even though to number such movements among the religions means to stretch the term "religion" almost beyond recognition.

When the ideologies are spread out in this way and their relationships begin to appear, some of us may be surprised to see how much of our thought and doctrine tends to be *monochromatic,* confined to one narrow wave-length or rather narrow range of wave-lengths, as if our minds were opaque to all the wider ranges developed elsewhere among mankind. This tendency to present one ideology, or one group of ideologies, is if it were the only one which had any light in it, gives us the conflicts of the sects and the schools. The tendency to be monochromatic is not quite so marked in many of the more recent writers; it is offset by the analogy which a number of interpretations, ancient and modern, exhibit to the band spectra of physics, where the lines of the spectrum indicate some complexity in the source which needs to be analyzed further. "Broad-line" ideologies are not very rare; if any entry in our list of 'isms is compared with its neighbors, examples of such fusions will occur. Illustrations, especially if drawn from the notable works of one's contemporaries, must be cited with some caution; the affixing of philosophical labels is often more dubious than the identification of spectral lines. But the fact that labels are sometimes too narrow and sometimes too broad, or in some other way do not fit very well, is no excuse for abandoning them. To abandon them would mean that philosophy must go back to topical analyses, or to historical sequences, or to personal complexes for the plan of its self-criticism, and miss the comparisons and contrasts which lend to the history of thought so much of its vitality and value. In fact the point about labels may be merely that philosophers quite typically do not like the labels they receive from other philosophers. Some of the most stimulating men have eluded their pursuers by writing their own labels and affixing them to their own works.

Labels or no labels, occultists attribute some of their secret knowledge to the direct intuition so characteristic of the mystics. Mysticism if it becomes ordinary or mild is likely to break down into supernaturalism, while supernaturalism when it is intense is caught up into mysticism, as into a third heaven. Border line cases or "band spectra" among the modern philosophies of the West may be illustrated from contemporary writers. Without claiming that there is nothing else to say about these men, and without discussing the points in detail here, we may say that Gerald Heard, in his advocacy of an "expansion of consciousness," appears to combine occultism and mysticism; John Oman, supernaturalism with idealism; J. A. Leighton, idealism with pragmatism; H. N. Wieman, pragmatism with evolutionism and naturalism; and M. C. Otto, aesthetic naturalism with humanism. If "religious realism" is discerned as a somewhat blurred line in the region of evolutionism and naturalism, other combinations come into view.

Sometimes the elements of the combinations lie farther apart in the scale, as when Henri Bergson combines mysticism with evolutionism, and John Dewey with his pragmatism is also one of the outstanding advocates of humanism. We might say that such work is like "dark line" spectra, and add that it is quite typical of liberal thinkers to show dark lines in the region of supernaturalism. W. E. Hocking and E. W. Lyman, for example, cover rather wide ranges in the central region of our spectrum; some of their views are not far from supernaturalism, but they seldom bring out clearly that one particular bright line. We might push the spectrum analogy even further, to cite opinions which, when they appear in contemporary philosophy, are so different from the main trends of their authors that they recall the "forbidden lines" of the physicists. W. M. Horton, for example, has some intriguing sentences of this kind.

The analogy may also be developed to include data on differences of intensity at various wave-lengths; this, being interpreted, makes allowance for the variations in psychological attitudes, in emotional content and drive, and in social enthusiasm and effectiveness. Such variations are familiar in different religions and philosophies, or in the same ones taken at different places and times. Thus Islam is more fiery than Judaism, and premillenarian Christianity is more intense than the easy-going types of orthodoxy. Among the philosophers, Royce took his idealism and James his pragmatism with evangelical zeal. One of the most frequent criticisms of religious and theological liberalism is that it lacks "dynamic." Critics who find humanism somewhat lax in its devotion to human betterment find the extreme forms of economic nationalism suprisingly intense.

One more service rendered by our analogy is that it puts into perspective some of the trends of our troubled times. These trends, let us say, are shifts up or down the scale, toward the "red" or toward the "violet" end. One wonders if the analogy can be pressed hard at this point, and if we are to understand that in the spectrum of the ideologies, too, we have a kind of "Doppler effect," so that the shifts mark recessions or advances, either of the Object, or of ourselves! At all events, the trends today are divergent. The past century has seen a very pronounced shift in the direction of the more liberal and radical views at the lower end of the sequence, the region of the highly penetrating rays of the sciences. The shift toward this end has been described by almost every interpreter of the signs of the times. But it is a great mistake to think that the shift toward this end is the only one which needs to be traced; there have also been marked movements in the other direction, towards conservatism and orthodoxy. Roman Catholic Neo-scholasticism, Protestant Fundamentalism, and the more recent movements of Barthianism and Buchmanism are all trying (shall we say, each according to its lights?) to bring God and man nearer together. And while we are speaking of shifts we ought to mention the well known tendency, on the part of Reinhold Niebuhr and some of his friends, to proceed "theologically to the right and economically to the left." One wonders if this double shift can be accomplished without interference and confusion.

Finally, all this may serve to raise the chief question for any discussion of religion. Is our philosophy of religion to be selective, emphasizing one particular line or combination of lines to the exclusion of others, or is there any consistent way, without being pluralistic and incoherent, to make it synoptic—to make it, in the root sense of the grand old word, "catholic"—with a purview extending literally "along the whole" range? If it is to be consistently synoptic, according to what principle shall it be synoptic? Shall it be the synopsis or synthesis of mysticism? Perhaps the mystical experience, though it is often confused and inarticulate, and only partially resolvable into intelligible doctrines, is really the full white light of religion, the light of which every doctrine is but a partial and isolated ray. Or perhaps there is some way, not merely of understanding the series of philosophies in terms of the different angles of incidence at which light from the Object falls upon mankind, according as mankind is inclined this way or that in different races, temperaments, and institutions, but also of adjusting or improving the prism so that it will transmit the light more evenly and bring the Object into clearer focus, without so much distortion.

In this book we seek answers to such questions. We shall need first a kind of spectrum analysis, in order to see what the series of ideologies discloses; accordingly, we turn in the following chapters to a critical study of the philosophies indicated. We shall consider in each case what the chief teachings are, how they are criticized by their opponents and defended by their adherents, and what elements in each of them may be worth retaining when the relationships of mankind and the Object are seen from another point of view. This point of view will be described in brief outline in the concluding chapter.

REFERENCES

[1] This chapter, with some alterations, is reprinted by permission from *The Christian Century*, 53, 1936, pp. 597f.

[2] H. N. Wieman and B. E. Meland, *American Philosophies of Religion*, 1936, pp. 10f. E. A. Burtt in his *Types of Religious Philosophy*, 1939, uses a classification partly philosophical and partly theological.

[3] Muhammad Iqbal, *The Reconstruction of Religious Thought in Islam*, 1934, pp. 48, 53.

CHAPTER II

OCCULTISM [1]

Occultism gets its name from its interest in "the hidden." The term, like others of our series, covers a wide variety of beliefs and practices, some of which have little or nothing to do with religion. Occultism is best described when it is contrasted with what in the West may be called ordinary science and religion; it accepts as authentic reports of occurrences which, although they are often regarded in the East as not very unusual, are quite generally rejected in the West as fantastic. For ages occultism has studied such alleged occurrences, insisting that some of its results are of religious importance. Historically the chief centers for these views are in ancient India and Egypt; there are notable contacts with the Greek world in Orphic mysteries, with Judaism in the Kabbalah, with early Christianity in Gnosticism, and with the modern world in Theosophy and some other contemporary cults. Occultism has been in some respects like a thread, running through the world's religions or close to them, and helping to bind them together. Philosophically it has much in common with mysticism, supernaturalism, and idealism. [2]

In obtaining its alleged knowledge, occultism often professes to use methods which go beyond the ordinary working of the "five" senses. Abnormal results are obtained by the aid of meditation or concentration, sometimes so intensified that it becomes hypnosis and trance. Sometimes the occultist's knowledge is like the mystic's intuitive insight, said to be a matter of immediate apprehension. Where the alleged knowledge is analyzed it is often said to be clairvoyant, as if objects were seen at distances or through barriers too great for ordinary sight, or as if events which have occurred in the past or are about to occur in the future were discerned as present. Again, the occult knowledge is said to come by telepathy, the transfer of perceptions or ideas from one mind to another without the medium of language or ordinary communication. Less frequently, the occultists trace their knowledge to clairaudience, the hearing of sounds beyond the ordinary range, or to telekinesis, the transporting of material objects by extraordinary passage through space. Such knowledge is sometimes said to come from discarnate spirits or to involve their intervention.

Occult cosmology portrays an elaborately structured universe. In some rather archaic forms of occultism the key to this structure is seen in the relations of the male and female sexes; in other forms the universe is understood in terms not so much biological as psychological, and mind, or something like mind, is regarded as more fundamental and important than matter. Most often there is a sequence or a hierarchy, at least vaguely describable in mental terms. Occultism often shares the ancient doctrine of the Logos, familiar in the West in the adaptation of it used in the first chapter of the Gospel of John to interpret the Christian incarnation. In general, the Logos is the principle of reason or reasonableness in the world; if it is not a Cosmic Person, it is the property whereby the world can be understood or described as reasonable, in intelligible language. This property expresses itself in the inherent reasonableness of particular things and the ideal possibilities of man's rational nature, so that even if the world is not actually a vast Mind, it is a system in which minds like ours can develop and can at least begin to comprehend what is around and above them. In occult cosmology, the cosmos is pictured in many divisions and subdivisions, in which favorite numbers like three and seven constantly occur. Special importance is ascribed to the planets, whether they are the planets known to astronomy or not. With or without the indwelling Logos, each planet is pictured as existing in a "chain" or sequence consisting of a number of successive "spheres" or stages of development. These stages are marked by different densities of the atoms of the planet; in the more rarified stages of its sequence a planet is "spiritual" and in the denser stages, material. Sometimes a planet is said to go in cyclic fashion through its sequences, in what is called a "round."

Corresponding to the stages of development of planets are certain kingdoms of nature, including the mineral, vegetable, and animal, and certain "planes" and "bodies" which particularly mark the development of human personalities in each planet. These planes are not places, but states of consciousness. They do not exclude one another, but interpenetrate. They are said to be discerned clairvoyantly by response to their characteristic vibrations. In the physical plane a person has the physical body, but even the physical body is permeated by its finer "etheric double," whose mysterious sense organs, as in the Hindu *Tantras*, are said to be certain "chakras" or plexuses, distributed in a row from the top of the head to the pelvis. Besides this, there are several other "bodies," each of which exercises special functions. The astral body is sometimes described as a kind of model of the physical body, and is said to be useful in clairvoyance. The mental body makes possible rapid passage from place to place. The causal body enregisters effects from each incarnation, thus making possible the reincarnation of an individual and the reading of past lives. The intuitive and spiritual bodies are still higher modes of existence.

In each planet or globe a number of successive races and subraces are said to be developed. Our own place in earth history is somewhere in the midst of this series; before us were the Lemurians and the inhabitants of the lost continent of Atlantis, and after us will be far more wonderful beings. Any individual, if in successive incarnations he manages to complete his course of development in one stage of a planet's history, moves on to the next stage there, and eventually moves on to the next planet of the planetary chain, and so on until emancipation is attained. This development of personality, viewed over several stages and planets, resembles a tide with a succession of waves. All these teachings are imparted by the aid of metaphors and an extensive use of diagrams and symbols.

In general, occultism pictures the world as developing under intelligent guidance, but if there is any one Supreme Intelligence for occultism it is, like the First Being for Plotinus, all but lost in the vast cosmic mists. Subordinate intelligences exist in myriads and are found in all grades—planetary spirits, guardian spirits for various parts of nature and for individual men, and even minor beings like fairies, elves, sylphs, and the like. The alleged data of psychical research concerning messages from the spirits of deceased persons are often accepted by occultism, but among so many intelligences or spiritual beings are accorded a rather incidental place. Somewhere in the hierarchy of spiritual beings places can be found for the personal deities of various religions, and practically all the myths of the world's folklore can if necessary be accommodated. In charge of various social groups and projects, and particularly in charge of the teaching of occultism, there are said to be adepts or Masters, who are sometimes represented as living in the fastnesses of Tibet and communicating their teachings by telepathy.

The goal of occultism is that its adherents should progress as far as possible, through successive planes and incarnations, toward adeptship or emancipation. For this long effort, meditation is regarded as of primary importance. The personality is progressively unified and adapted to the higher and more spiritual life. Often this process leads to marked refinement of habits and manners. Often it includes restrictions on diet, as in vegetarianism. Occasionally, as in the Yogic practices of Hinduism, breathing and other bodily functions are subjected to unusual and spectacular control. Occultism may easily lead to asceticism. Occultist groups often profess to guard their secrets from the uninitiated, and to scorn to make any unworthy use of their alleged powers. At the same time they warn outsiders against meddling with occult forces; these are said to be dangerous if employed without proper instruction from authorized teachers.

Among the non-religious affiliates of occultism alchemy has long been famous, especially as the precursor of chemistry. Other members of the curious group include astrology, palmistry, phrenology, and numerology; these attempt to discern past or future events by consulting data concerning the positions of the stars at the time of one's birth, etc., the lines of the hand, the shape of the skull, and the numbers connected with the events of one's life and the relations of those numbers to one another.

OBJECTIONS TO OCCULTISM

Important criticisms of the more religious forms of occultism are directed against both its methods and its content. In the first place, (1) its methods are often open to grave questions. Where occultism in its clairvoyance, telepathy, astrology, palmistry, etc., shows some results which it interprets as favorable, its critics sometimes make charges of deception and intentional fraud. Where this is out of the question, the critics say that only the favorable results are reported, and that negative instances are either neglected or reported only partially. Some favorable cases will naturally occur by coincidence and the law of averages; where the occultists claim percentages higher than this, the critics can raise questions about the theory of probability itself. Sometimes the occultists' statements are so general that they may be applied to almost any person or situation, and bear many different interpretations. Sometimes the sitters or clients unwittingly give more or less subtle clues and suggest answers to their own questions.

In the second place, (2) its methods, whether valid or not, are difficult. Comparatively few persons in the Western world are willing to subject themselves to such rigorous discipline in order to secure results which they regard as dubious. But (3) supposing the methods are devotedly pursued, they are, by the very fact of such devotion, open to the dangers of suggestion, particularly of autosuggestion. The human nervous system is exceedingly complicated and delicate and, especially under physiological strain or effort, can only with great difficulty, if at all, distinguish ideas which are grounded in authentic fashion in the outer world and ideas distorted by subjective conditions.

As regards the content of occultism, (4) it is said by its critics to be too primitive, and to go altogether too far in its support of ancient myths and magics. If occultism bows to this criticism and emphasizes teachings more favored in later Western civilizations, (5) it is still regarded as too remote, fantastic, and improbable. Western science has been too much occupied with other matters to submit to the occult disciplines or to be much interested in occult doctrines. Such doctrines are at their best regarded as imaginary overtones and at their worst as naive or base superstitions. A minor but sometimes potent objection is that (6) both the methods and the content of occultism are frequently presented in Oriental terminology which is very hard to correlate with Western theories about mind and the world.

In particular (7) the chief objections to the age-old

theories of reincarnation may be said to be (i) theologically, that they are not in accord with orthodox theologies of the Semitic religions; (ii) psychologically, that we have no memories of past lives and that accounts to the contrary are capable of explanations in terms of subconsciousness, autosuggestions, or even of telepathy; (iii) biologically, that reincarnation contradicts the principles of heredity, that the biological individual is disintegrated at death, and that another body, even if it were clear that it can be had, would mean another individual; (iv) sociologically, that the theory indicates a static rather than a dynamic society; (v) ethically, that it is unjust that we should have to be paying the penalty for sins in former incarnations of which we are not conscious; and (vi) methodologically, that opposing theories, much less fantastic, are more in accord with the caution of the laboratory sciences or with common sense.

OCCULTISM'S REPLIES

To the general criticisms the occultists are able to reply (1) that their methods, after all, are empirical. Sincere occultists depend upon experience, just as scientists do, and they invite empirical tests. It is true that their empiricism is mostly a matter of subjective experience rather than laboratory experiment, but they maintain that the one procedure is as empirical as the other. Many critics, in this and other problems, talk glibly of scientific method, without having thought much about what science is or what its possible methods are. If there is to be a thoroughly critical discussion of verification and proof, any critic, from Locke and Hume to the logical empiricists and beyond, can, if he cares to do so, entangle himself in strictures about our alleged knowledge until either he can not move a mental muscle, or else can move only in a kind of mental gymnastic which never comes to grips with the real world. If the game of criticism is pursued to the bitter end, the critics run out of fresh material and usually fall to criticizing one another; they get nowhere, and do not even recognize the status which we naturally have. Why then should we take the critical philosophies so seriously? The occultists do not know much about such investigations, but even if they know they do not think them important.

For the occultists, (2) their severe discipline is the counterpart of rigorous and specialized scientific training. As regards suggestion, (3) no one need try to avoid it, either when it comes from others or when it comes from one's self. In fact, any one of us would be isolated and lost without both kinds of suggestion. The point is not that one should avoid suggestions, but that one should avoid wrong suggestions. And the question as to which suggestions are the wrong ones is hard for any man, whether he is a scientist or not, to answer. The criticism that occultism leads to views which are primitive may mean only (4) that it runs true to human nature, but even if the criticism is sound it does not exhaust the content of occultism, for in many esoteric doctrines occultism reaches far beyond the primitive. The charge that occult doctrines are remote, fantastic, or improbable can be met, again, by (5) a countercharge of scientific dogmatism. Who knows where the proper limits of scientific data are? The data on transmutation of the elements, the principle of indeterminacy, and according to some reports the dependable results of experiments on telepathy and clairvoyance [3] show that in the past such limits have been too narrowly fixed, and that the sciences ought to be more than ever faithful to their ideal of an open mind and a free field for hypothesis, observation, and experiment, however unusual and unexpected the results may be. Once one begins to raise such questions, he can find, in religious ideologies which are in high favor, plenty of features which the empirical scientists regard as remote and improbable.

With regard to (6) the orientalisms, occultism regards some of these as incidental, and can point to the fact that all languages and all translations are to some degree incommensurable. Other orientalisms are to be welcomed and treasured; the Orient is very old and very wise, and rejection of its slowly garnered treasures of experience may mean mere brash provincialism.

In reply to (7) the objections concerning reincarnation, those who believe in it point out that other theories of life after death are also discredited, and withal are vague and elusive, where reincarnation is comparatively definite and concrete. Some other theories of the hereafter are grandiose and extravagant, whereas that of reincarnation, if certain rather simple presuppositions are granted, is comparatively reasonable. As against (i) the theological objection, a glorious array of names and religions can be marshalled from various lands and times in favor of some form of the reincarnation theory. It was evidently current in New Testament Palestine, and perhaps held by Jesus himself.[4] Among recent philosophers, no one has been more explicit than McTaggart; for him, the natural inference was that this life will be followed by others like it, each separated from its successor and predecessor by death and rebirth. He held that, if his theory was right, we should live many lives, perhaps many millions of lives.[5] Idealistic systems which regard individual personalities as like ideas in the Absolute Mind can easily think of that Mind as recalling its ideas repeatedly.

As regards (ii) the psychological criticisms, especially those concerned with memories of past lives, some say that we do not remember because we are so preoccupied with the affairs of the body; even if we could remember, we should be dreadfully encumbered by such an enormous accumulation of memories. Others point out that in ordinary life we remember only fragments of our adult past, and virtually nothing of our early infancy, although we have no slightest doubt of our existence at those periods. On the other hand, by using the proper methods of meditation, concentration, or hypnosis, occultists insist that memories of past lives can be recovered. And whether memories are recovered or not, it is declared that reincarnation offers the best explanation for apparently undeserved evils and misfortunes, and for the sense of familiarity with supposedly new places or persons which occasionally seems so surprising.

To (iii) the biological objections about heredity, it may be pointed out that no scientific theory can account in detail for all that occurs or fails to occur. To the objections concerning bodies, believers in reincarnation may reply on idealistic grounds, that bodies are not necessary; or, in terms of the "network theory" of society, that a personality is a functional differentiation within a social group rather than a means of identification of a biological organism. McTaggart declared that the supposition that the self has another body would fit the facts quite as well as the supposition that the self has ceased to exist.[6]

Various answers to (iv) the sociological objection are obvious; when changes in an individual personality in one lifetime are traced, there is not much that is static about it. To (v) the ethical objections, it may be urged that punishment fits crimes and not consciousness of them, and that all defect and imperfection should be met with the ideal of an improvement too great to be realized in any one generation. Finally, to (vi) the methodological objections, the answer, as for occultism in general, is to the effect that life is bigger than laboratories, and verification smaller than verity.

AN ESTIMATE OF OCCULTISM

The occult appears to be a more or less permanent penumbra of the circle of sciences ordinarily visible for

Western minds. From the point of view of such minds, much of the penumbra seems utterly obscure and doubtful, but the easy judgment that there is nothing to it is probably best recast into the statement that whatever there is, if anything, is for the time being and in the West conveniently neglected. But a philosophy able to meet all issues ought to have some means of accommodating light from any direction from which it may come.

REFERENCES

[1] Much of the material of this chapter has been published in *The Ayran Path* (Bombay), 8, 1937, pp. 443-8.

[2] On occultism, see A. T. Barker, ed., *The Mahatma Letters to A. P. Sinnett*, 1923; Dion Fortune, *Sane Occultism;* G. R. S. Mead, *Thrice Greatest Hermes;* G. Purucker, *The Esoteric Tradition*, 2 Vols., 1935.

[3] On telepathy, see J. B. Rhine, *Extra-sensory Perception*, 1935; *New Frontiers of the Mind*, 1937.

[4] *Cf.* Matt. 11, 14; 16, 13-4; 17, 10; Mark 9, 13.

[5] J. M. McTaggart, *Some Dogmas of Religion*, 1906, pp. 118, 134. For other suggestions, see W. R. Inge, *God and the Astronomers*, 1933, p. 292; J. E. Boodin, *God, A Cosmic Philosophy of Religion*, 1934, p. 33.

[6] J. M. McTaggart, *op. cit.*, p. 104.

CHAPTER III

MYSTICISM

Partaking always of the mysterious, according to some men shading off into utter darkness and according to others fusing our ordinary half-lights in a blaze of celestial glory, are the experiences called mystical. The experiences, properly speaking, are data for psychology; mysticism is an ideological interpretation of them which takes them to be of prime importance in our understanding of the world.[1]

On the psychological side, the transition from ordinary experiences to mystical experiences is gradual, so that precise distinction between the two is impossible; in general, the mystical experiences are immediately felt and recognized rather than clearly thought out or described, and they are felt as having some richness of content and personal importance. Many experiences which are regarded as at least sometimes mystical are not specifically religious; examples are the sense of companionship with nature; enjoyment of music or other forms of art; the sudden feeling of new significance of familiar scenes; the sense of relief from tension when a cause of dread is removed or a baffling problem solved; the sense of companionship with fellow members of one's own group; falling in love; and the feeling that one is performing one's duty or fulfilling one's function in society.

The religious mystical experiences are surprising and often inspiring. They are reported from virtually all countries, all periods, all cults—from the seers of the Upanishads and the Apostle Paul, from Plotinus and Pascal, from Meister Eckhardt and the sufis, and from many contemporary writers.

The characteristics of religious mystical experience have become familiar from a number of books, especially William James' *Varieties of Religious Experience*. What the mystics find is typically said to be ineffable, defying description in language. In spite of this, attempts are of course made to describe it, by symbols, metaphors, negations, and paradoxes, so that there is talk of things as diverse as the cross, pilgrimage, nothing, and "luminous darkness." In spite of the alleged ineffability and the confused attempts at description, the experiences are said to possess "noetic quality," and to impress those who have them as bringing immediate and certain knowledge concerning a reality beyond the range of perceptions and ideas, and affording insight into the mysteries of the universe and man and God. Sometimes they are accompanied by well defined bodily sensations and visual or auditory components. Often there is, at least for a time, a feeling of exaltation and of absorption into an overwhelming vastness which is felt to be the very being of God. But the experiences are typically transient and subject to marked fluctuations. Sometimes, though the experiences fluctuate, the sense of their authenticity and authority remains, and an experience once had may exert a potent influence for a lifetime. The experiences are frequently, but not always, said to be passive, and they are typically solitary. They may be attained by progressive stages; sometimes they are so standardized that instructions about the stages are furnished for those entering upon them. Religious mysticism is often preceded or accompanied by asceticism. Philosophically it inclines to monism, holding that dualities and other conflicts are resolved in the glow of the experience. Mystics usually profess a deep sense of ultimate reconciliation, security, and satisfaction, and feel that they are vouchsafed at least glimpses of an inner way to God and peace.

Mysticism as a philosophy seldom if ever occurs as a

fullfledged system, independent of other ideologies or on a par with them. It tends to articulate itself in their terms. Like a climbing plant, it thrives upon the sturdiness of others. We shall see that others which are anywhere near it in content and outlook lend themselves readily enough to its support.

THE CASE AGAINST MYSTICISM

No ideology of religion has been subjected to more constant and incisive criticisms than has mysticism; it is natural for most of us to consider the criticisms before we approach the position. At least a dozen criticisms can be distinguished and, for convenience of reference, numbered. We begin with a few which are directed against the more easily observed characteristics.

(1) Mysticism is said to be vague and so lacking in clarity that, as some ingenious critic has said, it might better be called "misty-cism." The charge of vagueness is brought both by the rationalists, who seek precision and definiteness of thought, and by the empiricists, especially scientists, who look for definite and measurable data. These critics call mysticism unclear, and also call anything else which is not clear to them "mysticism." In particular, the transiency and the fluctuations of mystical experience are held to render the experiences undependable.

(2) Allied with this is the criticism that mysticism is too emotional, that it is an overemphasis upon feeling, and primitive feeling at that, with altogether uncritical acceptance of its deliverances concerning God and the world and man.

(3) Again, mysticism is said to be psychologically abnormal, and to show depressive, pessimistic, or ascetic traits. It is said to be essentially a way of denial, a mechanism of avoidance and escape from what its critics regard as the realities of life. When mysticism tries to

justify itself, its attempts are said to reflect something of this abnormality, to be artificial, and to lack freshness, directness, or naturalness.

(4) Several of the great mystics have shown pathological symptoms, notably of hysteria. Sometimes there is paralysis, or contracture, and there are suggestions of degeneration, epilepsy, and delusional insanity.

When closer studies are made, facts come to light which tend to show that the mystical experiences are not so extraordinary. It is found that (5) groups of persons inclined to such experiences show certain characteristic traits. According to Starbuck, members of such a group appear to be slower in ingenuity and coordination; they tend toward conservatism and are more suggestible.[2] Thus the occurrence of mystical experiences can presumably be predicted from correlated psychological data.

(6) It is found, also, that mystical experiences can be closely imitated, if not duplicated, by the use of anaesthetics, drugs, or intoxicants, as well as by hypnotic concentration. Again, (7) some of the most marked characteristics of religious mystical experiences can be detected along other lines of interest, for example in aesthetic experiences, where vividness, rapture, and exaltation are familiar. Even in scientific work, the suddenness and the noetic quality of mystical revelation are at least approximated in the abrupt occurrence of long-sought solutions for problems, or to some extent in the more ordinary and lowly "hunch."

Encouraged by such observations and studies, the critics go on to challenge the grandiose interpretations which mysticism gives to its experiences, and to substitute explanations in terms of less wonderful physiology and psychology. In particular, (8) the interpretations which mysticism gives and the philosophies which these interpretations involve are modified in the direction of naturalism. For example, the mystic's seeing of lights and hearing of voices are put down as hyperaesthesia, extraordinary sensitiveness, especially to residual effects of past perceptions which are able to take over enough of the apparatus of the nervous system so that they appear as veridical perceptions. The reported experiences of levitation, of being "out of the body" and wafted through space, are traced to kinaesthetic sensations from the muscles, glands, etc., upon which the habitual sense of the body rests, and which by some internal disturbance have become blocked or distorted or doubled, just as we get modified visual perceptions by closing an eye or pressing an eyeball. The so-called "speaking with tongues" (if articulate language is really used, and not mere gibberish) may sometimes be traced to language actually heard at some earlier period and apparently forgotten. Gibberish, the more common form of glossolalia, is merely excited activity of rudimentary language mechanisms. The stigmata of St. Francis (the marks on his hands and feet, recalling the crucifixion of Jesus) have recently been associated with the purplish hemorrhages which, before adequate treatment was known, used to appear as complications of quartan malaria.[3]

The mystic's sense of bliss has been traced to relaxations of muscles and relief of tensions, and the ineffability of the experience to its disconnectedness and lack of articulation when ordinary perceptions and ideas are cut off and customary associations left incomplete. The mystic's so-called union with his object may be understood in these latter ways, combined with introversion and autohypnosis, and his sense of being possessed and overwhelmed may be due to "oculogyric compulsions" (tendencies to turn the eyes or concentrate the visual attention) due to an internal more than to any external condition.[4] The reported "sense of presence" may be explained by combining these with two other facts—first that one's sense of the presence of other persons in a room may be quite subtle, involving awareness of delicate changes in atmospheric pressure, etc., and second that a total experience may be "redintegrated" or set up again by the recurrence of a fragment of it or of a similar experience.[5] We must remember that in any of these cases, especially where there is illness or fasting, the threshold for curious suggestions is likely to be low, so that a very slight incident can set them going. As to mystical "revelations," it is noted that they vary in time and place, and incorporate materials familiar to the individuals concerned; Buddhists have specifically Buddhist revelations, while Christians have revelations in accordance with Christian traditions. In all these cases, psychologists use explanations in terms of the subconscious, or, when this is in disfavor, the even more naturalistic "automatisms."

(9) Associated with many of the foregoing, but widespread and important enough to be listed by itself, is the Freudian criticism that among the mystics a great number of case histories show evidences of compensations for sexual repressions and sublimations of such tendencies, so that, in disguise, they find their outlet in the socially more acceptable form of religious devotion. It is noted, for one thing, that some of the greatest mystics have been markedly influenced by friends of the opposite sex. In most of the biographies there are accounts of inhibitions, frustrations, and disappointments, with room for the inference that there were disturbances of sexual functions. Indicative of such frustrations, repressions, and sublimations on the part of some mystics is the fact that records of their experiences are crowded with erotic metaphors.

(10) Also very widespread is the criticism that mysticism is unethical. This may be urged on both practical and theoretical grounds. Practically it may be said that the mystics tend to live in solitude and to be self-centered and anti-social. Sometimes communities which

cultivate mysticism hold themselves quite aloof from common men and their needs. Theoretically the mystical position is sometimes assailed on the ground that it is so much given to absorption and union, or else that it allows so much relaxed disintegration of the personality, that it loses sight of the distinctions between right and wrong and all the sharp angles of the problem of evil.

(11) Mysticism is even challenged on grounds of religion, again in ways both practical and theoretical. As regards the practice of religion, it is held that the mystic contributes nothing to strengthen the personality through the forms of worship. He forsakes the ordinary tested ways of religious nurture for the extraordinary. On the side of theory, or doctrine, mysticism is indefinite. David Hume long ago made his Cleanthes say that the mystics are atheists without knowing it.[6] Mysticism is said to tend away from theism and its personal God, in the direction of pantheism. Some of the supernaturalist groups, who might receive considerable support from mysticism, can not overlook its occasional statements about the identification of the individual and God.

(12) Finally we should mention some philosophical criticisms of mysticism; these will become clearer in subsequent chapters. They are such as might be expected from the differences of outlook and opinion which divide the different schools, as well as from many minor differences between members of any one school. We noted that some of the philosophies afford support to mysticism; it is also true that most of them are able to criticize it, as naturalism does in providing physiological and psychological explanations for its mysteries, and supernaturalism does in opposing the mystic's conviction of his union and identification with God. In general the supernaturalists, together with the pluralists, criticize the frequent alliances of mysticism with mon-

ism. The systems which oppose idealism see in mysticism a peculiarly elusive example of those ambiguous views; on the other hand, the idealists regard mysticism as only inadequately thought through. Those pragmatists who do not like the fruits of mysticism criticize it for its results, sometimes also for its passivity, as well as for its traditional absolutism. Some evolutionists welcome it as a goal, while others reject it as too static. Some realists refuse to be mystical realists, and some naturalists abhor nature mysticism. Most naturalists, humanists, and communists, if not most Nazis, would be content to see religious mysticism gradually evaporate.

THE CASE FOR MYSTICISM

Mystics typically do not have much to say in reply to criticisms, but sometimes they have friends who speak for them. In the one way or the other the criticisms we have listed may be met as follows.

(1) Vagueness and indefiniteness do not necessarily mean falsehood, nor even inadequacy. To suppose otherwise is to disregard some of life's deepest experiences, as well as some of its most intriguing fields of exploration. There is a sense in which everything, even the most ordinary thing, is mysterious, and whatever clearness or definiteness there is about it is limited and perhaps superficial. To strive to make everything definite amounts to reducing everything to measurement, and the commonest facts of our inner life, to say nothing of faith, hope, love, goodness, beauty, or truth, need not submit to such reduction. As for transiency, it is better to catch glimpses of all this, to see it fleetingly, than not to see it at all—especially when, once seen, its influence may persist.

(2) The charge of emotionalism may be met first by showing how normal is emotion in other fields, as for example in aesthetic experience. With or without emo-

tionalism, the question of mysticism's emphasis on feeling turns largely on the status which is to be accorded to intuition. The advocates of intuition differ greatly; not all would confine themselves to what may be called a reasonable view. According to such a view, intuition is immediate apprehension, and may occur at levels of mental organization which are quite simple, as well as at others which are highly complex.[7] Some writers have discussed intuitions which belong only at one end of such a scale, and others have proceeded as if intuitions belonged only at the other; in any case, what is essential for intuition is not simplicity or complexity, but immediacy. Thus a vague feeling of unrest, or a perception of a rose, or an idea of a mathematical relationship may all be fairly simple intuitions. Structurally, as perceptions and ideas, they belong at the level of pattern-reactions. An idea, whether it is equivalent to a language-pattern or not, has a complexity of organization which is comparable. In the cases mentioned the pattern-reactions are taken in their immediate aspect, in their character of being immediately felt, but intuitions may also occur with respect to more complex units of mental organization, especially those units which involve stimuli which come by way of the distance receptors and responses in which the intervening space and time are conspicuous factors. For example, an end-reaction complex, like walking to get a distant object, combines several patterns, with preliminary or precurrent reactions (walking) leading up to consummatory or end-reactions (grasping the thing sought). Such a complex may be intuitively "seized" in its own intrinsic quality as a whole, or one may be aware of living through it as a whole, with means and end all fused together. Or, the end may be contemplated without regard for the precurrent reactions which lead up to it; such contemplation is familiar in aesthetic experience, and may have been the reason why Schopenhauer wrote that art is always at its goal. Similarly, the still more elaborate sentiments, like love, and valuations or ideals, like justice, comprising as they do whole chains of end-reactions and many patterns which have been developed in elaborate processes of conditioning, may be immediately apprehended or experienced, if not as wholes, then with more or less exclusive reference to the distant object, person, or idea which serves as an end. In a suitable situation, too, a whole personality, with a chain of means and ends, sentiments, and ideals, which spans a lifetime, may feel itself totally involved, especially with reference to another person, or to something cosmic, or to God. This is the natural locus of the mystical experience; it is the deep end of intuition, where the mystics maintain that personal things are personally discerned.

It should be noted that in none of these cases is intuition independent of ideation or intelligence. In fact intuition and ideation ought never to supplant, but always to supplement each other. And they may supplement each other in various ways. Sometimes intuition seems like a concentration or "emballation" of experience, from which ideas gradually unravel and become explicit and articulate, in communicable form. Evidently intuitions in some way contain ideas within them, perhaps somewhat as the circle contains its inscribed polygons. It is even possible to argue that intuition is an afterthought, and would not be discerned at all if one did not search for it and "re-mind" oneself that there is, or was, such an immediate feeling. But this only witnesses to the interrelations of intuitions and other mental processes, not to the unreality of intuitions. Perhaps the best answer to the questions about intuition and intelligence is that each serves as a cue for the other.

Just as intuition is thus not independent of ideation, so it is not independent of the organic functioning of the body, including the nervous system. There is no need to make it eerie or other-worldly; it is altogether too natural for that. And when intuition is regarded as natural, the method of mysticism can be defended against its critics, whether the content can or not.

(3) The charges that mysticism is depressive, pessimistic, ascetic, or world-denying may be discounted as hasty generalizations. It takes all kinds of mystics to make a world, and some of them have been buoyant and optimistic, and have derived from their experiences a freshened strength and heightened enthusiasm. Nor is mysticism always ascetic; Jakob Boehme married the daughter of the local butcher and by her had four children! Doubtless the mystic seems awkward and stilted when "facing reality" or confronted by some of the naturalness of the world, but so, often, does the metaphysician. It is passing strange to find the mystics criticized for lack of directness when their immemorial watchword has been immediacy; one suspects that the indirectness is in the interpretation rather than in the experience. And one who has not here or there realized the massive and majestic simplicity of some of the great mystics has not penetrated far into either life or nature. Even where there are confusions and as yet unorganized responses, these may be the very places in which to look for new possibilities of interpreting the richness of reality.

(4) Any high correlation between mysticism and pathological symptoms can be matched along other lines, where genius so frequently comes in fragile and unstable personalities. Perhaps sickness, too, has its uses in revealing in its own way some of the facts about the world. Bergson dismisses the pathology of mysticism as merely incidental to the profound upheaval which marks the mystic's magnificent attainment of what is virtually a new stage of evolution.[8]

(5) The fact that mystical experiences can be correlated with other traits means merely that they can be psychologically studied and analyzed, not that they are

invalidated by such investigations. If it be urged that an experience is judged by the correlations it keeps, and that mysticism goes with conservatism or orthodoxy, the question may involve the validity of religious conservatism or orthodoxy; we shall have to consider this question later, but whatever the answer is, it seems evident from other available cases that the mystical responses can be reconditioned and correlated with other systems of metaphysics and theology.

(6) As regards drugs and intoxicants, the mystics declare that such things do not produce experiences of a depth or height or delicacy comparable with theirs, and that their after effects are notably more vigorous and healthy. In fact, most of the criticisms of the mystical experiences to the effect that they can be stimulated by the influence of anaesthetics, narcotics, or stimulants can also be made of the more profound musical experiences. From many points of view one understands mysticism best when he thinks of it as a kind of music.

(7) The point just mentioned helps to explain why the effects of mysticism can be so nearly duplicated in the arts. And the fact that some features of the mystical experience can be matched in scientific work ought again to help to naturalize the mystical method rather than uncritically to outlaw its content.

(8) This point, in turn, helps to meet the criticisms to the effect that in the newer physiological and psychological sciences the mystical experience is being explained away. There is no doubt that scientific investigations weaken the elements which in mysticism have been taken to be miraculous; probably they also weaken the elements which have been interpreted as animistic and understood as if the mystical were incorporeal, quite of another nature than the mechanisms of the body. Another set of barriers to understanding will be passed when we learn that the mystical may be also the physiological and the mechanistic.

The question of agreements and disagreements among mystics of different faiths is widely discussed; the upshot seems to be that there are both resemblances and differences, and that emphasis on the one side or the other is largely a matter of interest. With all the differences which have been brought out—and they cover most of the doctrines ordinarily at issue between the great faiths—it can at least be said that all the mystics agree *that* there is something presented to men which is immediately appealing, commanding, and even overpowering. Perhaps this greatest common factor of mysticism is the mystics' chief contribution, and the question of content, the question just *what* the something is, the question in which the mystics differ according to heredity and environment, can be left to the schools to determine.

(9) The Freudian criticisms, which may seem quite devastating, are best met by admitting that they are partially right and then pointing out their exaggerations. Some Freudians trace everything in religion, as well as in other phases of life and thought, to the ups and downs of sex impulses. Freudianism has been a theory which lends itself easily to extremists, some of whom have gone beyond Freud; but on the other hand eminent psychoanalysts like Jung and Adler have been less onesided and dogmatic about the sex impulses.

Granting the sex impulses a prominent or even a dominant influence, one finds some critics of mysticism proceeding as if everything connected with sex were despicable, and others arguing as if repressions and sublimations were wrong. Among such views, the normal way is to take a middle course, regarding the sex impulses as naturally grounded in the cosmos, but remembering that some repressions and sublimations are indispensable, whether in society or solitude. It is easy to see that among the mystics are many abnormal cases, sometimes sex-psychopathic cases, but this is by no means the whole story. Wherever it is the story, we should be thankful that for such men and women, beset by tempests almost too great for them, sublimations are possible. Here again, as in the case of autosuggestions, the point is not that men should have no sublimations, but that they should have those which raise the level of personality and which square with the cosmos.

If the point in the Freudian criticism, instead of being that it reduces mystical experiences to something immoral, is merely that it reduces them to something natural, this may be to ground them all the more firmly in the nature of things.

(10) Here we come to the oft repeated criticism that mysticism is unsocial and unethical. This can be met in one way by showing that the critic is himself arguing from an inadequate view of society, forgetting that it involves a mutual or organismic relationship. It is well for the group that some of its members learn, if they can, to be seers; they may help to orient those of us who can not see in their way. The mystic's alleged disintegration may mean merely a lowering of compartment thresholds in order to place himself in the way of more integral experiences. A more practical method of meeting the criticism is to point to the many available examples of mystics who have been aglow with social enthusiasm and have engaged actively in social service. With regard to the theory of evil, the view which proclaims that evil is swallowed up in the all comprehending good is absolute idealism, rather than mysticism; it is a fair question whether there is a necessary connection between the two.

(11) Against the contention that mysticism is a menace to religion, so many witnesses can be called from among the pure and the self-forgetting that we need only refer to them, without pausing to listen to their age-long testimony. Surely it is not religion which mysticism endangers; it is at most only some types of ritual

and of theology. The pantheism of many mystics is one account of the testimony of immediate experience, but not necessarily the final account. And the stricture that the mystic makes himself one with God is magnified out of all due proportion and importance. There is no need to rebuke the mystic for impiety or blasphemy, and no need ponderously to show that what he avers is logically, psychologically, or theologically impossible. The fact is that the mystic—at any rate the Western mystic—even though he used the words, never meant the statement to carry the implications which his critics have seen in it. Is not the mystical experience ineffable, and do not words break down, and confess that they have no wings?

(12) We have seen that representatives of the various schools of philosophy are not agreed among themselves about mysticism; some support it, while others criticize it. To discuss the arguments in detail here would be to anticipate several chapters which follow. Let it suffice to say that there are several marked tendencies to favor mysticism and that it is ideologically stronger than many of its critics think. The reason seems to be that with all the differences of the philosophies and with all the vagaries of mysticism, mysticism reaches down to something which is fundamental and essential for philosophy. Mysticism on the surface is a climbing plant; but its roots strike into the same ground as those of the philosophies, and go deeper into the subsoil.

From occultism, mysticism can have more aid than it wants in the West and more than it needs in the East. Supernaturalism is one of mysticism's favorite vehicles, and on its own account is so accustomed to supplementing what it regards as the laws of nature that it has no difficulty in supposing that God has his own direct access to men's minds, with or without benefit of the laws of psychology. In fact, extraordinary ways of revealing himself to man are likely to be regarded as most in accord with God's supernatural power.

Idealism, with its doctrine of the primary and ultimate reality of mind, (either our minds, or the Universal Mind, or both) easily passes into a mysticism appropriate to it, especially when the Universal or Absolute Mind is held to be the ground and matrix of our minds. Much of the technique of idealism and its variant, panpsychism, consists in alleged dissolving of the distinctions which its opponents hold to exist between mind and anything which is not mind. As soon as these barriers are thought away, it is easy to suppose that the Cosmic Mind is immediately present to minds like ours; the Vedanta philosophy in its most famous version even goes so far as to identify the two. Thus mysticism is at least implicit in any idealistic view of the world, and it is often explicit. Generations of mystics have been nourished upon the Upanishads and the Vedanta, upon Spinoza and Hegel. In our own day it is no accident that men who share the idealistic tradition, as do W. E. Hocking and A. S. Eddington, are among the outstanding friends of mysticism. Hocking maintains that the mystical experience finds the center of reality, as love finds the idea of a person.[9] Eddington holds that science deals only with the metrical aspects of the world, but that the non-metrical aspects, which are more important, are most significantly revealed in experiences which may be credited to mysticism.[10] More theological in its setting is the mysticism of Rudolf Otto, with its emphasis upon religious experience as typically experience of the "numinous," the impending or threatening or "dreadful" reality.[11]

Pragmatism, too, has often been friendly. William James left a notable record of an experience which might be interpreted as nature mysticism.[12] The philosophy which he worked out amid the manifold varieties of religious experience maintained that God, a "More of the same quality" as our consciousness, has access to us through our subconsciousness, and that the mystic on his own ground is invulnerable.[13] Apart from the strongly personal views of James, any mystic may appeal directly to immediate experience of values, as does Rufus Jones; we shall see later that there are good reasons for regarding the value philosophies as akin to pragmatism. On the other hand, any pragmatist may hold that mysticism is to be judged by its fruits in the development of personality, and the judgment may be favorable.

Both creative and emergent evolutionism afford places of some honor for the mystical experience and its interpretation. Bergson sees in the early religions a static phase of development, devised by the life impulse as a kind of safeguard against an unrestrained use of man's newly acquired intelligence. This static religion is here and there supplemented by the far more adequate dynamic religion, the religion which bursts forth in the experience of the great mystics, who believe that they see what God really is.[14] Alexander thinks that the urge or Nisus of the world proceeds on its way toward deity, a level higher than anything it has yet reached, and affects the human mind by ways which are other than cognition.[15] Realism, strictly speaking, is an epistemology, a theory about knowledge, rather than a metaphysics, a theory about the universe; all that realism really needs to say about the universe is that there are objects independent of our minds. These independent objects may be apprehended or known in the mystical experience. Hence we find "mystical realism," affirming a mystical knowledge of nature, of God, or anything else which is regarded as its object.

Among the naturalisms, aesthetic naturalism reflects enough of the inarticulate experience of the artist so that it is haunted by mysticism as by a kind of memory or hope. Akin to religious naturalism is the cosmic mysticism of Wordsworth, Thoreau, Whitman, and John Burroughs. Even in humanism there is sometimes room for a kind of residual mysticism, whether by courtesy or as the last twinge of pathos for an abandoned faith. A social mysticism is entirely compatible with Nazism and not altogether antagonistic to communism; even a cosmic mysticism might follow where the Marxians take their Hegelianism seriously. In short, only an unrelieved naturalism has no place for mysticism, and unrelieved naturalism is seldom if ever reached. It is more a threat than a philosophy.

THE ABIDING CONTRIBUTIONS OF MYSTICISM

What are the deep roots, the abiding contributions of mysticism? We shall have to see later that much of the content of mysticism, like that of occultism, is open to serious question, and may even be dismissed as vagaries —may be cut off, as climbing plants are sometimes cleared away when the axe is applied to the roots of the trees. But beneath the surface are the deeper roots; there are certain presuppositions in mysticism which the centuries have not availed to eradicate, and which renew their strength as the seasons pass.

Let us distinguish among them, first, *immediacy*. We have seen something of this in discussing mysticism's method of intuition; we need now to discern in mysticism not alone the method, but the quality of immediacy. It is hard to make this clear, because there is no way of making immediacy mediate without forfeiting it; these words of mine to you have no advantage over other words which have been expended in such attempts. If each of us can not recognize it in himself, in his own experience of the present moment, it will hardly help to multiply words about it. Using just a few words, to indicate indirectly what is meant, we can say that the immediate is not quite an "ultimate"; it is rather an "intimate." It is not merely the subjective, such as may be discerned by introspection. It includes the subjective, or rather pertains to the subjective and something else. It is not merely the experiential, but, as it is sometimes called, the "existential." It is a quality of the subjective-at-work. It belongs to my experiencing things rather than to things which I have not yet experienced. I need not look for it now anywhere but here, where I am now, as I write, nor need you, if you read, look for it anywhere but where you are when you read. Perhaps neither of us can really look for it elsewhere, because it is so intimately a quality of his looking for anything, anywhere, at any time; when I turn from writing or you from reading, each of us changes the content but not the quality of his immediacy, as a man using a searchlight changes the picture but not the luminous beam. It may take the mediation of words or ideas to direct our attention upon immediacy, as upon intuition, but this does not supplant immediacy; the unique quality will as likely as not be transferred to the very words or ideas which are used in the attempt to reveal it.

We shall see that the idealistic philosophies have used such immediacy as a veritable key to the world, the basis for whole theories of knowledge and systems of metaphysics. They have relied on immediacy to dissolve the barriers and distinctions between mind and its objects, between self and not-self, between persons and persons, between human personality and Absolute Personality. The mystic himself has been sure that immediacy broke down the barriers between human personality and divine personality. All this may be very seriously challenged in ways to be indicated as we proceed. We shall see that many of our treasured thoughts of human personality, of its objects in the everyday world, and of the Object of our religious devotion may have to be challenged or changed. But nothing of this can quite touch the fundamental fact, the fact beneath the surface, in which mysticism has a root and for which, in the midst of all the ideologies, it steadfastly stands.

Take away the quality of immediacy, and we lose the freshness of living experience anywhere. Take it away from religion, and whatever is left can be expressed in words and written in books about philosophy and the sciences, or about language and semantics.

Again, the mystic has borne witness not merely to an immediacy about experience, but to a *totality*. He has not stopped halfway, but has given himself utterly, and has felt himself utterly overwhelmed. Sense, reason, and feeling alike have been swallowed up in an engulfing experience; the typical mystic reports that his very self has been absorbed into the Highest. There are, as we said, explanations which see all this in terms of psychology rather than of theology, but even if it is only psychology there is a point here which is too important to miss: it is that at least sometimes a personality reacts markedly as a whole. At least for once, and for the time being, a man's experience is unified. It is a point which the analytical psychologies like behaviorism, particularly as amateurs understand them, are likely to miss and which their opponents like the *Gestalt* or organismic schools are likely unduly to proclaim as some fresh discovery. It is a point which some of the philosophers have seen, but have interpreted in strange fashion, as when idealists make the totality of the self-conscious human personality an argument for a Cosmic Mind, or when pragmatists, who make plain the fact that ideas are instrumental in valuations and situations, restrict their relationships with the universe to attempts to conrol the environment. The point needs continually to be emphasized: whatever be the case with single perceptions, ideas, or emotions, there are experiences in which the personality reacts as a whole, and a man acts in his integrity. Even if man is a machine, he is an adding machine, which not merely prints single entries but sometimes casts a total. The mystic has perhaps been through no conscious process of integration, but he has kept his experience integral. The life is more than thought, and the man than his words.

This, by the way, has two corollaries worth noting. First, it is no wonder that the mystical experience can not be adequately expressed. To describe such inclusive experiences is to dissect them and disentegrate them, to break them *down* into language-patterns as the chemist breaks down a complex molecule with its distinctive properties into elements in which the molecular properties are no longer found. Second, no ideology can be judged by its ideas alone. The experiences of any persons who discuss questions like these are organized long before any one enters the discussion, in units more inclusive than the ideas or language-patterns they employ. An ideology may be a structure of ideas, but if so, it is embedded in a matrix of sentiments, valuations, selves, and personalities. It is impossible for any person to come to any discussion utterly without prejudice. The most that any one can do is to expose his prejudices on all sides in the hope that they will be well ventilated and suited to the cosmos. We can not blindly condemn the mystic until we have compared his prejudices with ours; when we do, we may find the same kind of personal matrix in the one case as in the other, and find that the mystic, in the method if not the content of his interpretation, has been true to the totality and integrity of personality, whereas the rest of us have found that totality so mysterious that we have been content to work with some of its fragments.

A third point emphasized in abiding fashion by the mystics is that man, so to speak, may approach the universe unafraid. Sometimes this confidence has come in curious ways, in uncanny insights or sudden visions, as when some of the old mystics thought they saw in a moment "the plan of all things" in earth and heaven. Their approach to the universe has been anything but the slow, cautious, positivistic, piecemeal work of the scientists. But science—what specialist does not know it?—is a thing of fragments. The whole is lost from sight by reason of preoccupation with the parts. Moreover, science is subject to the limitations of perception and of thinking; we need to remember that perception is selective and in correlative fashion at the same time inevitably "neglective," that we perceive things by distinguishing them against their neglected backgrounds. Thinking, as we shall argue later in more detail, shares that limitation, so that we are never able to think in descriptive fashion of the "whole universe" without perforce neglecting something as background and leaving it unexplored. But the mystics have not been distracted by the fragments nor hampered by any modest sense of limitations; they have in a way insisted that they "knew it all." We can not share their visions, particularly when we see the confused and sometimes infantile accounts they have given of details which the piecemeal sciences know so much more accurately. Nor can we share the mystic's audacity in disregarding limitations and, like the absolutist philosophers, rushing into statements about the infinite whole as if limitations did not exist. But the mystics at least have kept what the scientists and some of the philosophers have all but lost —a sense for the cosmos and for man's kinship with it. We shall meet something of this when we come to religious naturalism, where the attempt is made to regard the natural universe as the Object of religious devotion. All these points about the sciences and the philosophies we shall have to develop as we go on, attempting with the materials of the sciences to develop an adequate ideology of religion. The mystics, with a strength too great and too consistent to be disregarded, have maintained a certain steadfast confidence, which has sometimes envisaged the universe with a majestic sweep, and we ought if we can by our own means to make contact with such deep confidence and such cosmic grandeur.

REFERENCES

[1] On mysticism in general, see R. M. Jones, art. "Mysticism" in Hastings *Encyclopaedia of Religion and Ethics*, 9, p. 83: Evelyn Underhill, *Mysticism*, 1912, and *The Mystic Way*, 1913: C. A. Bennett, *A Philosophical Study of Mysticism*, 1923: J. H. Leuba, *The Psychology of Religious Mysticism*, 1925.

[2] E. D. Starbuck, in Sixth International Congress of Philosophy, *Proceedings*, 1927, pp. 91*ff.*

[3] E. F. Hartung in *Annals of Medical History (NS)*, 7, 1935, p. 90.

[4] S. E. Jelliffe, cited by O. L. Reiser, *Philosophy and the Concepts of Modern Science*, 1935, p. 210.

[5] E. S. Conklin, *The Psychology of Religious Adjustment*, 1929, pp. 150*f.*

[6] David Hume, *Dialogues Concerning Natural Religion*, Part III; edd. T. H. Green and T. H. Grose, 1874, Vol. II, p. 406*f.*

[7] See G. P. Conger, *The Horizons of Thought*, 1933, Chapter XXI.

[8] H. Bergson, *Two Sources of Morality and Religion*, transl. R. A. Audra and E. Brereton, 1935, p. 233.

[9] W. E. Hocking, *The Meaning of God in Human Experience*, 1912, pp. 354, 433.

[10] A. S. Eddington, *The Nature of the Physical World*, 1929, pp. 275, 323.

[11] R. Otto, *The Idea of the Holy*, transl. J. W. Harvey, 1925, Chap. IV.

[12] H. James, ed., *Letters of William James*, 1920, Vol. II, pp. 75*ff.*

[13] W. James, *Varieties of Religious Experience*, (1920), pp. 424, 511*f.*

[14] H. Bergson, *op. cit.*, p. 249.

[15] S. Alexander, *Space, Time, and Deity*, 1927, Vol. II, p. 377.

CHAPTER IV

SUPERNATURALISM: (I) ITS POINTS OF STRENGTH

When after considering occultism and mysticism we come to supernaturalism, the issues are more sharply outlined, as might be expected in a system which, while often found elsewhere, has made itself more thoroughly at home in the Near East, in Europe, and America. It is less like Hindu sculpture, so often done in high relief, and more like Greek sculpture, often done in the round.

Supernaturalism insists that man has to face not merely nature, the natural order of the world, but also something else. The view is essentially dualistic. Properly speaking, it sees not a dualism, an irreconcilable antagonism between its two principles, but only a duality, in which one of the two (the supernatural) is held to be the primary source and the ultimate destiny of the other. The twoness is not absolute, but the contrast between the two principles is sharp while it lasts, and its sharpness is not for us to remove. Just what belongs to the one or the other realm is not always easy to determine. Primitive races personified the forces of nature and thought of spirits or gods presiding over winds and waters, days and seasons. Children think of a Big Man up in the sky, theologians of a Divine Creator and Providence, and philosophers of a Great Mind behind the universe. Most frequently the fundamental duality is discerned between nature, conceived as impersonal, material, or mechanical, and a supernatural order of one or more beings conceived as personal, spiritual, and purposeful. Usually the supernatural is regarded as possessing, albeit in varying degrees, the characteristics of personality, such as feeling, knowledge, purpose, will, power, love, and goodness.

The possible combinations here include the various forms of polydemonism (belief in many demons, not necessarily evil, but slightly superior to men); polytheism (belief in many gods); henotheism (belief in a number of gods, among whom one is supreme); and monotheism (belief in one, the sole existent God). The variant of the last which is called deism differs from it in ascribing to its object a lower degree of personal characteristics; the God of deism is usually aloof from the world of nature and man, and markedly transcendent, in contrast to the God of theism, who is more highly personalized and, even though transcendent, is either also immanent in the world or at least capable of some intimate contact with man.

Often it is declared that the natural and the supernatural are known by us in different ways, as when the natural is said to appeal to our senses, or our senses and reason together, while the supernatural appeals in part to reason and in part to some higher faculty like intuition or faith in God as revealed in some special way. Oman maintains that the supernatural is a special kind of environment; it means the world which manifests more than natural values, values which stir the sense of the holy and demand to be esteemed as sacred.[1] Writers who emphasize the immanence of God sometimes maintain that the distinction between the natural and the supernatural is overdrawn, but there is no question that it is of great importance in the history and philosophy of religion.

Supernaturalism is so important among the ideologies that our discussion of it will occupy several chapters, of which this is devoted to a study of its general characteristics. It will be appropriate first to review some of the traditional strong points of supernaturalism.

(1) Among its strong points we find, first, the fact

that it is very ancient. It is so thoroughly ingrained in Western culture that we sometimes hardly discern it as an ideology; although of course it is a theory, a doctrine like others, it seems more like its matrix which is our life. It comes to us with the momentum of a long past. Until recently practically all human affairs developed in close kinship with it. Its traditions are interwoven with human history; the glories of antiquity, much of the glamor of the East, and the charm of the European Middle Ages can not be understood without it. The Renaissance seemed for a while to disregard it, but the classics which the Renaissance rescued from oblivion were conceived in its spirit, and the fine arts in which the Renaissance flowered gave it new glory. Romanticism drew upon its strength, and nationalism and internationalism alike have appealed to it for inspiration. Science has often been slow to break away from it, and every now and then looks back. Even neo-paganism reflects it. Supernaturalism is battle-scarred, time-honored. It comes with fresh appeals and with surprising strength, especially to any who dread the removal of ancient landmarks.

(2) Supernaturalism is not merely ancient, but also very widespread—so much so that in its favor may be cited whatever strength there is in the old argument "from the consent of mankind." The more nearly pantheistic or non-theistic faiths which do not regard supernaturalism as primary or ultimate are after all not far from it. It has been amazingly popular; if a census were taken of all nations and peoples and tongues the vast majority would be found to favor it. A factor in its spread has been its simplicity. In form, if not always in detailed content, it is easy for untold millions of simple folk to understand and accept. The simple folk far outnumber the sophisticated, but myriads of the sophisticated, too, have their own reasons for adhering to supernaturalism.

(3) For millions of men, supernaturalism comes with all the impact of an absolutely authoritative system, through men who proclaim themselves as chosen to be its vehicles to others. If it is not from the Lord giving the law to Moses or answering Job out of the whirlwind, it is from a Pope armed with the power of excommunication, or from Allah empowering Muhammad to condemn those who oppose him, or from a council or creed which has managed to invest itself with frightful prestige. Supernaturalism shines in glorious ritual or thunders in prophetic messages. Under milder conditions it may seek to commend itself to man's reason or to his emotions, but always it means to remain essentially irresistible, and to provide the conclusive answer to every deep question about the world. The answers are held to rest upon revelations, formulated in one or another inspired sacred book and authenticated by miracle or prophecy or both. Sometimes the inspiration is declared to be literal, and the books are believed to have been virtually dictated; this is the traditional doctrine of Hinduism, Confucianism, orthodox Judaism, orthodox Christianity, and Islam. In other cases the books are believed to be inspired as regards their main motives and religious values, as in Buddhism, liberal Judaism, and liberal Christianity. The personally founded religions trace their revelations specifically to historic figures; some of these men, like Guatama and Jesus, are regarded as in one way or another not merely human but divine. Either within the sacred books or in others influenced by them, the religions and sects have developed official systems of doctrine. In the West the most famous is Roman Catholic scholasticism, the intellectual product of the Christian Middle Ages. It is fashioned out of Christian experience, which is ascribed in the New Testament manner to the supernatural and given a natural basis and a strong common sense appeal in the philosophy of Aristotle. In the scholastic system,

47

revealed theology comes from its authoritative source in the church traditions, including the Bible, and fills out and completes natural theology, which man is able to reason out by the aid of authoritative works of Aristotle. Articulated with the rigor of deductive logic, the system is comprehensive and consistent enough so that on thousands of disputed questions it can face inquirers with what are held to be reasoned "proofs" of the accepted doctrines. In the nineteenth and twentieth centuries there has been in the Catholic church an impressive revival of this philosophy, known as Neo-scholasticism; it still follows the mediaeval system of Thomas Aquinas, but corrects a few minor defects and, without modifying its views of the authoritative traditions and the Bible, brings the words of Aristotle into considerable accord with the discoveries of modern science. Sometimes there is conspicuous support for scholastic doctrines in philosophies developed outside the Catholic church, as in the works of Bergson or more recently of M. J. Adler.

Other Christian systems dispute with Catholicism over some points of content, particularly the authority of the church and its extra-biblical traditions and the importance of the Aristotelian writings, but in general retain the authority of the Bible. The Protestants exclude from their Bible certain books of the so-called Apocrypha which the Catholics accept. Some Protestant groups place special emphasis upon the authority of the Gospels for the salvation of believers, and tend to let questions about other biblical books rest. Against the more literal interpretations, the so-called liberal Protestant groups, often aided by the pragmatic philosophies, set the authority of experience, as signally instanced in the experiences recorded as biblical, but often reinforced or modified by modern experiences and interpretations. As a reaction against such liberalism, the Fundamentalist movement has revived the literalist views, proclaiming belief in the Bible "from cover to cover" and assailing modern conceptions, both in science and ethics, as subversive and wicked errors.

The more recent Barthian and Buchmanite movements appeal more directly to Christian experience than to the authority of the Bible, but to a type of Christian experience which could hardly have occurred without dependence upon biblical revelation and authority. Thus Barthianism, allowing no foundation in natural theology and virtually disparaging human reason altogether, grounds everything on "the word of God," the fact that the utterly transcendent God has spoken to man, whose nature is sinful and whose efforts to attain worth or truth are futile.[2] The inspiration of the Bible is here so transcendent that it is, as we might say, "off the record" as we have it. The Buchman groups cherish direct experiences of guidance and ascribe them to fresh operations of the Holy Spirit, but the framework of their thinking is indicated by the official name, "The First Century Christian Fellowship."[3] The more recent designation as "Moral Rearmament" is an attempt to apply the teachings of the group more directly to contemporary problems.

The net result of these various authoritarian views is that supernaturalism is remarkably sure of itself. For vast masses of mankind, it is almost the hall-mark of religion. Its note of authority and finality is so lacking in most of the liberal systems that many a tired or disillusioned explorer like Cardinal Newman turns back to its security once more.

(4) If the appeal to authority fails, in an age which prides itself upon its empiricism, supernaturalism also may claim to be empirical. To be empirical means to appeal to experience, but to restrict the word or the method to laboratory experiment is, according to supernaturalism, to narrow it and spoil it. Any one whose laboratory is his life may prove all things and hold fast

that which is good. Thus supernaturalism can claim the empiricism of experience, if not of experiment, and point to its effect in personal life, in social processes, in historic events. Its claim is that any sincere inquirer may taste and see that the Lord is good, and that anyone who doubts supernaturalism should read the signs of the times.

In the perspective of Protestant history, the Barthians, the followers of Buchman, and many other sects appear as special groups each emphasizing some particular type or factor or definition of Christian experience. Thus the Barthian "existential moment," in which a man, ceasing to be a "spectator" of religion, steps forth into a new reality and becomes aware of God's word to his own soul with such decisiveness that time has nothing more to give him,[4] is quite comparable to the old-fashioned Christian conviction of sin, the experience of rebirth, and the mystical experience. The "life changing" of the Buchman groups is the old-fashioned conversion, and "guidance" is another name for what is usually called communion with God. In all these supernaturalist sects and doctrines there is more unity than appears on the surface, and all of them can, if necessary, with a united front bear what they proclaim as empirical testimony to supernaturalism as the philosophy of their religion.

(5) If scientific difficulties arise, supernaturalism turns out to be surprisingly flexible and convenient. In William James' metaphor, it furnishes overtones.[5] In another metaphor, we might say that before the doors of all philosophies, the sciences like a fleet of moving vans are unloading a great store of facts of all shapes and sizes, which somehow must be taken into the house of philosophy and arranged there in some livable order. In such a situation, a two-story house is likely to be more convenient than a one-story bungalow; what does not fit on the ground floor can be put upstairs; whatever

be the content of the natural world, salvation is more or less frankly proclaimed as a supernatural process. As a matter of fact, the oft repeated statement that there is no quarrel between science and religion comes almost always from those who live in two-story philosophies, of which supernaturalism is by far the best known. In such an ample structure, for example, water and wine and bread and protoplasm belong downstairs, among the facts of nature, of chemistry. But suppose water was changed into wine at Cana, or bread into flesh in the Eucharist this morning? Nature will have no place for such miracles, but the supernatural can welcome them. And such a two-story world is not merely convenient; it is, in a way, consistent. The two parts can be made to fit together, and each has something which the other lacks.

We must not omit to notice that supernaturalism draws no small strength from the force of its contrasts. It deals always with a higher principle, another world, and is often able to draw its lines sharply between the higher and the lower. The Barthians, although they do not allow man to construct a worthy natural theology as a pedestal for the supernatural, maintain that God is unknowable except as revealed, and God reveals himself altogether or not at all.[6] Revelation pierces history; the supernatural occupies another dimension than ordinary reality—one might say, a dimension which is prophetic, while that of ordinary reality is profane. It is the awful disparity between these which is signalized in the "theology of crisis," the "Kairos" or appointed time. The sharpness of the contrast is said to give religion driving power. Such contrasts work out in ethics in a set of definite standards for a bewildered world, and in a clear challenge to open conflict on behalf of right against wrong. In the characters it breeds there is a moral fiber and in the convictions it engenders an intellectual clearness which are as yet unmatched in rival systems. Not all supernaturalism shares the scholastics' clearness; the Barthians believe in a God who is not cosmologically but epistemologically transcendent, a theory of the creation which is religious but not necessarily physical or biological, a superhistory which is not interpreted history, a Christology virtually independent of the historic Jesus, and a person or ego distinct from the personality. Some of its contradictions Barth leaves in dialectical form, insoluble by reason. Paul Tillich, in a view called "belief-ful realism," tries to construe as having religious value the paradox of modern disillusionment concerning the present world as contrasted with traditional assurances about the goodness of the "Unconditioned." [7]

(6) Sometimes the convenience of such a view appears in what William James called "piecemeal supernaturalism." [8] Many a man who does not believe that Elijah made an axe swim or that Buddha flew through the air finds it harder to make up his mind about the miracles of healing or the salvation of his soul or the divine governance of the world, and may well wonder where to draw the line between acceptance and rejection. But supernaturalism admits exceptions. It does not have to be universal, nor account for everything; a man can pick and choose the particular cases which appeal to him. Such a piecemeal supernaturalism has the moral value of leaving something for us to do; the supernatural carries only a part of the load.

Nothing better illustrates the adaptability of supernaturalism than the fact that if such piecemeal supernaturalism does not appeal, one can do something quite different—he can turn from definiteness to indefiniteness, and hold supernaturalism in an abstract, general way, without being explicit about any particulars. It is sometimes easier here to do business on a wholesale than on a retail basis—easier to affirm that the world is dual in principle than to affirm, for instance, that any particular miracle occurred.

(7) Supernaturalism has known how to ally itself with other philosophies, even with some which have been its rivals. Thus occultism and supernaturalism may claim the same miracles and trace them to kindred sources. Often supernaturalism finds its consummation in what it shares with mysticism as the experience of absorption in the highest; sometimes it joins mysticism in disregarding or scorning the pronouncements of ordinary experiences or ordinary thought. Supernaturalism has flourished within the matrix of pantheism and absolute idealism, largely because such vast monisms are unmanageable and tend to crystallize again in the familiar images of the gods—witness the myriads of deities which have been carried along in Hinduism, and the fact that so many high Hegelians have somehow contrived to be theists. Supernaturalism and personalism are obviously close together. Conservative supernaturalism, with its reliance on the older doctrines of authority, does not need the help of pragmatism, but liberals who, especially since Schleiermacher, have turned to the authority of experience, are pragmatic without knowing it; they may even give up doctrines of transcendence and say that God is what he is experienced as being. In more popular fashion, there is abundant testimony to the fact that supernaturalism "works"; many men find that it is, as it was for William James, more satisfactory to believe than not to believe. And if any one doubts the claim, he is invited to make the pragmatic test for himself.

As regards evolutionism, supernaturalism can be dovetailed with it and made to supply answers to enormous questions which evolutionism itself leaves open. Some of these questions concern the ultimate outcome of the cosmic process; in the nineteenth century Henry Drummond and John Fiske gave their memorable answers, to the effect that the evolutionary series is like a ladder leading through the animal species to man and from man leading, or at least pointing, upward to God. The theistic evolutionists say similar things now. The evolutionists are typically more interested in outcomes than in origins, but if questions about the origin and primary source of everything will not be silenced, supernaturalism, while accepting the evolutionist accounts as far back or as far down as they go, can always preface them with a majestic "In the beginning, God."

From the days of Plato, there have been alliances between supernaturalism and realism; in fact, some alliance is necessary, for the supernatural to its devotees must be of all realities most real. Some of the naturalisms are not altogether unfriendly. Although extreme naturalism dissolves the supernatural, and aesthetic naturalism refines it into imaginative poetry, the more ethical and religious types of naturalism find it hard to set their own limits and therefore hard to deny the operation of something Other or something More. Even humanism can be non-committal about this, and only communism in its contemporary form rigidly excludes it. But history has shown that supernaturalism has a way of raiding the camp of its worst enemies and triumphantly bearing off their facts and experiences to serve as so much additional evidence "on the side of the angels."

(8) Whether drawing strength from the points we have indicated or disregarding them, supernaturalism makes a strong appeal to faith. Psychologically faith goes beyond mere belief. Belief is essentially acceptance of an idea into a person's effective system of ideas; faith combines with this a more emotional feeling of personal confidence, especially as regards another person or persons. The degrees of belief and of faith vary, and the variations give rise to much confusion of terms. Merely to entertain a proposition is not to believe it; belief involves some acceptance, even though the acceptance is only tentative and uncertain. From such tentative ac-

ceptance, belief and faith vary all the way to the utter confidence and deep conviction characteristic of saints and sometimes of scholars. The different degrees here reappear in various attitudes toward supernaturalism. For instance, Catholicism defines faith as acceptance of doctrine upon authority; the implication is that one either accepts the official system or one does not. In the long history of faith we find an amazing number of variants—among them, believing because it as absurd, believing in order that we may understand, unshaken faith, blessed assurance, faith as a means of synthesis of intellectual contradictions, a faith that inquires, adventurous religion, robust credulity, and the will to believe. It is impossible to describe all the variations of supernaturalism's appeals to faith; but the important fact is that whatever be the strength or the weakness of supernaturalism at any given time, it is always possible to appeal to a faith which reaches further out than strength has hoped or weakness has feared.

(9) Before the accounts of supernaturalism are made up, we must reckon in its favor whatever advantage accrues from the various arguments for the existence of God. These complicated questions are discussed in later chapters; our judgment is that something can be said for at least some forms of the teleological and the moral arguments.

REFERENCES

[1] J. W. Oman, *The Natural and the Supernatural*, 1931, pp. 23, 71.

[2] On Barthianism, see K. Barth, *The Epistle to the Romans*, transl. E. C. Hoskyns, 1933; *The Doctrine of the Word of God*, transl. G. T. Thomson, 1936; also several works cited below.

[3] On the Buchman, or Oxford Groups, see A. J. Russell, *For Sinners Only*, 1932: R. H. S. Crossman, *Oxford and the Groups*, 1934.

[4] J. R. McConnachie, *The Significance of Karl Barth*, 1931, 87. Such emphasis upon an "existential moment" goes back to S. Kierkegaard's contrast between mere "life" and a more deeply apprehended and religiously richer "existence." In contemporary German philosophy elaborate analyses of "Existenz" have been developed by M. Heidegger and K. Jaspers, under the influence of the phenomenology of E. Husserl (see below, p. 135 and n. On Kierkegaard, see his

Philosophical Fragments, translated by D. F. Swenson, 1936; and E. Geismar, with introduction by Swenson, *Lectures on the Religious Thought of Sören Kierkegaard,* 1937; W. Lowrie, *Kierkegaard,* 1938.

[5] W. James, *Varieties of Religious Experience,* pp. 513*ff.*

[6] J. R. McConnachie, *op. cit.,* p. 100.

[7] See W. Pauck, *Karl Barth, Prophet of a New Christianity?* 1931, pp. 108, 116, 199; H. E. Brunner, *The Theology of Crisis,* 1929, p. 41; J. R. McConnachie, *op. cit.,* pp. 108, 113. For Tillich, see *The Religious Situation,* translated by H. R. Niebuhr, 1932, pp. x, *ff.*

[8] W. James, *op. cit.,* p. 520.

CHAPTER V

SUPERNATURALISM: (II) ARGUMENTS FOR THE EXISTENCE OF GOD

In order to search out all available resources for a philosophy of religion, we must examine with some care the classical and other arguments for the existence of God. They are often neglected, but neglect is justified only if they are exaggerated, placed out of reach of any real argument, and regarded as unassailable "proofs." Considered as arguments, they are interlocked with one another, and with so many of the philosophies that any attempt to treat them separately is a dissection.

THE COSMOLOGICAL ARGUMENT

The cosmological argument seeks to point us from the world as made to a Maker, or from a world regarded as secondary and dependent to a Being regarded as primary and independent. The argument shows a number of interrelated features. We shall indicate them under four headings: (1) widespread popular views; (2) views based on doctrines of authority; (3) views developed by the aid of abstract concepts and categories from various systems of philosophy; and (4) support from scientific work.

(1) There is first a deep rootage in widespread popular beliefs. Far and wide among men, the world is taken to be a manufactured product, and hence is ascribed to a Maker. The belief seems to arise as soon as men begin to inquire about such great questions; it is so natural that it is at home anywhere. Occasionally in advanced

cultures, one finds another popular notion, that since this is a world of law there must be a Law-giver.

(2) In support of the argument can be ranged all authoritarian views and particularly the first chapter of Genesis, with its opening words, "In the beginning, God created the heaven and the earth." Those who accept this on authority take it to be the first, and as good as the last word on the subject; even those who regard the chapter as a reëdited Semitic myth find that it moves with a majesty rivalled by few documents in science or literature. The argument from authority is not quite as archaic as sometimes thought, because many conservatives now take the six "days" as epochs or eras and dismiss as marginal the chronology which used to place the creation in the year 4004 B.C. Believers who go on from the authority of the Bible to that of the creeds subscribe to the doctrine of *"creatio ex nihilo,"* that God formed the world out of "nothing."

(3) The cosmological argument has drawn some of its most impressive and convincing support from a group of abstract concepts, including beginnings, causality, existence, infinity, absolutes, possibility, necessity, and perfection. Volumes could be filled with examples of these discussions; we mention only a few of the most important. First, the cosmological argument appeals to thinkers who hold that questions about the beginnings of the universe can not be disregarded. Thorough consideration of any process going on in time is likely to raise such questions; we shall see that they appear whether, with the Aristotelians and some of the evolutionists, one is trying to avoid an infinite regress, or, with some of the mathematical physicists, one sets about extrapolating the equations of radiation or entropy backward to an initial state.

Consideration of a process in time raises not merely problems about beginnings, but also about causality. In primitive life, anything unusual or unique is likely to be taken as the effect of an unusual or unique cause, and anything tremendous or overwhelming is referred to a very powerful cause. As men's views of the world become systematized, the unusual events and the overwhelming events together tend to be ascribed to the same power, until gradually everything is ascribed to it directly as the primary cause, or indirectly through the operation of intermediate secondary causes.

Most of the ways of arguing from the operation of causes close at hand to that of a great cause have been elaborated in the mediaeval Roman Catholic, the so-called scholastic philosophy, with a good deal of help from theories about existence, or being, and infinity. Thus it is held that an efficient cause can not be the cause of its own being, since this would be to act before it exists.[1]

Although originally it is not altogether clear as a statement of creationism, the scholastics usually take Aristotle's reasoning about an infinite regress and the Prime Mover, and argue that if when dealing with efficient causes it is possible to go on to infinity, there will be no first efficient cause, nor an ultimate effect, nor any intermediate efficient causes [2]—so that, if we do not watch our logical steps, we shall have no world at all.

Orthodox Protestantism has added little to the thought of the scholastics on this subject, but the cosmological argument with its theory of causation has remained deeply embedded in every system. How deeply it was embedded was shown in the deistic movement, which tried in seventeenth and eighteenth century fashion to apply reason to religion. Although the deists differed somewhat among themselves, their name is to this day associated with the doctrine that God is the first cause of the universe, although he remains aloof from it.

Several versions of the cosmological argument which involve ideas of beginning and causality are further describable by the general statement that the existent world requires something to raise it or preserve it from non-existence. According to the scholastics, the transition from non-being to being is only explained by the action of distinct anterior being. Some ordinary beings can either exist or not exist; their non-existence is thinkable without contradiction. But if everything could cease to exist, at one time there could have been nothing in existence. If at any one time there could be nothing in existence, then there can be nothing in existence now, because that which does not exist only begins to exist by something already in existence. So, unless again we are to lose our world, something must exist necessarily, with its necessity in itself.[3]

The notions of existence and causality are combined by the scholastics in that of self-existence, or "aseity," which is attributed solely to God, and tends to establish God in what is regarded as an unshakable position in respect to the created universe and the cosmological argument.

In more recent philosophy, the personalists ground the problem of causality in the reality of a personal being,[4] and Whitehead detects in his organismic world God as the "Principle of Concretion."[5]

The scholastics excelled in arguments passing from effects which are contingent to a necessary self-existent First Cause, and as we shall see, in developing contrasts between a world of Aristotelian potentialities passing into actualities and a Being who is pure Actuality.

In the concept of infinity, unless it was of God's own infinity, the scholastics saw little more than a difficulty for the cosmological argument. Some maintained that infinite regress of a sort could be reconciled with the argument, and Thomas Aquinas ventured to say that Aristotle's eternal universe (which we may assume to have involved infinite time) would require a creator just as a temporal universe would.[6] In more recent discussions, the concept of eternity has been used, for example by a

Fundamentalist writer, who, by an old scholastic turn with the term "nothing," argues that something has always existed, identifies that something with God, and then says that the cosmos can not be eternally unfolding, or it would long ago have reached its present state; hence it must have been created, and by a being who never had a beginning.[7]

In the Hegelian philosophy, nature is a finite manifestation rather than a manufactured product, but it is conditioned by its opposite, an infinite reality which is Absolute Spirit. Edward Caird thought that the "proofs" of the existence of God, so far as they were significant, were simply expressions of the impossibility of resting in the finite, and of the implicit reference to an Infinite and Absolute Mind.[8] Seth Pringle-Pattison combined the concept of eternity with that of creation; he held that God became God only when he created the world, expressing his nature in an eternal act of creation.[9]

Theories which make the Creator or ground of the universe infinite and absolute easily bring in ideas of perfection, and frame the cosmological argument in a contrast between matter capable of receiving perfections which are not among its essential attributes, and an external cause capable of conferring those perfections. Sometimes the argument in terms of perfection does not point very clearly to a personal being, but ways are usually indicated for the derivation or importation of personal attributes. Thus for the scholastics self-existence, construed in terms of perfections, including intelligence and will, is personal.[10]

(4) Scientific thought sometimes shows some notable indications of support for the cosmological argument. For example, Le Maître's theory of an expanding universe may be used as a basis for the inference that there was an initial state in which a cosmic bubble or a cosmic atom began to burst;[11] the question naturally suggests

itself as to why such an event should have occurred. Crowther says that everything points with overwhelming force to a definite event or series of events of creation at some time or times not infinitely remote. The empty void was stirred and protons and electrons appeared. For it we have nothing more appropriate than "And God said, Let there be light." [12]

A new version of the argument, involving many of the concepts we have noted, is available in the relativistic cosmology of E. A. Milne. With some evident affiliations for epistemological idealism, he argues that time is an affair of the experiences of observers. For any observer there are singularities—one "pre-experiential," a "natural zero" of time, and another its counterpart at a limiting distance, where a nebula moving with the speed of light would not be observable. Between the two singularities is the universe experienced by the observer. By the "cosmological principle" we infer that the natural zero of time possesses to an overwhelming degree of probability, the properties of an epoch of creation. At the other extreme there are nebulae just decelerating into visibility. Any observer may speak of the natural zero in terms of a first cause, the calling into being of the things describable, and there are always places where the newly decelerated nebulae just appearing to him are the most recent examples of the process in which the first cause has inaugurated an infinity of experiments. Although the physicist gains nothing by the addition of God to the scheme, we seem bound to go beyond description and make the addition.[13]

THE ONTOLOGICAL ARGUMENT

Strictly speaking, all the arguments for the existence of God are ontological; ontology is that part of philosophy which discusses being, or "being in general." Any question of the existence of anything may be called ontological. The traditional ontological argument for the existence of God might better be called epistemological. If it were called by this name, the name would at once suggest that the argument has little or no popular appeal. It is essentially a philosophers' argument, and is based on certain deeply embedded theories about the status of our ideas in the world. It tries to show that at least one of our ideas, the idea of God, is such that it must necessarily carry with it the existence of its corresponding object.

To develop the argument fully would require a considerable segment of the history of philosophy. Each time the argument becomes prominent it has to be understood in terms of the intricate speculations of the period. If we begin with Anselm's statement, "I have the idea of a Being than whom nothing greater can be conceived; but a Being which exists is greater than one which does not exist; therefore the Being whom I conceive must exist," [14] we must understand the statement against the background of other statements of the realist Anselm, who shared the ancient beliefs in a graded scale of beings and held that one of them, the most universal of all, was most real. [15] His argument is best understood as a short-cut, an attempt to dispense with some of his presuppositions.

Descartes' situation was quite different, as different as the seventeenth century was from the twelfth. The Frenchman was tormented by doubts which Anselm could not have worried about, but which, for Descartes, threatened to engulf the mediaeval doctrines along with their ancient framework. Descartes saved his world from such dissolution by the heroic expedient of letting his doubts have something like full play until they were stopped by the indubitable fact of his own experience— "I think, therefore I am"—so that he could reason out the difficulty from that standpoint. Thus the Cartesian emphasis upon subjectivism was not that of an old theologian taking a short-cut in an argument; it was more like a soldier, sorely beset by a new and powerful enemy, intrenching himself, digging himself in for dear life. Descartes managed to find among all his doubtful ideas the indubitable idea of a Perfect Being. This idea, he reasoned, could not have come from his imperfections, which were all too evident to him in the fact that he doubted. It must come from a source adequate to it, and this could only be an existent source; in the idea of a *Perfect* Being must be contained the existence of such a Being.[16]

After Descartes, the emphasis on the subjective develops through the long works of Locke, Berkeley, Hume, Kant, and Fichte, and at length issues in an idealism which makes mind, and primarily mind such as ours, not merely the instrument by which things are known, but the only kind of reality which can be known. Kant makes mind construct the known world out of an utterly indescribable raw material, the "thing-by-itself," the source of our sensations. Fichte goes further, making the "ego" responsible not merely for the world as known, but for the "non-ego," everything except itself. Against such subjectivism Hegel revolts, insisting upon an objective idealism which makes all reality consist of experience, but an Absolute Experience, immensely greater than ours. In the Hegelian system the ontological argument, like many another factor in the history of thought, is transformed almost beyond recognition. Hegel is not so much concerned with making our ideas tell us what exists; he sees existence itself as a colossal Idea, which works itself out in Nature and then works itself up through Nature in history, or Spirit. Hegelian idealists have shared his confidence in the cosmic character of experience and have sometimes coupled with it a Kantian demand made by our minds that reality should be intelligible in order that we might have a world.

Royce combined both strains, the subjective and the objective; his philosophy was a series of attempts to pass from mind in us to Mind in the universe. It is no wonder that he saw possibilities in the ontological argument, and maintained that unless there is somewhere an ontological proof which holds, we are left with no logical proof for any existence and there need be no real world at all. We are actually using something like the ontological proof all the time. For instance, when any one argues that there is a real world, he knows that there is a world from the nature of the case, from the very definition of the world; similarly for past and future, for laws of nature, for the notion of order, for relations or a relational system, for individual entities, and so on.[17] In all these cases, we have the ideas and define the terms in such ways as unavoidably to give them ontological status when we consider them at all.

The most important use of the ontological argument in contemporary philosophy is that by W. E. Hocking, who in general follows Royce, and, in contrast to older writers who use the ontological argument to indicate something about existence, uses it to indicate that if we have certain ideas they must rest upon corresponding experiences of ours. These experiences may then be interpreted in their immediate reference to the existent world.[18]

A number of other idealist and pragmatist writers have formulated an ontological argument in terms of values, or valuations, which claim objectivity or objective reality with such appeal or such insistence that it is held that we should accede to the claims.

THE TELEOLOGICAL ARGUMENT

Teleology, from the Greek τέλος, end, is the study of ends and particularly of purposes. The teleological argument for the existence of God is an argument from the ends which can be discerned or inferred in the world, to the existence of a Being who has conceived the ends and tries to accomplish them. Discussion of the argument has gone on for generations; several meanings of teleology have been developed, not all of them of equal value as arguments for the existence of God. The views opposed to the teleologies are usually grouped under the term "mechanism," which is also variously defined.

The meaning of teleology which gives us the classical teleological argument is that any given event, *A*, is (the outcome of a series of events which is) dependent on the prior conscious intention of a Mind superior to ours. Let us call this *supervenient* teleology. If read without the expression in parentheses, the formula makes any given event depend directly upon the superior Mind as a "primary cause," but if the expression in parentheses is included, it allows some intervening events to act as "secondary causes." In either case, the great point is that events depend upon prior, conscious, and superior intention. There is no vagueness nor evasion; teleology here means superior intention and purpose, prior to the given event and consciously entertained. As we proceed, we shall see various philosophies attempt to construe teleology in other terms, but this primary meaning is the one which we must keep most clearly in mind.

The teleological argument may be analyzed along lines similar to those of the closely related cosmological argument, although the amount of attention given to different lines varies, and in the nature of the cases some new considerations appear.

(1) We find first, as before, a widespread and almost ineradicable popular belief; generations have been reared supposing not alone that the world as a made product requires a Maker, but also that the world, obviously showing marks of order or design, requires an Orderer or a Designer.

(2) In the matter of authority, there are in the Semitic religions scriptural texts and theological doctrines about God's purposes. These purposes are construed in terms of God's nature and, especially in Christianity, his love for the world, love which is sometimes brought into sharp relief by doctrines about his justice.

The scholastic doctrine has to be understood in terms of Aristotle, as Aristotle has to be understood in terms of Plato. Plato's "ideas," considered by the help of the original Greek word, are not our ideas; primarily they are not concepts, but forms, or patterns, or types, or prototypes. Plato's statements about them are by some interpreters taken picturesquely, as if the ideas were a system of substantial ideal models of the world, somehow quite apart from their imperfect copies in the things around us. By other interpreters they are understood more subtly, as logical characters or essences which are present whenever ordinary things elicit them in us, and whether exhibited or not are always available to us for our activity of knowing things, but are not substantial models of the things. In either interpretation it is a two-story world (in one, the English word "story" is understood in its architectural and in the other in its literary sense); at any rate there is enough ideal quality about the ideas to suggest that they somehow determine or help to determine what goes on in the ordinary world.

This suggestion of supervenient teleology is modified by Aristotle, who is too matter-of-fact to accept anything which looks like a two-story world, with one story beyond our ordinary ken. Plato might account for a table as an exemplification of its idea, the prototypal Table of some other realm, but Aristotle would proceed less poetically, with his four causes, or else with his doctrines of form and matter, potentiality and actuality. Of the four causes of the table, the wood was the material cause, the carpenter the efficient cause, the carpenter's idea of the table the formal cause, and his purpose to make it the final cause. In the other terms, the table is wood which was once only the matter or material for it, but now has the table-form. The wood was once potentially the table; the table is now the corresponding actuality. It is the potential table now realized, the material wood now in-formed. The relationship, we might say, is transitive; it can be extended in either direction. Going backward, the wood, the lumber in the table, is now the actuality of which the tree was once the potentiality, the material. Going in the other direction, the table is capable of further and higher uses; it is material for the merchant or home-maker, it is potential merchandise or furniture. At the lower end of the series is presumably pure potentiality, matter which is not the form of anything. At the upper end of the series is God, pure form, pure actuality, without any potentiality or possibility of becoming anything else. Especially in organisms, Aristotle discerned form and matter; there is in each organism an immanent form or entelechy (from the Greek meaning to have an end in itself) which makes it what it is and keeps it true to its specific nature. In man the form is the soul. Aristotle did not allow ordinary forms to exist or subsist by themselves, although after death the "separable soul" could do so. We find forms in the substances around us, where matter has been "in-formed" with them. In this respect his teleology is immanent; but beyond all the hierarchy of matters and forms, beyond all structures and all processes is God as Prime Mover, the Goal of the world.

The scholastic beneficiaries of the work of Plato and Aristotle fused these Greek ideas about the world with the Semitic supernaturalism of the Christian traditions, as if all the elements naturally belonged together. The Aristotelian forms now become substantial forms, more like Platonic ideas, only not mere prototypes, but ideas in the Mind of God, formal and final causes, God's purposes for the world, and God was believed to work them out as Creator and as Providence.

(3) In the development of the teleological argument some new concepts and various philosophical systems become prominent. After Aristotle, causality is interpreted especially in terms of final causes, with the suggestion that events still to come at the end of a series govern events of the present and past. Considerations of possibility appear in the argument when Leibnitz contends that this is the best of possible worlds. The concepts of unity and order take on peculiar meaning in the work of Kant. In his *Critique of Pure Reason*, he limited our reason to the work of building a world out of appearances, and declared it incompetent to prove the existence of God. In his *Critique of Practical Reason*, for the sake of the moral life, he allowed us to postulate or assume God, freedom, and immortality. Combining these views in his *Critique of Judgment*, he emphasized the unity and order under which we conceive the empirical contents of the world as if they had been given by some intelligence, to which, on practical grounds, since we have to live the moral life, we ascribe aim or purpose.

Kantian in derivation and spirit, although not quite up to the sweep of Kant's postulates about God, is the view that regards the world as telic because it responds to our human purposes and values. We may call this type of teleology *pragmatic:* according to it, any given event A is (the outcome of a series of events) dependent on the prior conscious intention of mind, not essentially superior to ours.

Kant's suggestions about unity reappear on a cosmic scale when Kantianism undergoes its Hegelian transformation, from mind to Mind. We may call this third type of teleology *organismic;* for it, any given event A

is the outcome of an organismic order of events, which are in mutual relationships within the ordering whole. The opposing view of mechanism is held to apply particularly to the parts, and, in contrast to telic processes, to be in some sense fragmentary; or reversible; or, derived from telic processes after they become automatic; or imposed from outside, in contrast to teleology which is internal.

This last difference recalls the difference in Indian philosophy between the Nyaya-Vaisesika system, which requires an eternal factor to keep the elements of the world together, and the more organismic, albeit dualistic and atheistic Samkhya system, in which there is a Self, *Purusha*, for whom things exist, and who profits by the design of things. *Prakriti*, its counterpart, is a systematized unity of parts, a teleological whole.[19]

The organismic view of teleology, with emphasis upon the concepts of wholeness and totality, is characteristic of the Hegelians, particularly Bosanquet, who declares that the teleology of the universe is wholly above and beyond any plan or contrivance of a consciousness, and refers to the perfection and completeness of relations within the whole.[20] In these organismic systems, the parts mutually condition one another, somewhat as in a complete dictionary of the English language each word is defined in terms of other words. But in the dictionary there is one word which, besides being defined in terms of some others, is unique in its relationship to all others. Without it, or the relationships which it indicates, they would not be what they are; they would be only a heap of disorganized fragments, and might not be even that. The unique word is the word "dictionary." So, in the universe, there is one fact which, besides being in ordinary local relationships with other ordinary facts, is in a unique relationship to all the facts. Without it, or the relationship which it brings to expression, they would not be what they are.

They might be only a chaos, they might even not be at all. The unique fact is the fact of mind in us. We must understand the dictionary with the help of the word "dictionary," and the universe with the help of the fact of mind.

Some theories of teleology belong in the idealistic tradition, but emphasize the evolutionary rather than the organismic character of the mind process in the world. Sometimes the process is described in terms almost as personalistic as those used in supernaturalism; God is referred to in terms of consciousness, mind, intelligence, or will, but immanence is stressed rather than transcendence, prior conscious intention is not quite so clearly affirmed, and the other personal attributes are not quite so vivid as in the traditional faith. In his *Development and Purpose*, L. T. Hobhouse maintains that in a system where the parts mutually condition one another, any part which is a cause must not merely determine what follows, but be determined by what follows. If harmony among the parts of the world is implied in the structure of our experience, it must be future. The analysis of the ethical life and of rational thought points to an element of value conditioning reality as a whole, and it is a sound hypothesis that evolution proceeds in accordance with a purpose.[21] E. W. Lyman holds that we must either beg the order and unity of the world, or acknowledge that the order and unity have their source in a creative intelligence, with a purpose which brings into significant correlation our experience of order, of potentiality, of ideal value.[22] Personalists argue similarly from the fact of purposiveness in us to a kindred purposive Mind in the cosmos.

Other writers in their attempts to discern teleology in the evolutionary process have shown less affiliation with idealism. In Bergson's earlier work it was not so evident as it is now that his thinking goes back in the direction of supernaturalism. In a well remembered earlier argument, he contrasts the eyes in the two widely separated phyla, molluscs and vertebrates. With all their differences in origin and structure, the function of the eyes in the two phyla, he says, is simple and similar. Hence, he argues, some impulse or agency must be involved, preserving simplicity and uniformity of function, whatever be the makeshifts of structure. Bergson is a finalist, not a mechanist, and hence must be counted on the side of teleology, although he insists over and over that the vital impulse works freely. He will have no finalism which is merely an inverted mechanism, no process which moves automatically toward an end determined in advance.[23]

Several other writers keep free from both supernaturalism and idealism; they describe the cosmic process as developing in orderly fashion, particularly in the direction of life and mind in us, but the emphasis is upon process, order, and structure, rather than upon personalistic agency. We may call this *evolutionary* teleology: any given event, *A*, is the outcome of a series of events more or less in accord with a natural tendency to produce such events rather than others. Samuel Alexander, in his emergent evolutionism, traced all higher developments to a "Nisus" which moves from Space-time through matter and life to mind and perhaps even beyond mind to "deity." "Nisus" is the Latin word for striving, and the progress of the Nisus, apparently now oriented toward deity, is telic without being consciously purposive.[24] One of the best known arguments for evolutionary teleology is that of L. J. Henderson. He sees in the facts of origin and maintenance of life in the earth (especially in the abundance of carbon, oxygen, hydrogen, and nitrogen, all of which occur in quantities far in excess of any which calculations of probabilities would lead us to expect) some natural connection between the inorganic and the organic. The universe tends to produce life. He thinks that the explanation is perhaps either an unknown mechanistic one, or one in terms of a tendency which works parallel with mechanism without interfering with it, so that matter and energy have an original property, which establishes conditions favorable to life and is to be described as teleological, although it must be remembered that design and purpose are not in question.[25]

It is obvious that by the time the discussion reaches this point, teleology is viewed very differently than in the traditional supernaturalism. In place of supernatural intentions, we now have natural tendencies; supernatural determinations, too, have shrunk to natural terminations. But the terminations, after all, reach ends which are at once so definite, striking, and non-random that they are not regarded as merely the results of chance. The game may be all natural, but somehow the dice are loaded in favor of life and mind.[26]

One step further is taken in Dewey's doctrine of "natural ends," as distinguished from our purposes or "ends-in-view." When we come to think of it, any given event stands out as a kind of terminus, with an aesthetic quality of finality about it. We say "That is *that.*" So we may say simply, for this *eventual* teleology, Any given event, *A*, is the outcome of a series of events. The terminal outcome when anticipated with a view to utilizing or controlling it becomes an end-in-view.[27]

The divergence of the various types of teleology may be illustrated by Darwin's theory of natural selection, with or without Spencer's survival of the fittest. These theories were very damaging to the older supernaturalist teleology, but they may be readily domiciled among the evolutionist teleologies, and even equipped with a more or less personalistic will to live in the struggle for existence. Or, like any other natural process, they may be interpreted in terms of eventual teleology. After all, the universe has come out at such and such a point in such and such a way, and some thinkers do not feel obliged to say more. Various types of vitalistic biology may also be correlated with types of teleology—interventionist vitalism with supervenient, and organismic vitalism with organismic.

As regards pragmatism, the teleological argument can appeal to the pragmatic enthusiasm for trying out reasonable working hypotheses, as well as to the satisfactions resulting from beliefs that the world is purposive rather than a random dance of atoms. Experiences of valuation are frequently regarded as grounds from which to infer a cosmic purposiveness. Lyman, for instance, maintains that the relevance of value to existence, the continuous process by which values find increasing embodiment in existence, and the processes by which disvalues are resisted, point to a conception of purpose as being needful for explanation, not alone in the human realm, but also in regard to the comprehensive character of the cosmos.[28]

(4) For us the most decisive point about supervenient teleology is its traditional appeal to scientific data.[29] Thus with regard to the data of the physical sciences, it is popularly noted that the stars do not collide, but keep in their "appointed" courses, and it is inferred that the Supreme Architect has spaced them out. More technically, in a universe which is held to be subject to the law of entropy and running down to heat death, the fact that it has not yet completely run down is traced to some purposive activity which offsets the law. E. W. Barnes seems to argue that heat death will come unless God intervenes, and therefore God will intervene.[30] The probabilities of distribution of electrons, as indicated in wave-mechanics, have sometimes been interpreted as if the electrons had a rudiment of purpose.

Arguments from the physical sciences have been used to help out teleological arguments in connection with biology, as in some discussions about the age of the earth. In the earlier orthodox days it was held that the earth and all the rest of the universe with it was approaching the age of six thousand years, and this stretch of time was certainly not long enough for chance variations to have produced the marvellous arrangements which we see in plants, animals, and man. Even Helmholtz's venture into the immensities, with its calculation based on the rate of shrinkage of the sun and its conclusion that the whole solar system was some twenty million years old, fell short; the theologians still needed the conscious intention and intervention of a Mind to direct the cosmic process and get it to its present state of adaptation in the time available. To this day, with vastly longer time scales available, it is sometimes held that the world of the sciences shows arrangements of individual elements for which the odds are many millions to one against origin by chance, and the only alternative is origin by design.[31] It is sometimes argued that living organisms and the non-living environment are so different that a Great Intelligence is required for their combination.[32] The harmony of the parts, which in the living organism is on a scale familiar and relatively accessible to study, has made teleological inferences vivid if not inevitable. It has been often pointed out that organisms seem curiously capable of temporarily overcoming the entropic law and raising energies to higher levels of potential than they would have in the inorganic environment.

There are a number of more specific arguments based on data of organic development; they are usually arguments for vitalistic biology, and while they argue for a supervenient or intervenient teleology on the part of a vital force, do not necessarily witness to the existence of the supernaturalists' God. These include a number of arguments from embryology—that tracts or organs are formed in advance of any actual use; that the manner of formation sometimes varies in different species, but

75

leads to similar results; that dissection of parts of embryos does not necessarily prevent normal development; and that in certain regions there appear to be centers of organization for surrounding cells.[33] After birth there are in many species striking data concerning the regeneration of lost parts and organic adaptation. For instance, an animal may come to produce from its internal resources substances typically obtained from outside, as when gas in the air bladder of a fish is secreted from the blood.

Arguments drawn from facts of protective coloration of some species and the camera-like adaptations of which the human eye is capable, are familiar. Fraser-Harris argues that since the living organisms have parts which are by man imitated in constructed tools, there is intelligence and purpose in the realm of the living.[34]

Other arguments are based upon intricate societal and inter-societal adjustments. One example is the adjustment of guests and hosts in parasitism, and another which is very much used is the cross-fertilization of flowers through the unwitting agency of insects.

Some of the biological data take us into the psychological sciences, where the unsolved riddles of instinctive behavior are capable of teleological interpretation. Support for teleological arguments may be drawn from animism's interpretations of psychological data, as in W. McDougall's "hormism." [35] Knudson has an argument from epistemology, that the amazing complexity of the parallelism between thought and things requires cosmic purposeiveness for its explanation.[36]

The applied sciences are drawn upon for a widely used argument, to the effect that mechanism is exemplified in mechanical devices or machines, and that machines are designed by intelligence.

The data of sociology and human history are often declared to exhibit evidence of design and of the continued working of a beneficent Providence. The

Bridgewater treatises even argued for teleology from the supremacy of conscience, the "inherent pleasure of the virtuous, and misery of the vicious affections," and "the capacity of the world for making a virtuous species happy." [37] Recent thought has been more matter-of-fact, but has frequently seen in the fact of moral achievement against odds evidence that God is in his heaven and that things may be made right in the world.

THE MORAL ARGUMENT

Like the Atharva Veda among the Vedas, Kant's moral argument for the existence of God was a late arrival, but it has won for itself a place among the classics. It was Kant's substitute for the other three arguments, which he held to be defective because, limited as they were to reasoning based on experience, they pretended to reason with absolute certainty about matters which lay outside the province of experience. But this limitation, after all, concerns the pure reason, and for Kant man has also something else to do; he must meet the demands of the moral life. Kant had a severe background, and for him the demands of the moral life crystallized in an exceedingly strong sense of duty, so overwhelming that he could see no escape from it. Duty, with its imperative, was categorical; it could not be evaded. But Kant could see in himself no strength to meet its inexorable demands, and could see in the theoretical reason no way to satisfy himself of the existence of a God to insure the outcome. Hence man's awful problem: he must perform his duty without being able to reason his way to a Power to help his impotence. Man has, in fact, only one resource; that is, in those capacities of reason which, even though they are not constitutive, are regulative. Such a reason will not help much in theory, but it may be just the thing, apart from theoretical questions, to help in practice. While theoretically we can not prove the existence of a God to give us victory in the relentless moral struggle, practically we can postulate or assume whatever is necessary to insure our success in the struggle.

Kant was convinced that practical reason, in order to meet the moral situation, must make three great postulates—the existence of God, the freedom of the human will, and the immortality of the soul. Specifically, we postulate God as the ruler in the kingdoms of reason and of nature, who will establish the harmony demanded by the moral consciousness between the theory of moral worth and happiness in the actual world. If we are to get the force of Kant's argument, we must see in it not the breath-taking assumptions, nor the goal of the moral life envisaged as happiness, nor the fact that he later changed his view and allowed reason a somewhat closer approach to God, but the strength of the original inner moral demand.

The moral argument lacks the age and something of the prestige of the others. Popular beliefs to the effect that there must be some reinforcement and reward for our goodness, as well as supports for the argument in the Bible and the creeds, are not very definitely developed in connection with it. Nor does it use many abstract concepts, unless notions about values be called abstract. Like the ontological argument, the moral argument gets its chief support from the philosophies.

Early Hegelianism in a large way justified it, but in doing so almost drowned it. With a less introverted sense of duty than Kant's, and with far more flair for huge cosmic concepts, Hegelianism thought less of cautious postulates and more of vast processes rounding out man's full personality within the Absolute Spirit. In the midst of so much theory, practice is almost a by-product; it is a stage on the way to complete realization, and complete realization is intellectual, rational. The later idealism is less rationalistic and is often phrased more concretely and warmly in terms of values; we require a great Person to save us from littleness and insure our self-realization. Notable indications of the trend away from rationalism are the Ritschlian theology, with its attempt to disregard metaphysics and ground ethical theism on value judgments, and Höffding's famous definition of religion as faith in the conservation of values.

In the later idealism the moral argument is notably developed by W. R. Sorley and J. B. Baillie. Sorley's procedure is first to indicate a place in the world for judgments of value and then to make an argument with respect to their ground. The question is not so much, Does God exist? as, How is the universe to be understood and interpreted? From his idealistic standpoint, Sorley insists that there is similarity and kinship between judgments of value and judgments of existence. Both involve universals; there is a universal element in all correct moral judgments, as in all judgments about existence. Both are regarded as valid, independently of any individual minds which entertain them. Persons are conscious of values and of an "over-individual" ideal of goodness, which they regard as having undoubted authority. But how could this eternal validity stand alone, and not as the expression of the thought and will of an Eternal Mind? God must therefore exist and his nature be goodness.[38]

Baillie is closer to the Kantian tradition, which he interprets in intuitional fashion. For one's belief that he must do his duty, no reason can be given or required. We are thrown back upon an insight arising from the demands of our moral and spiritual natures. Baillie sees that the essential concern of religion is the relation of value to reality, or of human life to its background; but for everything in religion which goes beyond the direct intuition of moral value there is required only the activity of faith.[39]

79

Other writers, less fully committed to the presuppositions and conclusions of idealism, take the facts of life
somewhat more empirically. The argument commonly
takes one of two forms: it proceeds either from human
moral values and goodness to God as their ground and
guarantor, or else from human evils and failures to God
as necessary to overcome them and turn defeat into victory. Here is a broad field for the contrasts of optimism
and pessimism. At one extreme we find the view that
human needs, in the very nature of things, are met by
reality that has engendered them. At the other extreme
we have poignant, lyric words from those who, like
Kierkegaard and Unamuno, have cried out of the depths
when their hearts were overwhelmed.

Pragmatism with its emphasis upon human emotions,
satisfactions, and volitions might have been expected to
bring powerful aid to the moral argument, but there are
not many direct indications of it; both pragmatism and
the argument were probably caught in too many cross-
currents. Some influences which helped to formulate
pragmatism are expressed in the later forms of the argument in terms of values.

Modifications of the old moral argument which may
be of considerable importance, corresponding to a similar modification of the old teleological argument, come
from the evolutionisms, with their tracing of a cosmic
process, tendency, trend, *élan*, or Nisus, moving in matter, life, and mind to the attainment, at the human level,
of valuations and personalities dignified by religious experience. In these philosophies the goodness of the
world, like its purposiveness, is often regarded more
as inherent than as intended, and the conclusions about
God are often quite different from those of the traditional moral argument. But the good in the world is
given positive status, and the evils at least serve to point
a contrast. In the work of H. N. Wieman, the "value-
making process," the "growth of good," is God.[40]

Sometimes the moral argument is given a rather intimate, direct, and personal turn; it is said that we would be convinced of God's existence if we ourselves were better men. This turn is not confined to any one school. Plato makes the claim that what is acknowledged by better men has more weight than what is acknowledged by inferior men.[41] The Fourth Gospel makes Jesus say that if any man wills to do God's will, he shall know the teaching.[42] Pascal urges men to understand their incapacity to believe, and to labor to convince themselves, not by increase of the proofs of God, but by the diminution of their passions.[43]

SOME NON-CLASSICAL ARGUMENTS

Besides the four classical arguments, at least a dozen others appear in the history of thought, and at least some of them strengthen the four. The best known is the argument "from the consent of mankind"—the fact that religious interests are so widespread, and the statement that no savage tribes have been found without at least the rudiments of a religion, if not of belief in God.

The scholastics developed the "henological" argument, to the effect that the diversity of things, which after all has a certain unity, must point to a unified cause beyond them. It is said that being, goodness, truth, unity, are transcendental perfections, beyond the limits which restrict other perfections. When one and the same perfection is found in different beings it is impossible that they should possess it independently; all must receive it from the same source.[44]

Allied with the henological argument is the argument from simplicity, that pure goodness is absolutely simple and uncaused, but at the same time real.[45] Thomas Aquinas had a complicated argument from motion to an unmoved Prime Mover. The argument was worked out with elaborate considerations of potentiality and actuality, infinites, and wholes and parts. Two of his other arguments concerned capabilities of being and degrees of perfection.[46]

Poets and artists often say that beauty is their religion, and experiences of beauty are widely held either to bear direct witness to the existence of God, or to strengthen beliefs forming for other reasons. These and other tendencies to interpret value in theistic terms may be summed up in an "axiological" argument, and may be expressed in pragmatic terms. It may even be urged that in case of doubt we should get into the struggle and by our valuations help to make God more real.

As examples of contemporary thought, two men who have been variously influenced by Whitehead have made some suggestions concerning the problem. F. S. C. Northrop argues on materialistic grounds for a "macroscopic atom" as a boundary condition of the physical universe, serving as a frame of reference for measurements and congesting all its parts into their observed relationships. This primary substance with a determinate conscious experience he calls the body of God.[47] A panpsychist view worked out by Charles Hartshorne argues that there must be an ultimate subject of change, a cosmic memory, and a world anticipation, and that God unifies all these into a single first principle.[48] God is nature as infinitely intelligible and profoundly lovable.[49]

Recurring throughout long periods are tendencies to interpret data of occultism as evidence for the existence of God. Sometimes the field of psychical research or "parapsychology" is held to yield something. For example, W. McDougall regards work on telepathy and survival, together with facts connected with mathematical prodigies, as strengthening the theistic hypothesis.[50]

Finally, to all these arguments is sometimes added one made up of the others and held to combine them with a synthetic strength of its own.[51]

REFERENCES

[1] D. Cardinal Mercier, *Manual of Modern Scholastic Philosophy,* transl. T. H. Parker and S. A. Parker, 1916-7, Vol. II, pp. 40*f*; *cf.* G. H. Joyce, *Principles of Natural Theology,* 1923, pp. 61, 83.

[2] D. Cardinal Mercier, *op. cit.,* Vol. II, p. 41.

[3] *Ibid.,* pp. 43*f.*

[4] B. P. Bowne, *Personalism,* 1908, Chap. IV.

[5] A. N. Whitehead, *Science and the Modern World,* 1925, p. 243.

[6] Thomas Aquinas, *Commentary on the Physics,* viii, Lect. 2; M. D'Arcy, *Thomas Aquinas,* 1930, p. 183.

[7] L. S. Keyser, *The Problem of Origins,* 1926, pp. 27*f.*

[8] E. Caird, *Introduction to Philosophy of Religion,* 1881, p. 133.

[9] A. Seth Pringle-Pattison, *The Idea of God in the Light of Recent Philosophy,* 1917, pp. 304*f.*

[10] G. H. Joyce, *op. cit.,* p. 70.

[11] See *Nature,* 128, 1931, p. 699; A. S. Eddington, *The Expanding Universe,* 1933.

[12] J. A. Crowther, in F. Mason, ed., *The Great Design,* 1936, p. 61; cf. E. W. Barnes, *Scientific Theory and Religion,* 1933, p. 191*ff.*

[13] E. A. Milne, *Relativity, Gravitation, and World Structure,* 1935, pp. 134*f,* 138*f.*

[14] See Anselm, *Proslogium,* ii.

[15] F. Ueberweg, *History of Philosophy,* transl. G. S. Morris, 1888, Vol. I, pp. 381*ff.*

[16] R. Descartes, *Discourse on Method,* Part IV.

[17] W. E. Hocking, in C. Barrett, ed., *Contemporary Idealism in America,* 1932, pp. 53*ff.*

[18] See *ibid.,* pp. 58*ff.*

[19] M. Hiriyanna, *Outlines of Indian Philosophy,* 1932, p. 279.

[20] B. Bosanquet, *The Principle of Individuality and Value,* 1927, pp. xxiii*f,* 118.

[21] L. T. Hobhouse, *Development and Purpose,* 1913, pp. 338*ff.* For an idealistic view, see W. R. Matthews, *The Purpose of God,* 1936.

[22] E. W. Lyman, *The Meaning and Truth of Religion,* 1933, pp. 285*f.*

[23] H. Bergson, *Creative Evolution,* transl. A. Mitchell, 1911, p. 39.

[24] *Cf.* S. Alexander, *Space, Time, and Deity,* Vol. II, pp. 368*ff.*

[25] L. J. Henderson, *The Fitness of the Environment,* 1913; *The Order of Nature,* 1917, esp. pp. 190*ff,* 205*f.*

[26] *Cf.* W. P. Montague, *Belief Unbound,* 1930, p. 73.

[27] J. Dewey, *Experience and Nature,* 1926, pp. 95, 101.

[28] E. W. Lyman, *op. cit.,* pp. 288*f.*

[29] *Cf.* F. Mason, ed., *op. cit.,* pp. 36, 60, 110, 231, 272.

[30] E. W. Barnes, *op. cit.,* p. 240.

[31] A. Lunn and J. B. S. Haldane, *Science and the Supernatural,* 1935, p. 260.

[32] G. H. Joyce, *op. cit.,* p. 145.

[33] See H. Driesch, *The Science and Philosophy of the Organism,* 1908, Vol. I, pp. 115-164. The work on "organizers" is mainly due to H. Spemann.

[34] D. Fraser-Harris, in F. Mason, ed., *op. cit.,* p. 272.

[35] A. C. Knudson, *The Philosophy of Personalism,* 1927, p. 304.

[36] See W. McDougall, *Modern Materialism and Emergent Evolution,* 1929, esp. Chap. III, and pp. 120ff.

[37] *The Bridgewater Treatises.* . . . 8 vols., 1833, Vol. I, 1, "Notice" and Part I, Chapter II; Vol. I, 2, Chapter X.

[38] W. R. Sorley, *Moral Values and the Idea of God,* 1918, pp. 70, 189, 293, 352f; *cf.* Sorley, in J. H. Muirhead, ed., *Contemporary British Philosophy,* second series, 1925, p. 260.

[39] J. B. Baillie, *The Interpretation of Religion,* 1928, pp. 85, 244ff., 345f.

[40] See below. Chapter XII.

[41] Plato, *Sophist,* 246.

[42] John, 7, 17.

[43] B. Pascal, *Thoughts,* transl. C. Kegan Paul, 1885, p. 99.

[44] G. H. Joyce, *op. cit.,* pp. 106, 109.

[45] *Ibid.,* pp. 114f.

[46] Thomas Aquinas, *Summa Theologica,* Part I.

[47] F. S. C. Northrop, *Science and First Principles,* 1931, pp. 108f, 120ff., 273.

[48] C. Hartshorne, in O. H. Lee, ed., *Philosophical Essays for A. N. Whitehead,* 1936, p. 219: *Beyond Humanism,* 1937, pp. 14ff.

[49] *Ibid.,* pp. 19, 23. See below, Chapter VIII, n. 29.

[50] W. McDougall, in E. H. Cotton, ed., *Has Science Discovered God?,* 1933, pp. 152ff.

[51] W. K. Wright, *A Student's Philosophy of Religion,* 1935, p. 371.

CHAPTER VI

SUPERNATURALISM: (III) CRITICISMS OF ITS POINTS OF STRENGTH

Supernaturalism is too firmly intrenched to be lightly set aside, but it is being subjected to a kind of war of attrition. At each of the strong points we have noted, it is opposed by critics who have not been able to destroy it, but who are well supplied with ammunition to keep it under steady fire.

(1) Of course supernaturalism is ancient, but in the eyes of its trained critics this fact points the way to its basic weakness. They see in its ancient features, admirable as these sometimes are, only a mask for the archaic and the primitive. Supernaturalism, they say, is unmistakably derived from the animisms, spiritisms, and mythologies of early man, if not from primitive manaism, with its attitudes and beliefs which treated objects of the environment as possessing mana, or mysterious, more or less diffused power. Such power was, in totemism, regarded as the peculiar bond between a tribe and its totem object. In magic it was thought to be transferred from a person to an object, or from one person to another person. When a man died, the power, often identified with his breath, went forth from his body. It was supposed thereafter to go its separate way, being in its new state what we have learned to call his "spirit"; the word for this, in several languages besides our own, is equivalent or akin to the word for "breath," as we can see in our word "respiration." The heroic deeds of ancestors were transferred to the ancestral spirits and celebrated in song and story by minstrels and mythmakers, with such lofty phrasing that the ancestral spirits came to be thought of as superhuman, as demons, demigods,

and at length as gods. The amalgamation of lesser spirits into greater spirits, or gods, was correlated with the absorption of conquered tribes by those which had proved to be superior. So supernaturalism, with all its glorious traditions, rests on the fancies, superstitions, compensations, and projections of primitive man, who did not know any better than to discern a man in the moon, hear an interlocutor in the echo, see the mirage as a reality, and create the gods in his own image. Mankind is like a lens, projecting upon the screen of nature a magnified (never a mere life size) human image of himself. The tendency, begun in primitive days, has been continued by force of habit and custom. It has been reinforced by the dread of the unfamiliar things, the lack of adequate knowledge of obscure drives and psychological traits, the ease of projection and personification to account for them or for anything unusual, and the all too human tendency to prefer bright pictures to hard facts. In Barthianism, particularly, the post-war psychology of depression is unmistakable, and has resulted in overheated emotions, exaggerated doctrines, and an overworked escape mechanism. The doctrines of supernaturalism are, as Hegel long ago pointed out, essentially pictures—not, as Hegel held, of some pure thought or lofty universal, but merely of man himself in some of his manifold moods or imaginings. If we take away the anthropomorphism from the gods, say the critics, the picture fades, and only the projection machinery, man in nature, remains.

(2) Much of the same criticism applies to the argument that supernaturalism has been so widespread and simple. Obviously such matters are not established by majority vote, especially when so many millions on the majority side are so naive. Moreover, supernaturalism is not as widespread as it formerly was; Leuba has shown repeatedly that its hold has been noticeably weakened in the scientific atmosphere,[1] and in connection

with the Russian experiment there has been an open, organized, and incisive attempt once for all to get rid of such a shield for economic exploitation, such "opium of the people." Its simplicity is, for the critics, too transparent. Its account of the world and God seems like a docile child's picture book; the time comes when, attractive and temporarily helpful as such brightly colored things may be, they have to be outgrown and the child has to learn to read plain, black, cold type. Men who have been reared in the picturesque supernaturalist theology have to grow up to understand the world in the cold symbols of the scientist. It will not do to urge a simple childlike faith; the childlike is here too childish. Nor will it avail to bid such men become as little children; the apostle met that argument when he wrote "In malice be ye children, but in understanding be men." And they are hardly men in understanding, who in the name of theological obscurantism disparage science and culture, dismiss high human achievements as "the enticing words of man's wisdom" and seek to turn young people from universities which have resolutely set out to understand the universe. Sometimes the emotionalism displayed reminds one of the problem child's "tantrum" when deprived of his picture book.

(3) Against supernaturalism's claims of authority it is urged that men have been too easily impressed or overcome by them. For one thing, conflicting claims are made in various religions and sects, no one of which, in the modern world, can seriously claim exclusive revelation. The Hindus, Jews, and Muslims, for instance, rely on authoritative books, but the books are different; the Christians accept the Jewish Old Testament, but add a New Testament of their own. Within Christianity, too, there are differences such as we noted, with some groups professing virtual monopoly of authoritative revelation. The Barthian theology holds that God has spoken, but in the framework and almost in the vocabu-

lary of Protestant dogmatics. The sinner who accepts this revelation attains the true, inward "resurrection of the dead"; but the billions of men in the other majestic faiths seem to be left in silence and condemnation. What, ask the critics, can possibly be left of a supernaturalism which is torn by such internal conflicts?

Of the different conceptions held within Christianity, those which affirm the authority of the Church and the Pope may be affected indirectly by criticisms levelled against the authority of the Bible, with its records of Christian origins, and attacked directly by criticisms of the apostolic succession and of the doctrine of infallibility. The apostolic succession is the long line of men in whom, in one generation after another throughout the centuries, the alleged revelation and whatever power goes with it has been entrusted, but any break or cleft or conflict in the line or any historical uncertainty about its early members must weaken convictions concerning the continuity and the transmission of the delegated authority. Questions are also sometimes raised about papal infallibility, and about the record of the Church in the long warfare of science with theology.[2]

The authority of the Bible is questioned on various grounds. First, other sacred books of other religions make similar insistent claims to literal inspiration and moral authority. When the books are compared, it is found that most of them are ancient and Oriental, and that they exhibit traces of literary usage foreign to us, but common to those lands and times. In the ancient East, traditions accumulated orally long before they were written down. When they were written down, compilations were often made, with materials from several sources combined without much indication of their origins. Interpolations were easy, either by accidents in connection with the transmission of manuscripts, or by design, where writers sincerely felt that they knew what former writers said or ought to have said. There was also an ancient form of "ghost writing," where books were written and instead of carrying the real authors' names, were made to carry the names of famous authors in more remote antiquity. From all these usages together we have in ancient texts a jumble of variant readings, with discrepancies and contradictions. The Bible, which we too often regard as a book, is really a collection of such books, a collection which required a thousand years to write, and which reflects situations as different as any collection of books stretching through ten centuries might be expected to reflect. There is a certain unity of theme about the books of each Testament, but the doctrine that there is complete harmony or "consent of all the parts" can only be saved by the declaration that defects which are now apparent did not exist in the original autograph manuscripts, which of course have long since disappeared. There are further difficulties about the "canon of Scripture"; how do we know that the books, on either the Catholic or the Protestant list, deserve to be included as sacred while other books must fail to pass muster? For all but the great experts among us there are also difficulties of translation, and on some of the most difficult passages the experts disagree among themselves.

If it could be settled to the complete satisfaction of every one just what the text of the Bible is and just what it means, there would still remain questions at issue between the Bible and the sciences. Of course a literature as extensive as that of the Bible contains statements with which the natural sciences, archaeology, and history, using their own methods, either agree or can be interpreted as agreeing. Astronomy may make plausible the darkness of an eclipse at the time of the crucifixion, or geology give a clue to the destruction of Sodom, or archaeology find Hezekiah's inscription in his aqueduct, or history corroborate the Roman occupation of Palestine, and so on. But these corroborations and coincidences, important as some of them are, are quite insufficient to establish many other biblical statements, some of which the same sciences serve positively to undermine. The process of reconciliation, again, requires so much ingenious apology that even when carried through to best advantage, it robs supernaturalism of much of its impressiveness. Sometimes in these matters we find even the staunchest defenders of the faith at odds among themselves; the Fundamentalists pit the Book of Genesis against evolutionary biology, but Mr. Voliva at Zion City regards the Fundamentalists as traitors because they accept the Copernican astronomy!

Traditionally the attempts to establish the authority of the Bible have set a great store by miracles and prophecies. On the side of the critics the tendency is to regard accounts of miracles either as products of the myth-making imagination, or, if the events as reported really occurred, to regard them not as infractions of the laws of nature but as applications of laws which at the time were not understood. For instance, an unusual event reported both in the Christian and the Buddhist scriptures may be put down as a myth which somehow crept from one tradition to the other. In ages innocent of scientific method it is almost incumbent on one religion to tell as remarkable stories as the next one. On the other hand, from what we know of psychotherapy it is clear that a powerful personality like Gautama or Jesus might easily produce in suggestible listeners positive physical benefits and sincere convictions that they had been healed. Similarly, some of the miracles alleged to have been performed before crowds may be accounted for in terms of collective hypnosis, rare or absent in the West but not impossible in the East. The whole subject of miracles is further complicated by the fact that not even the most acute student of the records knows how much the stories of miracles have grown in devout minds, and not even the most critical natural-

ist knows beyond the possibility of exception just what
the laws of nature really are.

With regard to prophecies, the tendency is first to
scrutinize the ancient books for mistranslations and variant readings, and then if necessary to read between the
lines to see that the prophets had a political and economic, as well as a religious message, and that the books,
written with such controversies and crises in view, need
to be interpreted in their settings. For instance, the
famous passage in the eleventh chapter of Isaiah, which
has been translated "a virgin shall conceive and bear
a son," and interpreted as a prophecy foretelling the
virgin birth of Christ, is now more accurately rendered
"a young woman shall conceive, etc." and interpreted
to mean that in the next few years a boy of the new
generation would appear as the deliverer of Israel. The
puzzling apocalyptic literature, like the Books of Daniel
and of Revelation, together with many non-canonical
books, are now seen to refer not to any end of the
world or consummation of the cosmic process, but to be
intended, at one or another of the recurring crises in
Palestine's history, for revolutionary patriots who at
that particular time must circulate their propaganda in
cryptic phrases and ciphers to avoid arrest and its consequences. It is no wonder, then, that 1914 was re-
baptized with the old name Armageddon, or that the
end of the world has not come in accordance with any
of the schedules prepared for it, from the days of William Miller to those of Judge Rutherford. Only a few
of the men of the ancient world could understand those
books in their own times; the books will now bear any
number of fantastic interpretations and reinterpreta-
tions. Sometimes, to be sure, some prophecies have apparently been fulfilled. Where this has occurred, the
critics dismiss it as due either to coincidence; or to the
outworking of deep general principles which the prophets, who were publicists rather than clairvoyants, were

able to discern beneath the surface events of their times; or to actions ordered in accordance with a known prophecy which it was believed would or should be fulfilled.

Other arguments against the literal authority of the Bible are urged on moral grounds. The most devoted champions of the authority of the Bible in matters of science can not sanction the adoption of some of the Old Testament standards of morality; and Christians who meet this by saying that the primitive Old Testament standards were supplanted in the New Testament may face the further difficulty of adaptation of those latter standards to present day situations—difficulties which sometimes make hard going for doctrines of literal authority there.

In some Christian circles the doctrine of the inspiration of the Bible is modified to meet the results of modern studies, and appears in new forms. First, as a halfway station between the literal and the liberal positions, we have the view that the Bible was literally inspired at the times it was written down, but with a kind of allowance or understanding that while it was peculiarly suited to those times, it could be reinterpreted later on. Beyond this, the liberals swing over to other views of inspiration—the poetic, that the Bible is inspired as great works of literature are inspired; the pragmatic, that the Bible is inspired because it is inspiring; and what we may call the filial view, that the Bible is inspired not as the answer to a letter is dictated by a business man to a stenographer, but as the letter is turned over to a son or a trusted assistant to be answered in the spirit in which the younger person has been trained up, but to be expressed in his own words. According to any of these last-named views, the Bible is thus the human record of a divine experience.

Along with such views of the authority of the Bible, there is, especially among the liberals, considerable emphasis on the authority of experience. But then the question arises, what experience, and whose? Granting that one's experiences are consistent, is he to follow them, or accept the diverse judgments which come from the experiences of others? Moreover, if it is a matter of experiences, it will involve emotions and sentiments, and the emotions and sentiments of one's pronounced opponents are often as strongly developed as his own. In such cases, argument is likely to degenerate to mere assertion and reiteration.

The alleged proofs of supernaturalist doctrines and the conclusiveness and finality assumed by supernaturalism turn out to be open to somewhat similar criticisms. The fact is that any so-called conclusive proof involves not merely logical procedures which are dependable, but psychological data which are much more variable. If we start with a world common to everyone and say that the data are whatever that world presents to us, we may go on to define evidence as data which compel belief. But belief, as we saw, is acceptance of an idea into a person's system of ideas, and what compels such acceptance by one person does not at all compel it for another. Inference, which is the development of ideas from other ideas, and proof, which is the result of some of the processes of inference, alike depend upon such systems and thus upon psychological factors and not alone upon logical principles. Conclusions follow premises by the rules of logic, but premises have to be believed by the rules, such as they are, of individual and social psychology. The center of gravity of supernaturalism is not in its proofs, or even in its arguments; it is in its premises, its presuppositions, its psychological attitudes. In a sense it is not the logical upkeep of supernaturalism that is difficult; it is the psychological initial cost. The initial cost seems to be that of making an assertion, which is sometimes elicited by an overwhelming experience, sometimes unopposed, but sometimes made tentatively and even timidly. The upkeep is then for one reason or another—perhaps no stronger than the principle of the chain reflex, by which one response tends to stimulate its own repetition—a matter of making the assertion over and over, until one becomes utterly committed to it and convinced of its truth.

(4) The remarks just made about the variety of experience express a major criticism of the supernaturalist claim to be empirical. Empiricism means an appeal to experience, but properly to controlled, clarified, and criticized experience. The differences between the empirical testimonies of the various religions and sects do not mean that any one of them has been very incisive or critical in its review of the others. They are all too much alike for that, in method and in content; their differences are local and often superficial, and they are not equipped to criticize one another in other than local and superficial ways. Real criticism must come from sources outside them all, and comes with most clearness from the naturalists. Sometimes when the supernatural has received credit for a given result, closer scrutiny is able to trace the result to natural causes, often to quite human factors in the experimenter; the criticisms of supernaturalism on such grounds are similar to those noted in the discussion of the relationships of the Bible and the sciences, and in the discussion of mysticism.

Any claim that supernaturalism can show empirical results in personal life has to meet the criticism that the results are induced by personalities or personal factors which are not supernatural at all, but only subtly natural. Social psychology is familiar with sympathy, or induced feelings; suggestion, or induced ideas; and imitation, or induced actions. Any of these may be of marked influence in religious experience. A person, particularly one who has grown up from childhood in a given group, will tend to have the feelings, ideas, and actions which explicitly or implicitly are shared by his group. More subtle than heterosuggestion, coming

94

from other persons, is autosuggestion, coming from one's self, anywhere from one's subconsciousness to one's "super-ego." There are, as we have indicated, two sides to the problem of autosuggestion, but at all events, testimonies of the supposed presence of God, answers to prayer, forgiveness of sins, immediate guidance by the Holy Spirit, in short the deepest and richest records of religion, have to be understood in a world where autosuggestion is potent, rather than as if there were no such process. In some ways more baffling than auto-suggestion is countersuggestion, the tendency to have a feeling or idea or perform an action which other persons try to prevent or which one tries to prevent for one's self. Some cases of conversion, attributed uncritically to the working of a supernatural Power breaking down a man's opposition, can be interpreted in this way, as well as in accordance with other kinds of suggestion.

(5) The alleged flexibility and convenience of super-naturalism is regarded by its critics as a weakness. It seeks to capitalize a fundamental duality, but duality is after all characteristic of a problem, and supernat-uralism, instead of giving us a solution of its problem, gives us an impressive statement of it. A two-story house is more convenient than a bungalow, especially for storing heirlooms, but there is also more chance of separating things which belong together. Critics can urge against supernaturalism that it is an unnatural di-vision of the world-principles which, if they are not actually one, are too intimately related to be separated in that way. The division between natural and super-natural tends to be identified with that between matter and spirit, but in the case of the latter duality the con-viction deepens that its terms are not opposites; men who never understood either matter or spirit simply took for granted that they were opposites. In the two-story house there is, again, more chance of losing things. When in the division of supernatural and natural, the

natural is taken as the field of the sciences, the tendency
is to think, as did J. A. Thomson, that science deals
with the known, and religion with the unknown.[3] But
with increasing knowledge naturalism tends to be self-
satisfied and declare its independence; a religion left
to deal merely with the unknown will have no way of
distinguishing its field from the unknowable, and, as
with Herbert Spencer, may dissipate itself into a thin
agnosticism. Sometimes also in a two-story house the
upper story fails to harmonize with the lower, and the
result is an architectural atrocity. Santayana years ago
called the world of orthodox supernaturalism "the
clumsy conjunction of an automaton and a ghost." [4]
Freudians think of it all as sublimation of repressed sex
impulses.

Where the adherents of supernaturalism see a system
which breeds sturdy characters and intellectual clearness, its opponents see too much passivity, too much
weak and satisfied reliance upon the supernatural and a
subjection of intelligence to its domination. Critics of
the Barthian mysteries find them shrouded rather than
solved by the dialectic. In the eyes of its critics, the
sharp distinction which supernaturalism sees in the
world makes its sturdy ethics too rigid and its whole
emphasis too eschatological and otherworldly. Other-
worldliness, if it does remember this world at all, is
likely to blacken it beyond recognition; we can not
afford pessimistically and morbidly to abase ourselves,
as the Barthians do, nor to think that emphasis on our
sins enhances the glory of God. Sometimes we escape
this, but on the other hand picture the attainment of
salvation as an immoral combination of a gaunt perfec-
tionist code for this world and, for the Christians, an
anticipated eternity of selfish ease. The Muslims in
their combination use different elements, teaching that
fiery devotion here will earn hereafter the opportunity
for sensual delights.

The conception of a supernatural sharply distinguished from the natural is also attacked as religiously defective. It may elicit our awe, but hardly our love. Especially in the Barthian hyper-supernaturalism, it is conceived as so different and so remote from the ordinary world that we are utterly unworthy of it and can know it only by sacrificing reason in favor of anomaly and paradox, while nevertheless we depend upon it and without it must be altogether lost. For many critics, such terrific contrasts and built up crises lose more for religion than they gain. Nature knows the blackness of the storm cloud and the white purity of the snow; but there are many softer tints, and sometimes the rain is gentle. On the world-scale, too, it is hard to clear Barthianism of provincialism and dogmatism in the face of the non-Christian religions.

(6) Piecemeal supernaturalism is in some ways less open to criticism than is the more sweeping variety; it has, in becoming piecemeal, already yielded to criticisms aimed at the uncompromising features of the older doctrines. The principal question concerns the evidence which is available and the exclusion of alternative explanations. Each single event for which a supernatural agent is invoked can be subjected to more and more incisive criticisms, and so even piecemeal supernaturalism can be weakened by attrition. And if one takes refuge in broad generalizations the critics will either charge that the generalizations are unwarranted or abandon him in the mists.

(7) Whatever may be the agreements and points in common, any ideology which differs from supernaturalism, by the very fact that it does differ, implies some criticism of it. Supernaturalism fails to avail itself of aid from some philosophies which might be regarded as kindred; for instance, occultism has at least tried hard to see a world of spiritual beings, and supernaturalism, even where it has not been polytheistic, has retained its

angels and saints. In such a situation one might expect an alliance, and one does find it in the spiritualist churches, but the vast majority of supernaturalists distrust the spiritualists, as well as more scientifically minded advocates of psychical research, and stand aloof from them, if they do not openly condemn them. Again, mysticism has claimed not merely to see God, but to share his life, and supernaturalism could hardly express its own ideal in more glowing terms. Here again one finds that each frequently reinforces the other, but the supernaturalists who are overwelmed by the doctrine of God's transcendence declare, as we have said, that the mystics are impious in making God immanent. Similarly, absolute idealism is too monistic for the old-fashioned dualistic supernaturalism, although philosophy, like politics, sometimes makes strange bedfellows.

Some pragmatists have, with William James, derived great satisfaction from the fact that for them supernaturalism, whether piecemeal or intact, brings satisfaction, leads to profitable results, or in short, that "it works." But close upon the heels of this follow the criticisms from other pragmatists, first that it does not work in the same way for every one. Critics can point to Goldenweiser's statement that supernaturalism was of real advantage to primitive man, because it placed him in emotional rapport with nature, provided him with a system of interpreting phenomena and realized all his desires;[5] but one can not claim that supernaturalism does all this for modern man. A second and more serious criticism is that for other pragmatists supernaturalism does not work at all; James' eager acceptance of it can be paralleled by Dewey's stalwart rejection. Dewey maintains that supernaturalism tends to deaden our sense of human responsibility;[6] we find it altogether too easy to cast our burdens on the Lord. It is clear that if truth is to be sought in terms of satisfactions, the satisfactions must be scrutinized with more than ordinary care. One must beware of subconscious fears, of desperate clinging to old beliefs because one does not know what else to do, of escape mechanisms, and compensations which in espousing supernaturalism uncritically follow the line of least resistance. Judged from the point of view of social effectiveness, too, supernaturalism has no clear case. It has often made men passive rather than active. There are too many evils in a world reputedly God's world, and too many injustices which, in spite of its prophets, supernaturalism has officially tolerated if not fostered. Some of these appear to be not even up to the level of a human agency at work in the world, to say nothing of a divine power.

Of course there is an answer for the disagreements among the pragmatists; it appears when we remember that both James and Dewey are led by their pragmatism into pluralism. Pluralism might even accept the supernatural as one factor operative in the universe, but would be likely to minimize the effect of that one operative in the midst of so many others. For monotheistic supernaturalism, pluralism would be anathema.

We saw that it is possible to reconcile evolutionism with the action of the supernatural as an initiating cause. But the tendency in evolutionism is to emphasize processes and outcomes rather than beginnings; to understand the world by the aid of principles inherent within it, rather than coming from outside; and to eliminate intervening causes unless, like the environment in natural selection, they bear the credentials of the natural order. Thus, although it is not always hostile to supernaturalism, evolutionism finds more in common with naturalism and flourishes best in that setting. As for realism, it is in some form implied in supernaturalism, but the realisms also are usually more at home with its opponents. Supernaturalism has not made many friends among these philosophies; it has been too self-reliant, too dependent upon its own authorities of the past, who could know but little, and if they had known probably would have cared less for the newer thought. When it has made friends, it has been at the cost of compromise; thus some neo-realists countenance the supernatural but are likely to put it, along with Plato's ideas, among objects not existent but subsistent. Aesthetic naturalism insists that supernaturalism be retained for its beauty's sake, but among the wistfully regarded figments of the imagination. Humanism is indifferent and tolerates supernaturalism where it can not get rid of it. Communism is officially neutral, but as regards many supernaturalist doctrines and practices it is contemptuous and bitter.

(8) Critics see in the faith of supernaturalism, when it is simple, too much that is infantile, docile, or obscurantist, and when it is complicated too much that rests precariously upon simple foundations. If among the many degrees of faith, they try to attain one which is reasonable about supernaturalism, they find that faith tends to run down hill, toward reason. Hence many of them wield the razor to which the supernaturalist William of Occam gave his good name, refuse to appeal to entities that are not necessary, reject the supernaturalist explanations as superfluous, and in their attempts to understand the world turn to the more compact naturalisms which, albeit with some stretching, can be made to serve.

(9) If on the one hand supernaturalism can be credited with whatever strength is found in the arguments for the existence of God, on the other hand it must be charged with their numerous weaknesses. In the next chapter we shall consider these weaknesses before attempting an estimate of the whole position.

REFERENCES

[1] J. H. Leuba, *The Belief in God and Immortality*, 1916; cf. *Harpers Magazine*, 169, 1934, p. 291.

[2] See A. D. White, *History of the Warfare of Science and Theology in Christendom*, 2 vols., 1896.

[3] J. A. Thomson, *Science and Religion*, 1925.

[4] G. Santayana, *Reason in Common Sense*, 1905, p. 211.

[5] A. A. Goldenweiser, *Early Civilization*, 1922, p. 133.

[6] J. Dewey, *A Common Faith*, 1934, pp. 47, 53.

CHAPTER VII

SUPERNATURALISM: (IV) CRITICISMS OF THE ARGUMENTS FOR THE EXISTENCE OF GOD

The chief criticisms of the arguments for the existence of God will be taken point by point in the order used in Chapter V.

AGAINST THE COSMOLOGICAL ARGUMENT

(1) Against the cosmological argument it may be said, first, that the popular views are uncritical. They probably arise from our half-conscious reaction to any dim suggestion that we might undertake to duplicate or imitate some portion of the world around us; the cosmological argument has in it a pronounced anthropomorphic strain. Moreover, while it is true enough that a universe which was made would require a Maker, this anthropomorphism begs the question. Perhaps the world simply grew, and if it did it does not necessarily require a Grower. As C. D. Broad puts it, "If you start with a sufficiently narrow and inadequate view of nature, you will require a God to get you out of it." [1] Many traditional theories of nature have assumed that nature is virtually dead, but this is only an assumption. Etymologically it is an unnatural assumption, for the word "nature" as we get it from the Latin means "that which is about to be born," and there is in Greek a similar association of meanings. The belief in a Creator is not universal; the Buddhists and Jains, especially, consider it utterly inadequate. With regard to the world of law and a Law-giver, there is of course an ambiguity; natural law means a prolonged regularity in events, and

does not require a Law-giver any more than it requires a lawyer.

(2) Besides the general criticisms which are directed against authoritarianism, there is for the cosmological argument in its Christian form a specific criticism which is quite incisive. It is that important passages in the Old and New Testaments do not agree in their accounts of the origin of the world. The Book of Genesis contains the classical Hebrew account, that "in the beginning God created the heaven and the earth." The Hebrew verb is one suggesting "to make," and the verse gives us the basic statement of the cosmological argument. But there is another account of the world's origin in the Christian Bible, and another book which opens with the very words "In the beginning." This is the Fourth Gospel, with its profound prologue: "In the beginning was the Word, and the Word was with God, and the Word was God." The passage marks the incorporation into Christianity of the doctrine of the Logos, or Word, or principle of reason, or reasonableness, which ancient thinkers regarded as the first of a series of emanations, proceedings from the Primal Source, or God. In the King James version of the English Bible the prologue presently continues, "All things *were made* by him; and without him was not anything *made* that *was made*." Then, after an interval, "as many as received him, to them gave he power *to become* the sons of God." In the Greek original the words which we have italicized are from the Greek verb γίγνομαι. The problem of the meaning and proper translation of this verb is complicated, and there is some justification for rendering it in forms of the verb "to make." But the primary meaning of the Greek verb is, without question, "to become." If it is translated as "to make" it brings the Greek into conformity with the Hebrew verb in Genesis, but at the same time stifles what might have been in Christian thought a profound philosophy of development. If this

philosophy had been worked out it might have weakened the Semitic cosmological argument and might even have provided a biblical basis for the supposedly anti-biblical philosophy of evolutionism!

The Church Fathers should not be blamed too much for their unmanageable doctrine of "creation from nothing"; they were driven to that appalling leap under pressure from the dualistic world-system of the Manichaeans, who held in Zoroastrian fashion that God was opposed by another principle, and had fashioned the world as it is out of such material. This meant that God had encountered limitations which for the Fathers were intolerable; hence they sought to avoid them by the dubious expedient of calling them "nothing." [2]

(3) The notion of beginnings is obviously framed from our experience of the various parts or fragmentary events of the world and their relationships. The first criticism of it is that perhaps we have no right to apply it to the universe as a whole. If we do thus apply it, we are next faced with Kant's famous antinomy; [3] our attempts to answer the problem involve us in contradictions. On the one hand, it is possible to argue that the world had a beginning in time. Unless there were such a beginning, up to a given moment an infinite series of successive states of things must have passed away; but this is impossible, since an infinite series could never have been completed. On the other hand, it is possible to argue that the world had no beginning. If it had a beginning, it must have been preceded by empty time, but no "coming to be" is possible in empty time. The cosmological argument usually adopts the first answer; many of its opponents adopt the second. As we shall see later in more detail, it is difficult if not impossible to judge between them.

If one chooses to answer the question as the cosmological argument does, ascribing the beginning to God, further difficulties arise. The theological answer may overawe the logical question, but it does not answer it. Logically, we may still go on to ask, What began God? and What began whatever that was which began God?, and so on, in an infinite regress which continually breaks away from Aristotelian attempts to stop it. If we say God had no beginning, or that the Prime Mover was himself unmoved, we are involved in antinomies which are no less puzzling for being remote.

The concept of causality has been subjected to two notable critiques. The older is the work of David Hume, to the effect that the idea of causation arises when our ideas interpret mere unvarying successions among our impressions. The more recent critique grows out of the Heisenberg principle of uncertainty or indeterminacy, and maintains that scientific determination of fine-scale causation in nature involves detection of coincidences, and that any attempt to detect these must involve measurements by the aid of light-rays which themselves disturb the minute electronic processes under investigation.[4] The cosmological argument may evade the criticism of Hume, not in the Kantian fashion by accepting it and constructing a mental world in accordance with it, but by saying, with Sorley, that the universe is created only once, and there is in this case no question about succession.[5] The argument may evade the more recent criticism, either by maintaining that inability to describe causation in detail is no ground for denying it, or by taking statistical determinations as sufficient.

If these criticisms are successfully met, the cosmological argument runs into other difficulties about causation similar to those about beginnings. Primitive ascriptions of unusual or overpowering events to causes distinct from their effects are reflected even in the refined arguments of the scholastics: all of these together, when applied to questions about the universe, may be criticized in two ways, one negative and the other positive. The first criticism says, with the naturalists, that ordinary things which are unique and overpowering can be accounted for in terms of the laws of nature, and that the utterly unique and overpowering universe of nature does not need anything distinct from it to cause it, but is quite self-sufficient and able to supply in its own behalf as much of an account as can be given of anything. In a second and more positive set of criticisms, a causal explanation of the world is sought, but sought in some process, principle, or power not outside the world and not clearly distinct from it, but immanent within it.

Some variants of the cosmological argument which involve concepts of being or existence and non-being or non-existence are discussed in neighboring paragraphs or in a later chapter. When the doctrine of God's aseity is analyzed, God becomes his own ground, and so to speak, stands behind the scenes for himself; or else we have the baffling antinomy that God does, and also does not stand in such a relationship to himself.

The personalists and other idealists interpret the relationship of the primary personal reality to the universe not so much in terms of cause and effect as of ground and consequent, and hence are somewhat removed from the traditional creationism, although they suggest similar logical difficulties. The pluralistic personalists maintain that it is beneath the dignity of human persons to have been created.

Scholastic and other attempts to escape from the dangers of infinite regress bring other criticisms and questions. How, for instance, are we to know when in passing along the series of effects, we are to make the "leap to infinity," [6] or elevate one member of the series to the unique dignity of an uncaused cause? [7] These criticisms apply to deism as well as to theism.

Appeals to infinity on behalf of the cosmological argument may easily be made to work either way. For example, it is sometimes said that no infinite being would limit itself by creating a world distinct from itself; but on the other hand Sorley held that to deny the power of the infinite to limit itself is to deny the infinity of its power, and to make the existence of the finite impossible.[8] Does an infinite God, then, create or not?

There are similar difficulties with respect to absoluteness. If God is absolute, how can he be troubled with a world? But if he is absolute, he must be absolute relatively to something, and what is this, if not the world? As Lovejoy says, such dual dialectic has dominated many generations.[9]

The scholastic doctrines which see God as actuality and the material world as potentiality, or which regard God as necessary and the world as contingent, are developed so subtly and with so many evasive meanings that they are difficult to criticize in any brief compass. Until we come to a more detailed discussion, much may be compressed in the statement that it is hard enough to fix the meaning of actuality, but that it is strangely futile to try to ascribe any other than arbitrary content to notions of potentiality, possibility, contingency, and necessity.[10]

In their bearing on the cosmological argument, the notions of necessity and existence, like those of beginning and causality, were elaborately criticized by Kant, but his criticisms are so involved in subtleties, in peculiar uses of terms, and in presuppositions, that an attempt to make all of them clear would require a book about Kant, rather than about God. Kant maintained that the cosmological and teleological arguments for the existence of God depended upon the ontological argument, and that the last named went beyond the range of certainty accessible to limited human reason. As we have seen, he criticized these arguments by "pure reason," apparently in order that he might by "practical reason" advance his own moral argument.

Kant also criticized the idea of perfection when applied to any transcendent reality. On practical grounds, too, it is strange to think of ascribing perfections to a Creator in view of the imperfections of the creatures and the evils among which their lot appears to be cast.

(4) When the contributions from contemporary science are studied in the light of the foregoing criticisms, they appear to come not so much from the sciences as from the scientists. It should also be noted that on scientific grounds the theories of the "expanding universe" are still in the debatable stage.[11]

AGAINST THE ONTOLOGICAL ARGUMENT

The ontological argument in the form given it by Anselm and Descartes has been criticized more constantly and incisively than any of the other classical attempts to demonstrate the existence of God. Some of the most telling criticisms have come from churchmen; the argument is rejected by Thomas Aquinas and other Roman Catholic theologians on the ground that it can be doubted, and requires an active faith. Some of the scholastic and many non-scholastic criticisms can be summed up in the statement that the argument from a definition holds only if the object of the definition exists, but does not avail to demonstrate that existence, even though the definition and the object are held to be unique.

In the *Critique of Pure Reason*, Kant put forth all his powers against the ontological "proof," with the idea that in disposing of it he was disposing of the old cosmological and the "physicotheological" (since in part called the teleological) proofs at the same time. In phrases which passed into the history of philosophy, he declared that our minds are not adequate in such a problem. Being, or existence, is no predicate which can be added to the other predicates of a subject of which we are thinking and thus increase the sum of reality. A hundred real, existent thalers (dollars), he said, do not contain the least coin more than a hundred conceived or imagined thalers. All propositions about existence, he maintained, are synthetic propositions; they affirm of their subjects attributes not contained in them or in our experience, but which go beyond them. They can not be demonstrated merely by reasoning. So the concept of existence as applied to God is, for Kant, regulative but not constitutive; it is useful for guiding our thinking, but ought not to be regarded as a statement about a reality beyond our range.

The ontological argument in its later idealistic and pragmatic forms has to face the criticisms levelled against these philosophies, considered in chapters devoted to them.

AGAINST THE TELEOLOGICAL ARGUMENT

Just as considerations which favor the cosmological argument can be made to support the teleological argument or to correspond to others which support it, so criticisms used against the one can be used against the other.

(1) With particular reference to the teleological argument, the popular opinion that the world as designed requires a Designer is declared to be weak and anthropomorphic. Because we deal with objects in our environment by purposive action is no sign that the environment itself has originated from the purposive action of a Mind greater than ours. Such arguments are declared to be the results of loose reasoning from analogy; or of reasoning from a particular to a universal; or the use of the method of agreement without the checks provided by other inductive methods; or the uncritical supposition that the rational explanation of a thing produces the thing itself.

(2) Against authoritarian views regarding God's purposes it may be urged that at all events those purposes are difficult to discern, and if discerned are often

difficult to justify. In the Bible and the creeds they sometimes seem archaic, over-emotional, provincial, and withal not conceived for the modern world. Almost as old as the teleological argument itself are the criticisms which place it in a dilemma: either the world as we have it is the expression of God's purpose, or it is not; but if it is, then God is responsible for the defects and evils in it, and if it is not, God is not in command of the situation. Hence God is either not all good or else not all powerful. The strongest of all arguments against teleology is the appalling array of the world's evils. Every theology and theodicy is tormented by them. It makes little difference whether we distinguish between the so-called natural evils, like earthquakes, and moral evils, like murders, or whether we lump them all together; singly or in groups, they are the hardest challenge that religion has to meet. Even the organismic systems which, as in the "composition theory," regard all evils as eventual goods have to deplore the fact that goods must be so disguised, and the systems which make evil an illusion have to put up with a world containing such deceptions. If, mastering all these difficulties, we suppose that the world as we have it is the result of God's purposes, then for God's own sake we must add that the purpose must include more than as yet appears, and thus draw upon faith, which means to suspend argument, and sometimes to suspend reason. In a time when nations are plunged into an abyss of tragedy which makes unnumbered hopes and loves seem futile, such faith is more than ever hard to maintain.

(3) When we examine the abstract concepts which are cited in aid of the teleological argument, we find that since purposes are on the whole harder to discern than causes, arguments in favor of them are likely to be more arbitrary. If one sets out to criticize the cosmological argument, there need be no doubt that ordinary natural events have beginnings and causes; the question is

whether we may affirm the same of the universe as a whole. In the case of the teleological argument, it may be doubted whether ordinary natural events occur as results of purpose, and also whether the universe as a whole does. Here again we face difficulties recalling the Kantian antimonies. It is possible to assert that any event occurs in accordance with a purpose and also that it does not. One can "make up" purposes, even purposes for God, more easily than causes, and assign them to anything from the fall of a sparrow or the jump of an electron to a World War or the precession of the equinoxes; on the other hand one can deny purposiveness to any of these. Similar assertions and denials can be made with regard to the universe as a whole.

Further difficulties appear when we see that just as in the cosmological argument one account of beginnings or causation can always be made the beginning of a fresh question, so in the teleological argument a statement that a process occurs with a view to a certain end can always be made the occasion for a new question concerning an end or purpose still more remote. Corresponding to the problem of the primary cause we thus have the problem of the ultimate end, and, again, a theological answer may not suffice for a logical question. Even a "logical" answer like Aristotle's may be arbitrary.

We said that against the cosmological argument, some critics urge that the universe of nature is self-sufficient, and either needs no first cause or, so to speak, carries its own. As used against the teleological argument, the point about self-sufficiency has special importance. Just as the supernatural cosmologists commonly assume that nature is dead, the supernatural teleologists assume that nature is bad, and that only a purposive universe can be good or afford opportunity for us to achieve good. But it is as reasonable to argue that such good as there is in the universe is inherent as that it is intended and imposed from without.

Arguments about "final causes" are rendered less impressive by the newer work in psychology. This work has taken most of the mystery out of our ordinary purposive activity with its reference to future ends, by tracing it, for instance, to the action of distance-receptors which enable us to react to objects before actual contact; then to the process of conditioning, which enables us to substitute one stimulus or response for another and thus for example to substitute a word or a (purposive) idea for a distant object no longer actually seen; and then to the action of chain or circular reflexes, which makes a response to one stimulus furnish a new stimulus to a further response, and so on. By a combination of all these, a stimulus from an object seen or conceived as at a distance can elicit a response which leads to a secondary stimulus and a secondary response, and so on in sequences long or short, eventually leading in consummatory fashion to the object which was once seen or thought of afar off. So a final cause is a peculiarly persistent pattern in the sensitive tissues of the cerebral cortex; it is a pattern which is already in the neuropsychological organization, working like any other cause, prior to an effect which is subsequent to it in time. We have to distinguish between objects or goals which are not actually attained until some time in the future, and the *representations* of those objects now by present ideas whose significance or meaning is future. The representations, thanks to the principle of circular reflexes, operate as stimuli, and at length produce consummatory effects which now are still future. There is no need to make an unearthly mystery of this process. Whether it is variable, adaptable, or even consciously apprehended or not is beside the point. Granted, as all theories alike must grant, the complexity and intricacy of the nervous system and its unique function, these final causes can be just as mechanistic in their operation as other causes, and any crucial distinction between cosmic principles of mechanism and teleology must be sought elsewhere. When our purposes are traced to their roots in distance reception, processes of conditioning, and the peculiarities of circular reflexes, it appears easier to suppose that the environment in space and time around us is the matrix in which our purposes develop than that it is the result of a purpose so enormously greater than ours.

Leibnitz's statement about the best possible world, as well as other more modest statements about possibilities, are all inadequate in view of the fact that we do not know how good or how bad any possible world may be. For that matter, we do not even know how good or how bad the actual world is, or may possibly be.

Arguments based on ideas of wholes, or the whole, and parts are open to the charge of vagueness, because attempted distinctions between wholes and parts turn out to involve differences of degree between wholes, parts, and their relations which are hard to make precise. It is easy to argue glibly that the whole is prior to the parts, or the parts prior to the whole, or even that each involves the other, without arriving at any very clear ideas about the universe, and without having achieved any convincing argument for purpose.

Many other ideas embedded in the great philosophical systems have to be judged ultimately by considering the systems themselves, as we shall in the detailed studies in other chapters. If with the Kantians or pragmatists we argue that the universe is telic because it conforms to our purposes, we establish either too little or too much. It is hard, and perhaps impossible, for us to find anything that is fully amenable to every purpose of ours, and equally hard or impossible for us to find anything that is not amenable to some purpose. In the former respect, purpose is like Croesus; if it insists upon going to war, it wrecks its own empire. In the latter respect, it is like Midas; everything it encounters is changed into what it is supposed to want.

With reference to organismic systems, the distinction sometimes found between organic, telic action as irreversible and mechanistic action as reversible is open to serious question. The newer views indicate that any process is as likely as not to be irreversible, either because of entropy, or because space and time are measured locally and inadequately, or because the whole universe is itself an "organic mechanism," in which any amount of local or temporary recurrence can not mean the complete reduplication of former occurrences. It is noticeable that with all the current emphasis upon "events," there is no word "revents." But no matter how such discussions turn out, it does not follow that "reversible" processes are not intended, nor that "irreversible" processes are conscious.

We need especially to remember that even if the universe is identified with a great Mind, it does not necessarily follow that the Mind is God's, or that it is at all worthy to be an object of religious devotion; it might be the mind of a joker, a dilettante, or a fiend. For pluralistic idealism the situation is worse still; the universe may be the deliberation and dispute of jokers, dilettantes, fiends, and gods together!

Bergson's point about the current finalism being only an inverted mechanism is true enough, but it may easily confuse the problem of mechanism and teleology with that of fatalism and freedom. Mechanism does not necessarily mean absence of contingency; a mechanistic world might exhibit novelty and be as variable, as indeterminate, or as "creative" as any other. Nor does teleology necessarily mean contingency; a world which is telic might, for that very reason, be set and invariable.

Evolutionary teleology succeeds in bringing to our attention the fact that we as persons have somehow appeared in the midst of the world process and the opinion that, whatever else is to be said about it, it has at least produced us and whatever good we can discern or achieve. This, as we shall see later on, is of very great importance for a philosophy of religion, and we shall try to develop it in adequate ways. Only it should be pointed out here in the first place that this is not equivalent to the old-fashioned supervenient teleology, and in the second place that Henderson's chemistry and calculations of probability, and Dewey's theory of aesthetic finalities or natural ends can be so criticized as to make them say virtually no more than that the world process has come out in the way in which it has come out. Teleology must beware of tautology.

When teleology is pared down to its eventual form, everything that is said about it may be said in terms of mechanism. For mechanism, too, any given event is the outcome of a series of events, and, like any other event in any other series, it may be interpreted as if it were an end for the universe. The teleological interpretation singles out a given event and regards it as in some special sense an end of the universe, but mechanism may single out the same event, and, since it also has issues and outcomes and ends, interpret the event as one of its own.

(4) Concerning the so-called scientific confirmations of the belief that the universe is purposive, opponents trace them here also not so much to the sciences as to some of the scientists. It appears further that where some scientists are outspoken, others are guarded and evasive. Arguments are not always urged with scientific detachment, and terms are not always used with scientific accuracy.

When it comes to detailed data, sometimes elevated to the status of evidence, without exception there are alternative, mechanistic, and "dysteleological" interpretations. Thus the mechanists are able to point, to be sure, not to actual collisions of stars, but to some possibility of disturbing approaches at long intervals—only, of course, to be told by the teleologists that God has purposely arranged the near approaches. It is a poor teleology which will not work both ways. The equivocal character of teleological interpretation is seen especially in connection with the law of entropy; Whitehead uses entropy to show that God staves off universal heat-death,[12] while Northrop finds no purpose to prevent heat-death.[13]

It is well known that Helmholtz's and similar estimates of the age of the solar system and the earth have been vastly lengthened by the discovery of subatomic sources of energy. The result has helped the mechanists by increasing the length of time over which chance might operate.

Considerations based upon alleged probabilities are beset by many difficulties; especially when the resources of the theory of probability are brought to bear upon the cosmos, there is vast uncertainty as to the number of cases which should be considered, as well as the number of favorable cases. If the probability is to be expressed as a fraction, we know neither the denominator nor the numerator. All that is certainly known is that some events have occurred and that as regards the probability of others we deal with large numbers. At the same time there are some indications that in the processes of nature we have not a flat dead-level probability, but one in which the range of possible happenings is progressively narrowed, and the probability of future favorable cases correspondingly increased. For instance, take the familiar illustration of an army of monkeys "monkeying" with a mountain of type and by chance setting up the books in the British Museum. If this is thought of in terms of the relations of individual type characters and the finished product, the probability is of course vanishingly small. But if first we allow the monkeys the probability of setting up a vast number of combinations of individual letters, and then, without throwing down these combinations, setting up from them a much smaller, but still vast number of lines, and then, without throwing down the lines, setting up pages, and then books, and so on, we have a process which moves in a series of steps. So far, the probabilities are not lessened, because the probability of even two events occurring together is the product of the probabilities of each of them occurring independently, and the probability of all the events we want occurring together is unimaginably small. But now let the illustration be amended: first, allow the monkeys, not somehow to discard combinations of letters that do not make words (since this would require from the monkeys too much intelligence even for sorting demons), but allow the monkeys to discard combinations at random; second, *allow us to make sense of whatever combinations they retain*; third, allow to the monkeys and to us similar processes in the case of more elaborate combinations of words in lines, lines in paragraphs, and so on; fourth, at each step allow the monkeys to set up enough combinations so that after the discard at that step there still will be vast numbers left for further combinations; and fifth, allow the British Museum collection to change somewhat as the monkeying goes on. By these strange provisions, the probabilities of duplicating the British Museum collection might at least be increased, even though it is hard to take the illustration seriously.

Now there are some indications that the universe, in its production of matter and life and mind at successive levels, is more like the amended illustration with all its fantastic conditions than it is like the unamended illustration. We have to remember that the illustration is made up to clarify a cosmic situation which is impossible adequately to illustrate, because it is unique and in some ways unlike anything else we have to interpret. But the cosmos seems to be, like the type-setting, a kind of "stepped" system, like a step-pyramid narrowing toward the top. Although something is discarded at each level as it proceeds, vast groups of structures and processes become relatively fixed there; the ground thus won does not have to be lost or retaken; and the fact that we are here well toward the top in a process which has undergone many changes means, so to speak, that the process can be construed in terms which suit us. In other words, it never was very improbable that what has happened would happen.

Arguments derived from the facts of adaptation of life to matter have to confront the facts of maladaptation; survival and success are all too often offset by extinction and failure. Within the individual organism there is the same story; the harmony of the parts, especially in the human organism, seems curiously subject to injury and destruction.

As might be expected, just as vitalistic biology favors purposiveness, so mechanistic biology favors mechanism, and opposes the traditional supervenient teleology. Vitalism appears to be losing ground in general biology, although it is still strong because it has so much ground to lose. The mechanists think that the teleologists make a false mystery of life; it is the nature of the environment to produce life and sustain it.

The wonders of embryology appear to be telic, but this is when one thinks of them with reference to the future of the *individual* concerned. When one thinks of them from the point of view of past generations, they represent a shortening of processes and in some sense a recapitulation of ancestral embryonic structures, and embody nothing more startling than that complex processes, as well as simple ones, tend to run along established grooves. They tend to be modified by new conditions, and to come out somewhere, anyway.

The best mechanistic interpretation of the results of interference with embryos appears to be a combination of principles we have already noted—that the parts of an organism mutually support one another and tend to supply one another's deficiencies; that at any given level of development the possibilities of further development are narrowed but the probabilities of typical development heightened; and that in all embryos the tendency is to go through stages characteristic of the species. If in interference with the embryo the process of development is cut back to a prior level, the inhibitions once imposed by the later levels as they developed are removed and the process automatically starts over again from the given level. Interpretations in terms of vitalism and supervenient purpose are unnecessary, and peculiarly defective when it is noted how many of the mutilated embryos die.

The mechanistic interpretations of the regeneration of lost parts are similar, and the defects of teleological interpretations are similarly evident when it is noted that the process of regeneration is virtually confined to lower phyla, and that there some of the experiments in transplantation have produced uncanny monstrosities.

The teleological arguments from organic adaptations are met in ways that have been indicated, by considerations of the vast new time-scale, and by discount for maladaptations and failures to survive. Darwinism has brought its own problems, and often suffered from inadequate formulation, but there is no doubt that the principle of natural selection seriously weakened the old argument from design.

The principles of natural selection, sexual selection, environmental influence, and animal instinct are held to account for the societal adaptations of animals, such as they are. It is not that these are altogether understood or always estimated in the same ways, but it is held that the explanations are to be sought in natural facts rather than in supposed supernatural factors.

Arguments based on the wonders of epistemology lose their point when one regards the world of nature as capable of molding mind in its own matrix and keeping in contact with it during the process.

In human affairs, the argument from applied science that all machines are teleological needs a broader horizon, with a more adequate choice of examples. Instead of being made to refer to an artificial machine like a printing-press, the argument needs to envisage a "natural machine" like the sun-earth system. Here, as in an artificial machine, a portion of the available energy passes along one channel or set of channels and toward a more or less unified end-result, for instance, as Henderson has it, in the properties of living organisms, but it is at least not evident beyond dispute that the end was conceived in advance.

In human sociology and history the facts and interpretations of animal adaptations recur, with the addition of human habits and customs and the development of entirely human purposes which, when granted as natural, help to account for the human world as we have it and intend to have it without being magnified into distorted projections regarded as the purposes of God.

AGAINST THE MORAL ARGUMENT

The first criticisms of the moral argument may well be criticisms of the ideas about ethics which are involved in Kant's formulation of it. These include the dualistic view of man's nature, the theory of happiness as the reward of virtue and goal of his effort, and the rather calculating view of God as the insurer of such happiness.

The demand that there shall be a power adequate to enable us to do our duty, and even to crown our performance of it with a measure of happiness, may be satisfied without involving the existence of God. Kant, bachelor that he was, failed to do justice to the human social group. Some present-day thinkers make the group God's instrument or agent or revelation; others virtually identify the group with God; still others declare with Dewey that men get along better if they realize their responsibility for their own destiny and do not invoke any God at all. All agree in making the social group more prominent in the framing of any moral argument about anything.

Kant's moral argument in its original setting is really an enormous sight draft, made by a rather curious representative of the inhabitants of a pigmy planet upon the stupendous universe. In order to know whether the draft is good or not, we must know more about the resources of the drawee, and more about the original indebtedness, if there is any, than the moral argument or the Kantian philosophy can tell us.

It is to be feared that this applies to many representatives of overwrought philosophies of values, some lyric and some tragic. The contagious enthusiasm of some of the optimists, as well as the "moral demand" of others who, like Unamuno,[14] refuse to be consoled without God, needs a fuller account of the universe in which the demand is made. The moral demand that there shall be a God is not necessarily wrong, nor surely doomed to disappointment, but the mere fact that it is deeply motivated and reiterated does not of itself assure its satisfaction.

As in the case of the teleological argument, so with the moral argument, the worst difficulty is the myriad evils of the world. Over and over the gigantic dilemma recurs: if there be a God, he must be either not omnipotent, or not perfect, and in either case how can we be assured of the validity of our moral values, or the issue of our moral struggle? Shall we say, with Mill, that God is finite,[15] or with Brightman that he is limited by something "given," [16] or with Dean Inge that there are difficulties in discerning the purposes of the Creator? [17]

The view that we must "be good to see good," however admirable its expressions and its consequences, is in this context open to the subtle dangers of autosuggestion and wishful thinking.

AGAINST THE NON-CLASSICAL ARGUMENTS

The argument from the consent of mankind must not be pressed too hard. Vast numbers of so-called religious beliefs are crude and primitive, and what one tribe regards as a god may for another be quite ungodly. Furthermore, a counter-argument could be constructed from the *dissent* of mankind; as McTaggart points out, it is impossible to find a religion which no one has doubted.[18] More to the logical point, of course, is the fact that such matters are not decided by majority votes.

The henological argument, with its use of the concept of unity, is open to the criticisms which beset every monism. The facts of the world are obviously very diverse. At best, any conception of unity which is consistent with their diversity must involve such remote abstraction from the facts that what is left for content of the unity is all but unrelated to the facts which are to be explained by it. Several arguments of Thomas Aquinas are either outmoded or implied in some of the classical arguments.

Any argument involving aesthetic judgments is difficult to estimate, but it is at least evident that such judgments show wide variations. Philosophies of values and other pragmatic views are criticized in Chapter X. Northrop's macroscopic atom, as a kind of physical rendering of Whitehead's "Principle of Concretion," is open to criticisms frequently made of Whitehead's work. Some of them, along with criticisms of Hartshorne's panpsychism, will be noted as we proceed. Judgments concerning the data of occultism, even those data admitted within the field of psychical research, of course differ very widely.

The suggestion of a combination or synthesis of the arguments looks promising, although there can be no guarantee that a group of arguments, instead of mutually supporting one another, may not weaken one another. Logicians might dread an infinite regress of single arguments, first order combinations of these, then second order combinations made up of single arguments plus first order combinations, and so on. A more serious difficulty is that the strength of such a synthesis has to be felt rather than demonstrated. In order to be demonstrated, the synthesis must be analyzed into its constituents again.

PROVISIONAL CONCLUSION REGARDING SUPERNATURALISM AND THE ARGUMENTS

Supernaturalism merges so easily into theism, and theism has meant so much for the history and philosophy of religion, that any attempt at constructive work in the latter field must be much concerned with it—if not with the letter of its doctrines, at least with the deep interests which it represents. With all its weaknesses and extravagances apparent, there is still something in it which needs to be conserved. Just what this element is which the world can not afford to lose will be discussed from time to time as we proceed; in particular we shall, in our concluding chapter, take up again the projection theories and the element of contrast in supernaturalism.

With regard to the arguments for the existence of God, it seems clear from what we have seen that no one of the arguments, taken by itself, is conclusive, and very doubtful if all of them taken together are conclusive. Yet they represent centuries of thought upon the most important problem presented to the human mind, and if we can not give them the benefit of the doubt we should at least be careful not to dismiss them for less than they are worth.

They need to be understood, not as they have sometimes been employed, but as they have arisen. It has seldom if ever been any one's intention that any one of the arguments should stand alone, either for its religious content or its logical strength, or even that all of them together should be independent of other elements of experience. They have usually not been the grounds of faith, nor even indications of the ways in which God was being sought; they have been "talking points" for faith already otherwise grounded, when it has been called in question by other men or other portions of experience.

It is often said that they do not convince any one who was not convinced already, and as often noted that their inadequacy does not shake the faith of religious persons who declare that God's existence does not need any proof. Probably each of these statements is too extreme. The arguments may either help or hinder belief in God; they are so diverse that the chances are that some do the one thing and some the other.

Sometimes one of the arguments supplies what another lacks. It is, for example, no very telling criticism of the teleological argument to say that it supplies a contriver rather than a creator, when the cosmological argument is at hand to supplement it at that point. On the other hand, sometimes they fail to support one another. The cosmological argument is doubtful on account of difficulties with the notion of causality, and the teleological argument is doubtful on account of somewhat similar difficulties with the notion of purpose; neither argument helps the other in its extremity.

The soundest example of mutual confirmation appears to be in the evolutionist interpretations of the teleological and the moral arguments. This will need to be discussed more fully later, but we can see the essential ideas from here. The cosmic process eventuates, for us, conspicuously in some events of life and mind, and there are indications of a long-range tendency or trend toward such events. And whatever the trend is and whatever are its hazards, it issues at least in part in some righteousness and makes some goodness.

This, we should hold, is the chief net result of the arguments. The other major contentions, while not disproved, are involved in such difficulties, especially with regard to anthropomorphism and the limitations of our thinking, that no great help for religion can be expected from their traditional formulations. We shall return to some of these points in our concluding chapter.

REFERENCES

[1] C. D. Broad, in *Hibbert Journal*, 24, 1925, p. 47.

[2] See A. Seth Pringle-Pattison, *The Idea of God . . .*, p. 306. On the concept of "nothing" and several others discussed in the following paragraphs, see our Chapter XV.

[3] I. Kant, *Critique of Pure Reason*, II, ii, 2.

[4] See A. S. Eddington, *Nature of the Physical World*, p. 220.

[5] W. R. Sorley, *Moral Values and the Idea of God*, 1918, p. 319.

[6] E. Caird, *Introduction to Philosophy of Religion*, pp. 134, 137.

[7] M. Iqbal, *Reconstruction of Religious Thought in Islam*, p. 27.

[8] W. R. Sorley, *op. cit.*, p. 487.

[9] A. O. Lovejoy, *The Great Chain of Being*, 1936, p. 50.

[10] See below, Chap. XV.

[11] *Cf.* E. Hubble, in National Academy of Sciences, *Proceedings*, 22, 1936, p. 626; H. Shapley, in British Association, *Report*, 1938, p. 383.

[12] A. N. Whitehead, *The Function of Reason*, 1929, p. 22.

[13] F. S. C. Northrop, *Science and First Principles*, p. 10.

[14] See M. de Unamuno, *The Tragic Sense of Life*, transl. J. E. C. Flitch, 1926.

[15] J. S. Mill, *Three Essays on Religion*, 1874: Theism, Part II.

[16] E. S. Brightman, *The Problem of God*, 1930, p. 113; *A Philosophy of Religion*, 1940, pp. 305ff.

[17] W. R. Inge, *God and the Astronomers*, 1933, pp. 227f.

[18] J. M. McTaggart, *Some Dogmas of Religion*, p. 46.

CHAPTER VIII

IDEALISM: (I) THE CASE FOR THE WORLD AS MIND

Throughout the nineteenth century in Europe and America, thinkers who rejected supernaturalism found the chief rational support for religion in the philosophy of idealism.[1] This term, familiar enough when it refers to our ideals, here technically means emphasis on mind (sometimes described as "experience"), in one or all of a number of ways which we shall examine. There seems to be no way to an adequate treatment of the great idealistic philosophies which does not encounter some difficulties; part of the strength of the idealisms has been in their subtleties and profundities. In the literature, "mind" is treated in abstract, highly generalized fashion; it refers rather indifferently and non-committally to an individual's mind, to the minds of a group of individuals, to a World Mind, or the Mind of God.

The philosophy of idealism may be usefully diagrammed in an egg-shaped or ellipsoidal form; the two foci are epistemological idealism and metaphysical idealism, with the region of the latter very much larger than that of the former. Epistemological idealism is emphasis on mind like ours in a theory of knowledge; metaphysical idealism is emphasis on Mind, usually superior to ours, in a theory of the universe. When the term mind is taken abstractly, epistemological idealism opens out into metaphysical idealism; this is historically, in the West, the course of thought from the subjectivism of Descartes to the objectivism of Hegel.

The old story of the Arab, the tent, and the camel fits this development quite well. The Arab is philosophy, as represented by one philosopher after another.

The tent is experience, or mind, and the camel is the external world. The story helps to show how philosophy from Descartes to Hegel was forced to accept into experience more and more of what had been called the external world. Descartes with his partiality for subjectivism sets up the tent, with no difficulty about the camel. The camel presents himself more insistently to Locke, and wins a ready permission to stick his nose in the tent; for Locke, secondary qualities like color involve the activity of our minds, while primary qualities like solidity and extension belong to objects out in the world quite independently of our experience. But having gained this much, the camel next edges his head and neck in; Berkeley is ready to accommodate not merely secondary qualities, but also primary qualities within experience. The camel is unwilling to stop there, and gets his forelegs into the tent; Hume is forced to declare that our ideas of causation, too are merely the mind's way of dealing with unvarying succession. By this time the Arab, in the person of Hume, is uncomfortable (except when he can go out to dine or play backgammon with his friends), but presently the camel makes another advance and gets his hind legs inside; Kant insists that even time and space are subjective, and that out in the objective world is only the *Ding an sich,* the thing-by-itself. Kant is more content with this than Hume; he makes himself at home with the camel in the tent and will hardly even look outside. Then at last the camel gets his tail inside; Fichte tries to show that even the *Ding an sich* is subjective. But this is too much. The philosopher is crowded out of the tent, but only to find that the open sky is a greater tent above him; Hegel passes from subjective to objective idealism, from emphasis on our minds to emphasis on the world process, but finds that the world process itself is essentially Experience.

Thus idealism in Europe passed from its epistemological to its metaphysical forms. In India in the development of the Upanishads the course may have been the other way.[2] At all events, the resemblance between the two kinds of idealism is close; everything is held to be organic to everything else, and, no matter where one starts, sooner or later to involve everything else, in a world which is essentially mental.

We shall attempt first a kind of anatomical dissection of the content of idealism, picking out various interconnected strands in epistemological and then in metaphysical idealism. Cunningham says that the central thesis of epistemological idealism is that the object of knowledge is exclusively what at that moment it is known to be.[3] We find, however, that within what we call the epistemological approach this statement can be read in different senses, and that these senses can be distinguished with some clarity if we take as the central thesis of epistemological idealism the view that mind not unlike ours constitutes the world. Taken in this way, epistemological idealism can be anatomized to show three sets of variants, together with combinations of them—(1) according to the meaning of the term "constitutes"; (2) according to the number of minds involved; and (3) according to the mental process or function emphasized. The three sets of variants for the most part are cross-classifications, allowing permutations and combinations almost without number, all of them emphasizing mind and belonging within idealism.

We may illustrate the different meanings of the term "constitutes" by three answers to the question, What constitutes a university class? In one sense, persons constitute the class; students and teacher are the materials of which the class is composed. Similarly, it is maintained in one type of epistemological idealism that mind or consciousness or experience is the stuff of the world. This view, associated with Berkeley, is called mentalism; the world, even though experience shows that it is independent of our minds, is made up of bits of experience. In a second sense, the university administration constitutes the class; the administration takes previously existing materials like buildings, chairs, and tables, together with the students and teacher whom it has gathered, and the registration and program and recording machinery it has arranged, and organizes or disposes all these in certain ways to form the class. Somewhat in this sense, idealism maintains that mind constitutes the world by assembling the existing non-mental materials and imposing upon them an order of reality which is mental; this is Kant's view of the activity of our minds and the nature of our world. Mind imposes its arrangements upon the raw materials which come as phenomena within its purview, successfully enough for ordinary purposes and even for mathematics and science, but with no guarantee that our understanding also holds for objects which are noumena, independent of our minds, and with special distrust of the classical reasonings about God.

In a third sense, the instructor constitutes the class by imparting himself to it in such a way that the members, entering without special proficiency in the subject, are gradually molded, in a larger development of the instructor's own proficiency, and are transformed so that they themselves could be teachers. This sense of "constitutes" corresponds to the English Hegelian view that our mind or experience by broadening its field and penetrating beyond itself finds itself more and more in the Absolute Experience. It differs from the original Kantian view in the degree of order sometimes said to be imposed upon the raw material in the act of constituting it. For Kant the raw material is, let us say, real, but utterly unqualified and indescribable, since all describable order comes from mind; for at least some of the English Hegelians, the universe without mind may in quite realistic fashion have independent non-mental features or qualities, but those features, whatever they may be, are negligible compared to features illumined and transformed by mind, features which mind has made its own.

Whichever meaning of "constitutes" is chosen, the epistemological idealists differ in another way according to the number of minds which are involved in constituting the world. If only one mind is involved, we have the curious position of solipsism, according to which the individual's mind constitutes the world. If more than one mind is involved we have either what we may call collective idealism, where the minds cooperate with one another in the common task, or pluralistic idealism, where each mind constitutes its own world. The difference between the two last-mentioned forms is one of degree, impossible to fix with precision. The term pluralistic idealism is often used for the cooperative effort which might better be called collective idealism.

The third set of variants, any of which may be developed in combination with any of the other two, concerns the mental process or processes emphasized in the work of constituting the world. These may be, for instance, sensation and perception, as for Karl Pearson;[4] perception and ideation, as for Kant; assumption, as for some of the pragmatists; projection or projicience, as for Lloyd Morgan;[5] feeling, as for Bosanquet; emotion, as sometimes for William James; intention or volition, as for James and Dewey; action, as for James, or action and control, as for Dewey; appreciation, as for Balfour;[6] valuation or self-movement, as for Urban;[7] or unification, as for Bosanquet, when he emphasizes the function of the self or personality as a whole. When emphasis is on the personality as a whole, with or without stress upon any particular mental process, we have personal idealism or personalism. This list of mental processes carries us beyond the traditional range of epistemological theory, making it include what are often called valuational and other considerations, but in recent idealism no precise line can be drawn. The fact that emphasis is placed upon different mental processes gives us our clearest definition of pragmatism. If we call sensation, perception, and ideation the cognitive processes of mind, and other processes like emotion, volition, action, satisfaction, control, and valuation non-cognitive, then pragmatism is emphasis upon the non-cognitive processes of mind.

Recalling our egg-shaped diagram and the statement that epistemological idealism opens out into metaphysical idealism, we turn to the large end of the cosmic egg. Metaphysical idealism is emphasis on Experience or Mind in our theory of the world. It is sometimes called "spiritualism." We find here also several sets of variants, cross-classifications, allowing permutations and combinations. The first set concerns mental processes stressed in characterizing the cosmic Mind—we have intellectualistic systems like Hegel's, voluntaristic like Schopenhauer's, teleological like James Ward's, pragmatic like Dewey's. If combinations of these and other qualities which are regarded as vaguely or conspicuously personal are included, we have some variety of metaphysical personalism which often amounts to theism. Next, we have various theories as to the number of cosmic Minds. Some say there is only one, and are monists or monotheists; others say there are many, and are pluralists or polytheists. Again, there are variants as regards the relationship of the cosmic Mind and the world. The absolute idealists identify the two and insist that reality is totally and completely Mind, whereas the relative idealists trace some distinctions. Absolute idealism when it gives its object some degree of personal qualities becomes pantheism; if it stops with a bare modicum of psychic quality like mere awareness or dim consciousness, it is some form of panpsychism. Relative idealism, which distinguishes between the Cosmic Mind and its world, if it ascribes personal qualities to that Mind, usually becomes either monotheism or polytheism and is closely affiliated with supernaturalism.

The number of possible permutations and combinations of these variant forms of the idealisms, epistemological and metaphysical, is beyond counting. Some have been developed in India more fully than in the West. The Vedanta philosophy in its advaitist or nondual form may be said to identify the knowing self, the external universe, and the Absolute Reality, or Brahman.[8] The West finds it easier to take this in segments; we can understand the reduction of the external universe to the self, as in solipsism, and the identification of the universe and the Absolute Mind, as in absolute idealism. Many possible combinations of various kinds of epistemological with various kinds of metaphysical idealism remain undeveloped. Leaving them now and turning, as we might say, from the anatomy or morphology of idealism to its physiology, we shall pick out the currents of argument now most actively flowing from the epistemological toward the metaphysical pole.

We shall distinguish eight principal types of argument for idealism. There are epistemological and metaphysical elements in all of them, and the two sets of elements open into one another, much as the St. Lawrence opens out into the Atlantic and the tides there ebb and flow. The first five types of argument depend primarily and conspicuously upon the status of our minds and their processes. These arguments are (1) from the inconceivability of objects outside experience; (2) from the alleged priority or superiority of mind to its objects; (3) from considerations of problems of truth and error; (4) from the organizing and transforming effects of mind upon its objects; and (5) from the continuity between mind and its objects to an identity of quality between them. Less epistemological are (6) arguments from resemblances between processes in mind and in the world of nature, (7) reinforcing arguments and (8) synthetic arguments.

(1) The first idealist argument, from the alleged inconceivability of objects outside experience, is one of the subtlest in all philosophy. In its historic form it corresponds to our first meaning of the term "constitutes," and recalls the idealism of Berkeley, with his contention that "to be is to be perceived." To get the full force of it we must turn from perceptions to concepts, and try to imagine an unexperienced world. Of course, the very act of thinking of such a world involves mind, and any world that is thought of involves mind. We can not conceive a world without conceiving it, nor have a world without having it. We never have the "out of thought," but only "the thought of the out of thought." We can conceive no cessation or essential limitation of the activity of mind. From any world which we have or can have, mind is ineradicable, and what is here ineradicable the idealist takes as fundamental and essential. We might compare an object in a non-idealistic account of the world to a cake of ice; the idealist points out that just as we do not have ice without water, so we do not have objects without experience. The Berkeleian mentalist goes further and says that just as ice is formed of water, so objects are formed and made up of experiences; the panpsychist says they are made up of experiencers. If we stop short of mentalism and panpsychism, we may say at least that objects are minded objects, the world of objects is a minded world, and the reality of the world of nature is that of ideas in mind. Putting it in terms of experience and existence, existences are items in experience.

The argument from the inconceivability of non-experienced objects easily leads to solipsism, but most idealists manage to modify it before reaching such an impasse. No one can conceive objects without conceiving them, nor conceive them as altogether independent of his mind and having nothing to do with it, but one can conceive them as having existence external to his individual mind, and as thus grounded either in a community of minds like his or in a Mind more comprehensive and enduring than all our minds together.

Sometimes the idealistic argument is put in terms of valuations, rather than perceptions or ideas. Sorley argued that judgments of value are no less objective than judgments of existence. When we refer to "the good," we mean a good which transcends the experience of any man or body of men. But it would not be good unless it were good for some mind; hence a transcendent good must pertain to a transcendent Mind.[9]

In general, the procedure in the arguments from inconceivability may be described in four or five steps. First, in the case of any indicated object, the idealist insists that it is an experienced or minded, perhaps valued, object. Second, he then recognizes in the world an indefinite array of objects similar to the indicated object. Third, he insists that there must be a correspondingly indefinite range of experiencing or minding or valuing these objects. Fourth, he then argues that this indefinite range of experiencing or minding can take place only in a Cosmic Mind. Fifth, frequently he identifies this Cosmic Mind or Experience with the God of religion.

(2) Some of the arguments for epistemological idealism which are based on the priority or superiority of mind to its objects correspond to our second meaning of "constitutes"; mind imposes restrictions and regulations upon an otherwise indescribable, non-mental world. The priority or superiority may be logical, so that mind is declared to be necessary for a rational world or a world that is "intelligible"; it may be valuational, so that mind, or a world with mind in it, is given preference to any world without mind; or it may be metaphysical, so that the reality of mind is said to antedate

or crown the world or in some other way to serve as basis or climax for it.

So far as the definite features of the world are concerned, the Kantians usually combine these three types with the understanding that the mind is restricted to its phenomena, or what it receives from the otherwise unknown thing-by-itself. The Kantian view is difficult to distinguish from some others which do not accept its limitations to phenomena. In general, idealistic attempts to escape these limitations have taken two forms, one of which centers round the subjective pole, with emphasis upon the priority of mind, and the other round the objective pole, with emphasis upon mind's superiority to anything other than mind. They may be called loosely the Fichtean and the Hegelian idealisms.

At least in one phase of his work, Fichte tried to abolish Kant's distinction by making the mind or ego posit everything, including whatever was non-mental, or the non-ego. In such a view the priority of mind is so much emphasized that even the indescribable non-mental thing-by-itself has to be derived from it. It may be observed that since any factor which is said to be indescribable is at least referred to by our minds, the Kantian view is difficult to state without opening the way for the Fichtean; in other words, the priority argument easily avails itself of whatever strength there is in the inconceivability argument.

Without attempting too much where refined distinctions and subtleties are endless, in this region of initial emphasis upon the subjective one many trace the starting point of the idealism of Bradley, who argued that the differentiation of object as well as subject takes place within immediate experience,[10] and an important point of the phenomenology of Husserl, who claimed to discern the ground of all the sciences in an intricate analysis of meanings and essences which are present in immediate experience.[11] Sometimes the priority is described in terms of activity, as in Gentile's view that mind is productive of the objective world of experience.[12] Often there is said to be an activity of will or process of valuation, and the world is declared to be what it is in response to ideal demands; in such statements idealism and pragmatism support one another.

Much of the strength of arguments from the priority of mind depends upon the way in which they manage to elude solipsism and open out into metaphysical idealism. The term "mind" or "experience" is used in such a general sense that it need not be confined to minds like ours and may be understood to apply to a Mind of another order.

The view that mind is prior to its objects is basic in personal idealism or, as Bowne called it, personalism.[13] It is sometimes not very prominent there, because personalism aims to give a concrete and rich, rather than abstract and poor account of the world and in so doing incorporates and stresses many other qualities and characteristics of mind and features of the idealisms. In fact, so many elements are rather loosely and generously combined in personalism that it serves as a kind of synthesis of all idealistic theories of knowledge, philosophies of values, cosmologies, ethical loyalties, aesthetic appreciations, and religious experiences and interpretations of them. Elements from supernaturalism, mysticism, evolutionism, and sometimes realism are also freely included, so that any complete account of personalism becomes a complex affair. But the central teaching is the priority of personality.

Sometimes personality is conceived in terms of substance, and again in terms of activity. Sometimes the view is monistic, and again it is pluralistic, as for Howison, who held that reality is essentially a society of persons, with one supreme among the others.[14] Sometimes it is absolutistic, and very sure of itself; at other times it is put forward more modestly as a matter of reasonable faith. Usually the emphasis falls not on rationalistic clearness or consistency, but on valuations as more fundamental. At all events, it is said to be in the experience of our own selves that we find the solution of all the basic problems of philosophy—problems which fail of solution when we start with a world devoid of personality, but are solved when the fundamental reality is seen to be personal and to prescribe or include the elements which are otherwise so irreconcilable.[15] Interpretations of nature in terms of cause and effect, for instance, are traced to our personal experiences of having caused events to happen. Physical energy is interpreted in terms of volition. We noted that Brightman traces the evils of the world to something "given" in the personality of God as our sensations are in a way given to us.

Like other idealisms primarily epistemological, personalism opens out into the larger metaphysical idealism, with the argument, the assertion, or the faith that the world of nature is essentially the activity of a Person.

The views that mind is prior to its objects and that persons are primary realities are also involved in theories of "social immediacy,"[16] to the effect that minds are known to one another directly, and for this knowledge do not need sensations of bodily movements, language, the projection of one self into another, or other secondary processes and helps. Theories of social immediacy draw support from metaphysical theories of interpenetration and are quite consistent with psychological and sociological theories which regard each individual mind as a differentiation within society, like a knot in a network of experiences or events.

Theories of social immediacy are invoked to afford immediate recognition of a World-Mind. Here W. E. Hocking combines several idealistic strains. Of central importance for him is the "reflexive turn," whereby each of us is self-conscious. Each of us, moreover, is aware of nature as the object or group of objects known to other minds. It is in submission to nature that each of us finds his mind and the minds of others receiving their characteristic developments. Nature which thus immediately becomes self is immediately apprehended as a Self, an Other-Mind, which is in reciprocal and essentially mental relationships with our minds. In worship we discover this Other-Mind to be God. Hocking, as we saw, also uses an adaptation of the ontological argument, combining this with his "mystical realism." [17]

The other attempt to escape from the limitations of Kant's theory of knowledge was not subjective, but objective, and attains its greatest prominence in Hegel, who sees mind in us as at once the climax and the clue to the whole cosmic process. For Hegel the whole process goes on in accordance with a triadic "thesis, antithesis, synthesis," which may be interpreted crudely as a progressive combination of opposites, although Hegel called it their identity. All minor triads are comprised in the super-triad of Idea, Nature, and Spirit. First in the cosmic development comes the remote, abstract, basic, formal realm of Idea, where the cosmic principles go through their triadic forms and stages without being embodied in any actual world. The process is logical, rational, but lacks an object, an opposite, something over against it by which it can be better defined and further developed. Part of its own tendency, however, is that it should go out beyond itself, realize itself, make itself more real than ever, precisely by developing such an other, or antithesis. This antithesis to the realm of Idea is the world of Nature, inorganic and organic. But any antithesis, in turn, is incomplete unless it gains a higher unity with its original thesis, a higher unity which fitly expresses the nature of both. So Nature is not complete until something grows out of it which combines the characteristics of a rational set of principles like the Idea and of embodied existence like Nature around us and thus illumines both, showing at last what each imperfectly contains. This great synthesis is Spirit, attained in the rise of man and civilization. In the light of man and civilization as at once climax and clue, we may think of the whole cosmic process as having the basic characteristics of an Experience or a Mind. Within it all, man's personality wins in the Absolute a fulfilment which constitutes religion. There are two interpretations of such fulfilment, the one in popular, picture-like doctrines about God, and the other in the more adequate although vaguer concepts of philosophy.

Life would be too short for an attempt to show in full detail all the variations upon the great Hegelian theme. In fullness of development and richness of content, it almost rivals scholasticism and the Vedanta, without the authoritarianism of the one and the Orientalism of the other. In it Spinoza seemed, though dead, yet speaking. Sometimes it made headway not so much by its argument as by its moving emotional quality: it was as if deep called unto deep in the Hegelian formula. Even the fragments of Hegelianism are titanic. Shorn of its philosophy of Nature and much of its philosophy of Spirit, it was imported, as Neo-Hegelianism, into England and America, where it dominated nineteenth century liberal philosophy of religion and influenced a whole generation of the elder philosophers of today. A mere touch of the Hegelian formula in the work of Karl Marx and his followers has furnished a philosophy of history which after a lapse of generations has been potent enough to serve as the intellectual theme of one of history's most stupendous upheavals.

(3) The Hegelians, often also under marked Kantian influence, have developed most of the remaining idealistic arguments. These include some which are based on considerations of our knowledge of truth and error.

For the most part, idealism has adopted the coherence theory of truth, to the effect that any statement to be true must "hang together" with all our experiences and that true knowledge of the world is a body of statements which, like the words of the dictionary in our illustration, mutually sustain one another, without need of other support, such as might be afforded by a realistic correspondence with an independent reality, or by pragmatic consequences in gaining control of the environment. The coherence theory takes us back to the views of Descartes, that certainty can be attained, and can be attained by examining one's own experience until ideas become clear and distinct. Taking this much from Descartes, the idealists conclude that if we keep at our problems long enough, we can think them through coherently and eliminate error. But if we are to "think things through," things must be thoroughly accessible, and they can be thoroughly accessible only if they are mental. If there is anything non-mental, we can not penetrate it, can not think through it; anything non-mental will remain an irreducible surd, out of our range and the range of certainty. In other words, we can solve our problems only as we can dissolve them in mental terms, leaving nothing non-mental to be foreign to us. So the coherence theory of truth and the metaphysics of idealism serve one another.

Arguments based on theories of truth and error are the most difficult in the whole armory of idealism. Among them are included Bradley's views as indicated by his title *Appearance and Reality*, Royce's "argument from the possibility of error," and, we might add, McTaggart's theories of exclusive and sufficient descriptions. No brief formulation of them can exhibit their elaborate sequences and quick turns; Cunningham's chapters on these men should be read as an introduction to their writings. Let us here say merely that Bradley, taking for granted that our minds can never be satisfied, so long as there are inconsistencies or contradictions in our thinking, maintains that our ordinary relational thinking is shot through with such defects. He then saves our knowledge by a theory of judgment, which makes it consist in attaching qualities or predicates to existent reality as the one subject of all propositions. So we can have at least a general knowledge of reality. By the principle of inconceivability, reality must be at least sentient experience, and if it is to meet our demands it must be complete and self-contained, a harmonious unity, an absolute whole.

Royce argues, in part, that the recognized fact of our ignorance implies a logically possible type of experience, but that, again by the principle of inconceivability, any possible experience must be actually a part of some experience, and that such an experience must be complete and organized. Hence any distinction in our minds between truth and error points to a Mind which knows both and knows the difference between them.[18] McTaggart's argument includes a definition of a sufficient description as one that absolutely identifies a substance; a "principle of determining correspondence" which obtains sufficient descriptions from certain relationships between parts of substances; and a theory of selves and the perceptions of selves in terms of wholes and parts, which is said to bring selves and perceptions under the principle and thus to show that the only substance is spiritual substance.

(4) In another type of argument, corresponding to our third meaning of "constitutes," the emphasis falls not so much on the inconceivability of objects apart from mind or on the priority of mind as on its unique organizing and transforming status when once it has appeared. These views have in common with those of Bradley and Royce an interest in knowledge as pertaining to a totality, but they emphasize the unified and organismic features of such a totality, particularly the

mutual interactions of parts. Where such organization or wholeness appears to be incomplete, they emphasize the tendency toward it, and argue from the imperfection of data and premises, *"a contingentia mundi,"* [19] from the fragmentariness of the parts to the ideal completion of the whole. The organismic views avail themselves of a mutual influence of interacting parts in a world where no external relations, but only internal relations are held to be real; [20] they do not suffer from Hegel's obscure statements about identity. Since the influence is to be mutual, mind need not be afraid to admit that there is an objective world, or even a material world. If we start with a material world, the function of mind is still so transforming and so significant that idealism can take care of itself.

The most important idealist of this group has been Bosanquet. His cardinal principle is that of non-contradiction, which he interprets to mean the spirit of totality or the whole. He finds this variously exemplified in the activity of thought, including in the complete account feeling and will, aesthetic experience, the concrete universal of logic, coherence as the criterion of truth, individuality, nature, life, individual and social mind, freedom, and value. Mind appears relatively late among the other wholes, but at its level we can describe more precisely than ever the tendency toward totality in the whole. The task for the finite individual mind is by self-transcendence to penetrate its surroundings, organizing them in the unity of self-consciousness and thus transmuting its experience. The high-water mark of this penetration, and the content of it, is the Absolute. The Absolute is spiritual, although it is not a self or person. [21]

Whitehead's philosophy, although it includes Platonic features and is almost a supernaturalism, is usually regarded as an organicism, with an outcome not unlike Bradley's. Examining the implications of immediate experience, with the aid of highly abstract logical and mathematical techniques, Whitehead analyzes the world into various kinds of objects, into events, and at length describes it in terms of actual entities or actual occasions.[22] Each of these occasions is made up by its prehensions of all other occasions in the organismic whole. Time-systems and space-systems are systems of prehensions. Such prehensions are a prelude to the apprehensions of our minds; each actual occasion, although not conscious, has feeling and "subjective aim." Logical induction would not be valid without this fundamental mutuality and organicity of the world's events. The actual occasions, always coming into being and perishing, are not self-sustaining; the sustaining factors are found in "eternal objects," or Platonic ideas, which have "ingression" into the occasions, and also in God, the ground antecedent to transition, the Principle of Concretion. God is the ultimate irrationality, determining why the world is what it is rather than something else. In his primordial nature God envisages all ideal possibilities, and in his consequent nature enjoys their fulfilments.[23]

A number of systems, while remaining idealistic and sometimes belonging among the organismic idealisms, emphasize a process of evolution in the world or the World Mind. It is not always easy for idealism to accommodate evolutionism, because evolution requires time, and idealism prefers to picture its Absolute as timeless. But the problem has not been without answers; Bradley concluded that there are degrees of truth and reality,[24] and others closer to the data of evolution have interpreted the universe as a series of levels of development, with a hierarchy of sciences appropriate to them. For instance, J. S. Haldane maintains that the evolving universe, on grounds of consistency and unity, can be nothing else than a manifestation of one Spiritual Reality or one God.[25] The emergent evolutionism of Lloyd Morgan has enough idealistic elements to be studied in this connection.

With a realistic epistemology, J. E. Boodin develops a view which he has called "cosmic idealism." He takes account of much of the detailed data of evolution, and regards God as the law of the whole. The God-stream of energy, like music, surges through cosmic space and time. We are obliged to think of it as creative thought and creative personality, however much it may exceed our capacity.[26]

Seth Pringle-Pattison, sometimes numbered among the personalists, thinks of man in his organic relationship to the world as an organ of the universe; in man's conceptual thought and values the universe beholds and enjoys itself, and we must judge the universe here at its highest development rather than by anything lower in the scale.[27] This way of judging the universe, by its production of mind in us, is a favorite among writers who combine idealism with evolutionism.

(5) Sometimes the emphasis on the mind's contribution to the world is stated in terms of an indispensable continuity between mind and world, and this continuity is then interpreted as indicating an identity or common character for the two. Thus Royce found in our ideas both internal and external meaning, the internal meaning especially in our purposes and the external meaning in the outer effects of our purposes when realized, or our hypotheses when rendered precise. But internal meaning passes over continuously into external meaning, and the two should not be sundered. Since internal meaning and external meaning are thus continuous, the world outside our minds may be regarded as continuous with mind and at least enough like it to share its essential quality. Its purpose is our whole meaning and its knowledge our ultimately true knowledge.[28]

The argument from continuity to identity is the chief reliance of panpsychism, which, in spite of some difficulties of definition, may be regarded as a form of idealism. According to the panpsychists, since no one knows where to draw a line between psychic qualities in us and qualities which are held to be continuous with them in the world around us, we may regard all objects as having some degree of psychic quality.[29] The psychic quality and its degrees are variously named; by various writers it is said to be selfhood, value, consciousness, feeling, and so on. Montague regards consciousness as a form of potential energy.[30]

(6) In connection with other idealistic arguments, some importance attaches to the fact, emphasized by Royce, that there are resemblances or analogies between mental processes and processes in nature around us. For instance, both sets of processes are often irreversible, and within each there is mutual influencing of one part by another part. In each there are rhythmic repetitions, new developments, processes of trial and error, and survivals.[31] Royce also developed an elaborate argument to show that our mental process of interpretation has its counterpart and larger meaning in the cosmic process.[32]

(7) The foregoing, more or less official arguments for epistemological and metaphysical idealism come largely from the schools and from the professional philosophers; some of them could hardly thrive anywhere else. But the case for idealism is not complete until we have counted other considerations which have given it additional strength. These include not merely aesthetic idealism, emphasis on the artist's mind or consciousness or experience in a work of art, and ethical idealism, emphasis on man's loyalty to his ideals of goodness, but also any experience or aspiration of the so-called higher or spiritual life, any conviction or faith about God, and anything which leads to belief or hope in immortality. There are notable affiliations with mysticism, especially in emphasis upon immediate personal experiences. Pragmatism has probably given to idealism in the form of increased vigor a good return upon idealism's original investment in it. Quite recently idealism has received

unexpected support from some of the scientists. Eddington as we saw, has marked off the field of science as the metrical, determined by our pointer-readings and measure-numbers, which give us no primary reality, and has left the more important non-metrical aspects of the world for more direct and frankly mystical ways of knowing. Jeans, with an epistemology which recalls Berkeley's, notes the conformity of physical data to our interpretations and gets the impression that nature is the thought of a Thinker, apparently a Mathematician.[33]

(8) The full strength of the idealistic argument is not developed until one notes an increment coming from a "synthetic argument," the effective, organic combination of all the others. It has been evident from our discussion that epistemological and metaphysical idealism can be separated only by dissection, and that the arguments we have listed shade off, overlap, interlock, and often depend upon one another. In the view of its adherents, idealism synthesizes not merely arguments, but life's divergent ideas, interests, and values—subject and object, reason and feeling and will, goodness and beauty and truth, matter and life and mind, all declared to be harmoniously unified in the view that the fundamental reality is Mind. Persons with minds can speak for themselves and refuse to be reduced to anything other than mind.

Pantheism, in the West associated with the Stoics and Spinoza, may be regarded as in part a reinforcing argument for idealism and in part a synthetic argument. Sometimes it brings little suggestion of the idealistic philosophies; in the history of religion it is affiliated with mysticism, and in literature among the nature poets it is close to other aesthetic experiences and expressions. On the other hand, on its more philosophical side it is a high reading of absolute idealism, synthesizing many of its elements and arguments in a rich, personal or quasi-personal view of the universe and way of life in it. A "colorless pantheism" verges upon panpsychism. Pantheism differs from Christian Science in that it does not deny the reality of matter nor make matter an illusion or an error; it is content to accept matter and regard it either as identical with the spiritual being of God, or as an aspect of that being. A variant sometimes encountered is panentheism, the doctrine that everything has its being in God. Doctrines that God has his being in the universe are best dealt with as immanental supernaturalism, or as some variety of evolutionism or religious naturalism.

REFERENCES

[1] On idealism in general, see R. A. F. Hoernle, *Idealism as a Philosophy*, 1927: A. C. Ewing, *Idealism, A Critical Survey*, 1934: and, of the books cited below for details, particularly that of Cunningham and that edited by Barrett. For British idealists, see R. Metz, *One Hundred Years of British Philosophy*, 1938.

[2] *Cf.* R. E. Hume, *The Thirteen Principal Upanishads,* 1921, pp. 51*f.*

[3] G. W. Cunningham, *The Idealistic Argument in Recent British and American Philosophy*, 1933, p. 377.

[4] K. Pearson, *The Grammar of Science,* 1911, pp. 41*f.*

[5] C. L. Morgan, *Emergent Evolution,* 1927, pp. 49*f.*

[6] A. J. Balfour, *Theism and Humanism,* 1915, pp. 74*ff.*

[7] W. M. Urban, *Valuation, Its Nature and Laws,* 1909; Urban, in C. Barrett, ed., *Contemporary Idealism in America*, pp. 105*ff.*

[8] See S. Dasgupta, *History of Indian Philosophy,* Vol. I, 1922, Chap. X.

[9] W. R. Sorley, *Moral Values and the Idea of God,* pp. 152, 352*f.*

[10] F. H. Bradley, *Appearance and Reality,* 1908, p. 459.

[11] E. Husserl, *Ideas: General Introduction to Pure Phenomenology,* transl. W. B. Gibson, 1931. Husserl has notably influenced Max Scheler and Nikolai Hartmann. Scheler emphasizes emotions and values, particularly love. Values, which exist in their own right, are apprehended immediately as pertaining to an objective reality and exhibiting absolute religious content. Hartmann sees our attempts to meet the world beset by doubts and the necessity of choices between alternatives, neither of which seems adequate, but finds in a phenomenological account of our experience of the real world, including an analysis of self-existent moral values, a more comprehensive solution of the problem, a solution involving moral freedom. Husserl has also influenced M. Heidegger and K. Jaspers in their developments of "Existenz" philosophies akin to those of Kierkegaard and Barth.

[12] G. Gentile, *The Theory of Mind as Pure Act,* transl. H. W. Carr, 1922, p. 43.

[13] B. P. Bowne, *Personalism*, 1908.

[14] See G. H. Howison, *The Limits of Evolution*, pp. 256, 277, 289, 332ff, 359.

[15] A. C. Knudson, *The Philosophy of Personalism*, pp. 237ff, 344, 366, 371, 377. See E. S. Brightman, *A Philosophy of Religion*, esp. pp. 224ff, 251ff.

[16] See G. A. Coe, *Psychology of Religion*, 1916, Chap. XV.

[17] W. E. Hocking, *The Meaning of God in Human Experience*, p. 278.

[18] J. Royce, *The Religious Aspect of Philosophy*, 1885, Chap. XI.

[19] See G. W. Cunningham, *op. cit.*, p. 115.

[20] See A. C. Ewing, *op. cit.*, pp. 43ff and Chap. IV.

[21] B. Bosanquet, *Principle of Individuality and Value*, pp. xxxvi, 267f, 337; Cunningham, *op. cit.*, pp. 115, 129.

[22] A. N. Whitehead, *Process and Reality*, 1929, p. vii; *An Enquiry Concerning the Principles of Natural Knowledge*, 1919, pp. 61-99; *Process and Reality*, pp. 27ff.

[23] A. N. Whitehead, *Science and the Modern World*, 1925, pp. 97, 101, 220, 243, 249; *Process and Reality*, 1929, pp. 29, 35, 47. On the whole subject, see D. Emmet, *Whitehead's Philosophy of Organism*, 1932.

[24] F. H. Bradley, *Appearance and Reality*, 1908, Chap. XXIV.

[25] J. S. Haldane, *The Sciences and Philosophy*, 1929, p. 181.

[26] J. E. Boodin, *Cosmic Evolution*, 1925, subtitle; *God, A Cosmic Philosophy of Religion*, 1934, p. 35; Boodin, in D. C. Macintosh, ed., *Religious Realism*, 1931, p. 484.

[27] A. Seth Pringle-Pattison, *Idea of God*, pp. 111, 156, 176, 243.

[28] J. Royce, *The World and the Individual*, First series, 1900, Lect. VII, esp. pp. 273, 288, 299, 306.

[29] In his book, *Beyond Humanism*, C. Hartshorne follows Charles Peirce and A. N. Whitehead in developing a panpsychism of "organic sympathy" or "societal realism." He uses the argument from continuity (pp. 115, 273f) and shows significant affiliations with the four preceding idealist arguments (*e.g.* on pp. 121, 170, 184, 187; pp. 23, 26, 132; pp. 46, 116; and pp. 23, 184, 208). There is also frequent and marked reliance upon arguments involving identity, generalizations, universals, infinites, order, possibilities, wholes, absolutes, completeness, perfection, freedom, and other categories and concepts which we shall examine in Chapter XV.

[30] W. P. Montague, in Aristotelian Society, *Proceedings*, 21, 1921, pp. 36ff; *The Ways of Things*, 1940, pp. 482ff.

[31] J. Royce, *op. cit.*, Second Series, pp. 315ff.

[32] J. Royce, *The Problem of Christianity*, 1913, Vol. II, Chaps. XI-XIII.

[33] J. H. Jeans, *The Mysterious Universe*, 1932, pp. 157-165; *The New Background of Science*, 1933, pp. 284ff.

CHAPTER IX

IDEALISM: (II) THE CASE AGAINST THE WORLD AS MIND

The philosophy of idealism is so cleverly knit together, so comprehensive, and sweeps along with such impressive power, that at first it seems difficult to penetrate it with objections. But sometimes a single obstacle placed in its way slows it up enough so that its details may be examined and some of its weak points made evident. The obstacle most frequently used for this purpose is the realistic epistemology, the view, held with minor variations, that there is a world independent of our minds. It is understood that the realist answer is an argument and an emphasis rather than a proof.

(1) The argument that objects can not be conceived without involving mind did not altogether avoid realism, even with Berkeley; he held that the world was experienced as external.[1] While a world conceded to be external to our minds might not be independent of them, realists ordinarily think of the one concession as involving the other. In a sense, it is as hard to avoid realism as idealism; for while it is true that if reference is made to a world which is not experienced, no description can be given of that world, there is still the formal *reference*, and the fact that the reference is to an object of reference, even though the object is not described, is as ineradicable as anything which the idealists can claim. Cunningham maintains that this first type of idealist argument shows a fundamental ambiguity between knowledge and the object of knowledge, and that there is a phenomenalism which can be saved from solipsism only by bringing in a dubious universal consciousness.[2] Ewing says that we can think of an object existing inde-

pendently of our consciousness only as it would be if it were present to a mind; nothing can be an *object* without a thinking subject, but this does not mean that nothing can *exist* without a thinking subject.[3]

One of the best known replies to the idealists comes by recognizing but not taking too seriously what R. B. Perry calls "the egocentric predicament." [4] We can not know the world without knowing it, any more than we can eat food without eating it, but this fact, stated in various ways, gives us only a tautology, redundance, or reasoning in a circle; it does not add anything to our knowledge and does not mean that things require to be known. The predicament is only a harmless natural condition of the knowing process; there is no point in developing it into a whole epistemology, and much less in exaggerating it into a whole metaphysics.

Again, to call every object minded is like defining every chair as painted or dusty; it is "definition by initial predication," [5] calling a thing by the first predicate which occurs. It does not sufficiently distinguish between accidental and essential properties. Moreover, the idealist gains nothing by underwriting each object by an experience which precisely corresponds to it.[6]

(2) Many of the realist criticisms of the first idealist argument, the argument from inconceivability of objects apart from experience, apply with equal force to the second, from mind's priority or superiority in relation to its objects. The idealists here impose their own interpretations upon the shock and impact of the material world and the reflex responses to it which men make as animals do. Arguments from the priority of mind, if they remain within the Kantian phenomenalism, are not free from Kant's own kind of realism, which had to acknowledge a thing-by-itself as independent of our minds in the very fact that it was by itself. The post-Kantian arguments for the priority of mind to its objects, where they have disregarded Kant's thing-by-itself or have derived it

from mind, seem to get along more consistently, but disregard of it looks like evasion, and derivation of it from mind, even if not preposterous, may be compatible with independence. Even if mind does originally confer objectivity upon its world, the objectivity may be irrevocable, the reference thus set up permanent, and the relationship now one of independence. The contention that only an idealist view is intelligible or explanatory means that only such a view satisfies an idealist's theory of what intelligibility and explanation are.

The phenomenologies which profess to discern the ground of the sciences by analyses of meanings and essences given in experience are elaborate and imposing, with an array of terms, distinctions, and allegedly inescapable conclusions which baffle most attempts to understand or criticize them. There are words and distinctions enough so that a phenomenologist can argue that his philosophy is an objectivism as well as a subjectivism and that it does justice both to realism and to idealism. But in its method and outlook, or rather inlook, the affiliations of phenomenology are unmistakable. Like Locke, it begins by virtually insulating mind from the natural world. Like Kant, it then requires that from mind thus insulated shall come an authoritative account of the world, although the account is now not to be one of categories imposed by mind upon the raw material of sensation, but of discerned possibilities of experience. Phenomenology is so introspective, not to say introverted, that it runs great risk of being arbitrary, and so strained in its struggle with subjective "tasks" and "problems" that some of its alleged profundities are almost certainly artefacts. Whatever is authentic in it can be better understood in terms of a logical realism freed from such dubious psychology. As a philosophy, phenomenology and its allies show too many signs of inbreeding. It needs fresh contacts with the universe.

The idealist charge that all realistic theories rest upon prior personal values and motives may be admitted and answered by saying that the realist admits his motive, which is to reckon adequately with what to him seems unmistakably to be in a world independent of him.

Personalism quite definitely includes realistic elements. Knudson says that the otherness which personalism attributes to individual consciousness implies a distinction between knowing and being.[7] According to Brightman, we must assume some explanation for experiences of the self in the realities which lie behind it; the fact that we have to start with self-experience is the fault of the universe.[8]

If the theories of social immediacy are taken from the point of view of any individual, he must ascribe some objective status or independent reality to other minds, and thus not altogether escape realism. The only ways to avoid this realistic account of other minds would be, on the one hand, a solipsism so extreme that no one would isolate himself in it, or on the other hand, a fusion or merging of individual minds so extreme that no one could quite lose himself in it. And, the realists can go on to ask, if other minds are to be accepted as real, certainly some of their experiences are to be accepted as real, and in the case of any such experiences which are not one's own, one still has some of the old difficulties, which are not removed by calling them mental.

The whole theory of social immediacy may be challenged by the statement that the interaction of minds assumes the conditions of interaction, including physical, chemical, and biological relations. If social immediacy is admitted to be primary, it is strange that it comes dragging so much machinery with it. The impression that it is primary may, like the mystic's experience, be due to some subtle autosuggestion or redintegration.

With such difficulties in the theory of social immediacy as regards our minds, it is certainly precarious to attempt to extend the principle to God's mind. Our relationships with one another are conditioned by the fact that we belong to the same species, and often in mental life very markedly by the fact that we speak the same language. We have neural structures and mental processes that for all practical purposes are the same for all. But any extension beyond these limits is open to grave question. Unless there are similarities of structure which do not easily appear, or unless immediacy of a type which is close to mysticism is legitimate and authentic, the argument for social immediacy can hardly strengthen religion.

Criticisms of Hegel have been legion—his formalism, his arbitrariness, his extravagant assertions, his obscurities, his playing fast and loose with the principle of identity, his scientific inadequacy, his confusion of logic and cosmology, his ponderous ideas about mind and man and God and the Absolute, have all been made prominent by his opponents, in criticisms which apply in considerable measure to his successors.

(3) The idealist arguments about certainty, emphasizing the coherence theory of truth, are sure to draw the fire of the realists. The latter insist that a certainty altogether mental and subjective would be incapable of adequate testing. It would account for truth, but not for error. Against error, clearness and distinctness of ideas, even of coherent ideas, offers no adequate defense. A man or even a number of men may have such a coherent system all worked out, and yet be utterly insulated from things as they are and have no means of checking their system by reference to an independent criterion. For realists, this criterion is correspondence, the matching at least of the order and relationships of our ideas with the order and relationships of things. The procedure of comparison in order to eliminate errors need not necessarily have elements from mind on the one side and

elements from the world on the other. It is better not to cut across the grain like that, but to cut along it, or across the time-lines, and compare my mind's interaction with the world at one moment with my mind's interactions with the world at another moment, or with other minds' interactions with the world.

In Bradley's tortuous arguments about the defects of the "relational level" of thinking, he tries hard to involve thinking in fatal contradictions, and in his more constructive treatment he has much to say about the demands and satisfactions of thought and about the harmony and unity of the whole or the Absolute. All this serves to raise fundamental questions about the nature and limitations of our thinking; our discussion of them is best deferred until they can be taken up more systematically in Chapter XV.

Royce's arguments concerning possible experience depend at fundamental points on work done by Berkeley and Kant and criticized in preceding sections. From the point of view developed in Chapter XV, it may be said that he describes possibility, where it would be more accurate not to attempt to describe its content but to leave it undescribed. According to the same point of view, it may be agreed *that* there is absolute truth without any committal as to *what* the absolute truth is— whether it is organic, or belongs to a Mind, or is known by any other descriptive term, affirmative or negative. McTaggart's argument has been carefully criticized by Cunningham;[9] it may also be criticized at a number of points touched upon in our concluding chapter.

(4) The argument from the organizing and transforming effects of mind after mind's appearance in a previously non-mental world makes at least a formal concession to realism, although it is as impossible as ever for realism to describe the characteristics of such a non-mental world. Sometimes by the idealists the objective reality of "nature," meaning everything in na-

ture apart from mind, is conceded; again it may be conceded only that there is a non-mental reality, without any attempt to say what it is. But some concession certainly is made, and it can be so great that the choice between idealism and realism is determined by the degree of emphasis on the one element or the other. This is particularly true with evolutionary views which exhibit the world as passing from non-mental levels to levels characterized by the presence of our minds. Sometimes it requires considerable search and weighing of the statements of evolutionist writers to determine whether their views and preferences are idealistic or not. Cunningham says that the argument *a contingentia mundi* assumes that the object of knowledge is empirical and fragmentary, but with a transempirical reference, an implication about experience itself and the surrounding order.[10] This reference, we should say, is precisely of the sort that professes to lead, but can really only point beyond thought's horizons; concepts of wholes, totalities, absolutes, and perfections are all subject to the natural limitations of our thinking.

Whitehead's philosophy is often criticized for some ambiguities and inconsistencies, but more seriously for its abstruseness, its retention of Platonism and quasi-supernaturalism, and its virtual panpsychism.

(5) Under suitable definitions, the transition from internal meanings to external meanings of our ideas may be psychologically quite unbroken, but to argue from this as continuity to an identity between mind and world is to assume meanings for both continuity and identity which disregard the horizon principles outlined in Chapter XV. Moreover, if continuity must imply identity, it is not clear how any new entities arise in the world, nor how evolution can be real.

Against panpsychism in this connection it may be urged first that consciousness in us is often held to be the result of conflict and may be regarded as a discontinuous interruption of unconscious psychological or biological processes. But granting, in the face of such difficulties, that there is continuity between our consciousness and the objects around us, any "consciousness" or psychic quality which can be attributed to such objects must be extremely tenuous and practically negligible; it is better to put it out of its misery. The best way to accommodate all the factors involved here seems to be to distinguish as the evolutionists do between genetic continuity and generic discontinuity; this allows mind to be at once continuous in its derivation from life and matter, but discontinuous in qualities and kinds of processes involved. Other panpsychist arguments are open to criticisms which are brought against the corresponding arguments of idealism.

(6) Arguments from analogy are quite generally, although sometimes too hastily criticized in accordance with the cautions familiar in the logic books. As such books say, the fact that two processes resemble one another in some respects is no sign that they do in other respects, nor that the first respects are important or essential; the problem needs a more thorough study than the idealists have given it. In general, it is plain that idealism is not so close to the scientific attitude as is its rival, realism. The scientists who are observing stars or cells can hardly be expected to remind themselves that they are dealing with mental facts or phenomenal experiences. Nor can those who observe the effects of atoms or electrons, even though they do not actually see such objects, be expected any longer to agree that they are dealing with ideal concepts or mental counters. On the other hand, attempts of the idealists to use scientific data and of scientists to argue for idealism have often been unimpressive. James Ward was most effective as a critic of nineteenth-century naturalism and agnosticism, but the idealism which he offered in their places had the usual presuppositions about minds.[11]

Nowadays to reduce the data of physics to mathematical formulation does not necessarily mean to find consciousness lurking in the interstices or to be confronted by a Mathematician; it may mean merely mathematical instead of physical realism. And if the physical sciences have seemed to strengthen idealism, the social sciences have also seemed to weaken it by providing a more clearly empirical substitute.

(7) The reinforcing arguments for idealism from the fields of aesthetics, ethics, and religion are usually open to other interpretations by philosophies opposed to idealism. Realism also has some powerful reinforcing arguments of its own. One is an "industrial argument," citing the stubbornness of matter, particularly as encountered in industrial processes. Epistemological idealism is a poor argument to use on a workman in a mine or blast furnace. It is also lame in an earthquake or a blizzard, and perhaps at its weakest in an astronomy class. To many minds the greatest and most conclusive argument for realism is the fact that the universe is so overwhelming.

(8) Synthetic arguments are always difficult to estimate, but in this case it can be said that they amount to little more than the argument for personalism, which is itself a kind of synthesis of the others. And synthesis is also a game at which more than one side may play. The combined effect of all the arguments *against* idealism appears to grow more and more formidable with the passage of time and the current trends of opinion.

Against pantheism, two great arguments have been urged for centuries—the fact that if made explicit it must ascribe to God only attenuated personal qualities, and, on the other hand, must include within the being of God the evils of the world. The latter is sometimes met by theories which make evils incidental or illusory, but these theories are not very convincing. Sometimes pantheism is said to tend toward fatalism and pessimism.

It can usually be made to show some of the defects attributed to mysticism.

Besides the foregoing criticisms based on opposition to particular arguments and tendencies within idealism, there are others which apply in more general fashion to the philosophy as a whole. (i) In the first place, it has the marks of an ingrowing philosophical tradition, where each generation of thinkers, whether in India or Europe, depends too much upon its predecessors and lacks fresh contacts with empirical sources which are above suspicion of prejudice. (ii) It looks as if epistemological idealism, although it developed a little earlier in the West and was first attached to supernaturalism, is now not much more than an approach to metaphysical idealism, and has been magnified and elaborated for its sake. The rise of the river of epistemological idealism has not been due to water from its own springs; it has been a tide backing in from the ocean. If the whole of idealism is represented in an egg-shaped figure, the attempt is made not merely to stand the egg on end, but to enlarge the small end for that purpose. If any one brings up the story of Columbus here, it should be recalled that Columbus stood his egg on end only by smashing it beyond repair.

(iii) Some idealist groups criticize others, especially for being abstract and intellectualistic. (iv) Another set of criticisms carries the charge of abstraction further, insisting that in idealism mind and similar terms have been treated in such a general way that the whole philosophy is vague, confused, equivocal, and ambiguous, if not contradictory.

(v) Psychologically, idealism has seemed too introverted, introspective, and over-reflective. It is like going into an old-fashioned ice-cream parlor lined on all sides with mirrors; there are so many reflections and reflections of reflections, so many rows of tables and processions of customers that it is hard to single out the plain hard facts among so many illusions built upon them. The idealist has taken the apparatus of mind, which was meant primarily to be directed upon the external world, and in quite myopic and distorting fashion has directed it upon its own delicate processes, and even upon the "possibility" of those processes. Then, without any too accurate knowledge of these processes, he has strained every argument to make mind as he understands it central and essential to the cosmos.

(vi) In thus magnifying mind to cosmic proportions, idealism has been anthropomorphic, and has tended unjustifiably to interpret the universe in human terms. Our point of view is of course anthropocentric, as it is egocentric; but though man may occupy the center of the cosmic circle, he should be careful about spreading himself to the circumference. As the universe has been studied in modern ways, much of the older idealism has seemed increasingly presumptuous, if not absurd and impossible. Sometimes the whole movement to emphasize the place of mind in the world seems like a survival of some early modern protest against Copernicus and his downward revision of man's estimate of himself. (vii) Many critics have found idealism too tender-minded and sentimental, and, particularly in its absolute forms, inadequate to face or deal with the ghastly evils of the world.

(viii) It is a question whether idealism really succeeds in getting rid of materialism; Santayana charges that there is a materialism latent in it, and says that if matter does not exist, something else exists which is just as material.[12]

(ix) Other critics have seen in it no great help even to religion; its conclusions are too vague and ambiguous to be of much value for the more sharply etched forms of theism, or to inspire the definite codes and courses of action to which the theistic faiths are committed. Wieman and Meland think that the need for idealism is decreasing; for a long time it mediated between supernaturalism and naturalism, but that this function, now that neo-supernaturalism and religious naturalism are available, is no longer necessary.[13]

(x) Open to all these criticisms, idealism has tended to be dogmatic in statements concerning unity, ultimates, absolutes, infinites, and similar concepts and terms, with scant attention to the more matter-of-fact arguments of opponents like the pluralists and relativists. In particular, idealism has disregarded limitations such as those which we shall study in Chapter XV as "horizon principles." Yet with all its dogmatism, idealism has not hesitated, whenever it has been forced into a tight corner, to appeal to ignorance, with the plea that the finite can not comprehend the infinite or to sheer intuition, with the plea that all thinking and all description is ultimately inadequate.

(xi) Lastly we many mention certain faults of style which are often conspicuous, and which seem to be intrinsically connected with the philosophy. Idealism has sometimes been so ponderous that it has tended to collapse of its own weight, and again so subtle that it has tended merely to evaporate. Sometimes a critic gets the impression that it makes its way by overwhelming or suffocating, rather than by convincing, its opponents.

AN ESTIMATE OF IDEALISM

In spite of all the criticisms which have been brought against it, idealism, like the supernaturalism which for some it supplants, has been far too widespread and too commanding to be lightly dismissed. Such many-sided systems, entwined in the feelings as well as the thoughts of generations, are hardly susceptible of proof or disproof; approval or disapproval is all that one can bring to bear upon them. On the other hand, when all the criticisms, specific and general, are considered, we find them preponderant; metaphysical idealism rests too directly upon epistemological idealism, and epistemological idealism is in principle borne down by a universe now known to be far more overwhelming than Kant's starry heaven or Hegel's Nature. All the great philosophical systems are perennial, if not immortal; but idealism seems destined to inevitable decline. There may be no way to avoid this, but if some interests which idealism has helped to develop go further and further into decline with it, then the world must feel the pinch of spiritual poverty. These major interests are often and variously described; let us call them man's faith in himself, and in his personality as having some cosmic status and significance. Whatever be the fate of epistemologies, these interests seem worth retaining: we shall later on suggest a way in which this may be possible. Even if experience and reality do not coincide, the possibility still remains that they are analogous, and that understanding the one will help us to understand the other. Even if the world is not a Great Mind, the mind may still be a little world, the growing point of reality, and a microcosm of the whole.

REFERENCES

[1] G. Berkeley, *Three Dialogues Between Hylas and Philonous*, iii; ed. A. C. Fraser, 1871, Vol. I, p. 325.

[2] G. W. Cunningham, *Idealistic Argument*, p. 377.

[3] A. C. Ewing, *Idealism, A Critical Survey*, pp. 14, 21.

[4] R. B. Perry, *Present Philosophical Tendencies*, 1910, p. 129.

[5] *Ibid.*, p. 128.

[6] A. Seth Pringle-Pattison, *Idea of God*, pp. 199f.

[7] A. C. Knudson, *Philosophy of Personalism*, p. 36; cf. p. 376.

[8] E. S. Brightman, *Personality and Religion*, 1934, p. 28.

[9] G. W. Cunningham, *op. cit.*, Chapter XVII.

[10] *Ibid.*, pp. 381, 508.

[11] James Ward, *Naturalism and Agnosticism*, 1899, Vol. II, Lects. XIV and XX.

[12] G. Santayana, *Character and Opinion in the United States*, 1921, p. 184.

[13] H. N. Wieman and B. E. Meland, *American Philosophies of Religion*, 1936, p. 343.

CHAPTER X

PRAGMATISM

Toward the end of the nineteenth century pragmatism developed under the wing of idealism by shifting the emphasis away from perceptions and ideas to non-cognitive processes such as emotions, volitions, and satisfactions.[1] It was easily recognized as a new name for some old ways of thinking; it belongs in the succession marked by Kant's reliance upon the postulates of the practical reason, Schleiermacher's emphasis upon feeling, Lotze's dictum that mechanism is universal in extent but negligible in significance,[2] and Ritschl's revolt from metaphysics and grounding of Christian theology in value-judgments.[3] Nor was pragmatism without affiliates in its own contemporary world; Eucken's glowing activism, Bergson's philosophy of creativity and spontaneity, Höffding's treatment of religion as essentially faith in the conservation of values,[4] and many elements in the personal idealism of the time moved along related lines. In less academic fashion, any one who prefaces a statement of his views by the words "I like," or "I prefer to think," is a pragmatist without knowing it.

Among the affiliates of pragmatism, special mention should be made of philosophies of values. In our account of idealism we noted that emphasis upon the processes of mind may single out valuations as particularly important. The fact that men prefer certain features of the world to other features, or strive for certain ideals against forces which oppose those ideals, or estimate their experiences in terms of value-judgments may be made the center of gravity for a whole world-view. This interest has inspired an extensive literature and development of value theory or axiology, which has been particularly serviceable to supporters of the moral argument for the existence of God, to personalists, and to pragmatists.

Typical of such philosophies is the statement of Dean Inge that appreciation of value is as integral a part of our experience as the judgments which are based on sense perception. Goodness, beauty, and truth are absolute values which stand in their own right, guaranteed by the testimony of our whole personality. The distinction between fact and value is real in the world which is our normal environment but not in the higher world of spirit, where value reigns supreme, apprehending facts in their ultimate significance. Our citizenship is in heaven, in a spaceless and timeless world in which all the intrinsic or absolute values are both actual and active. In this higher world we find God and our own eternity.[5]

If we consider pragmatism apart from such affiliates, it appears most clearly as a philosophical expression of "the yeast that is America." The strongest arguments for it have always been its freshness and its practicality. As a philosophy with a name of its own it goes back to Charles Pierce, but first becomes well known in the work of William James.

The fascinating story of William James is now available in R. B. Perry's splendid volumes revealing the thought and character of that never-to-be-forgotten man.[6] Many and varied were the strands which united in him and diverged from him, but as we need to see him here James was an idealist who could not brook the absolutism which Royce and the others had received from Hegel, and who had scant patience for the finely spun epistemology upon which the traditions were made to depend. Its absolutism, James thought, was equivocal in the face of moral problems and any "logic-chopping" was curiously misplaced in a world beset by compelling need of practical action and living religion. Gradually accustoming himself to judge philosophies by their fruits, or lack of fruits, James tossed traditions aside and developed his own highly individual views. He was impetuous, vivid, vital, with a measure of unabashed opportunism and inconsistency—an artist working in the materials afforded by philosophy, a kind of philosophical Rodin or van Gogh or even Wagner. As his new ideas took form, James swung further and further away from the old, abstract, theoretical controversies; if they made no practical difference, let them be abandoned, and let the issues of philosophy be joined along new lines of consequences in human satisfaction and well-being.

There is a sense in which, after all, this shift of emphasis is only a belated recognition of what goes on all the time in all of us. Reason in itself may be coldly rational, but it never gets a chance to operate that way; the cold light of reason is always somewhere above the absolute zero of emotional heat. We all seek satisfactions all the time; the fact is obscured, because we do not always formulate our goals clearly and so seek satisfactions that are vague; or because we sometimes manage to pit long-time against short-time satisfactions and serve ideals which are so remote in realization that they seem unreal; or because the satisfactions which we seek are shared by so few persons that they are unrecognized by many. But we all seek satisfactions all the time; pragmatism in emphasizing this simply meets us on our own ground and "catches us where we live." This is one reason for its strong initial appeal; in this sense we are all pragmatists, so naturally that at first it is hard to think of belonging to any other school.

This seeking of satisfaction is, however, only the first step in pragmatism, and has to be distinguished from the next and more decisive step. The next step is not a simple method, an emphasis upon satisfactions and consequences, but a remarkable theory of truth. The shifting of emphasis to satisfactions meant the virtual abandonment of the old quest for absolute certainty, and the substitution of practical working solutions in a world where, if only for the adventure of it, we should be willing to run the risk of being wrong. But pragmatism is not quite content with the new emphasis without the old terminology. So it says not merely "Get some satisfactions," but goes on to say, "Call those satisfactions by the name *truth;* look for truth nowhere else, and do not use the word in any other sense." It is this second step which differentiates the pragmatic philosophy from what in the first step is the mere pragmatic method. Those who take the second step will not merely work for satisfactions and if possible attain them, but in so doing will declare that they share in the actual making of truth.

For instance, take the problem of the existence of God. Suppose we find, as many do, that any attempt to get an answer in the traditional way is inconclusive. But the answer one way or the other, does make a difference. If we follow William James, we shall find more satisfaction with the belief in God than without it; and we shall therefore regard the idea of God as true.

This statement must be carefully distinguished from some others which verbally resemble it. We must not say that because the idea of God satisfies us, therefore God exists, even though the pragmatic teaching is sometimes thus construed; such an interpretation confuses the whole pragmatic point of view with the lines of the traditional problem. The pragmatic view is that the idea of God brings us satisfaction, and that therefore it brings us truth, in the only permissible sense of the term truth. Our satisfactions do not make God exist in reality, external and independent of us; our satisfaction makes truth. Truth is not in correspondence as for the realist, nor even in coherence, as for the idealist; truth is in consequences, personal consequences.

One should also distinguish between pragmatism and the view expressed in Hans Vaihinger's phrase, "the philosophy of as if." [7] Vaihinger emphasizes the rôle of assumptions which are known to be false, but which nevertheless yield conclusions which appeal to us as truth; but pragmatism could not regard assumptions as false if they lead to what it regards as truth.

James, after an attempt to show by a study of reflex action that even in our discussions of theism we must take account of motor and coordinating as well as of the sensory or receptive functions of the nervous system, wrote the famous essay "The Will to Believe." He maintained that in the question whether God exists or not there is no possibility of a rational decision, and yet the question is of such importance and urgency that we are simply forced to make a choice between the two alternatives, even if it is a choice on emotional and practical, rather than rational grounds. We may, then, believe or not believe. If we believe, we do it by exercising our right of choice, choosing one answer rather than the other. But suppose we are not inclined to do this, and so do not believe; in this case we have also made a choice, only we have made the other of the two possible choices. So we make a choice anyway, and if this is the case, we have the right to make, and might as well make the choice which yields the greater satisfaction.

Sometimes the argument shifts to the ground that we have the right to believe when our belief itself helps to create or make real the thing believed in. James illustrated this by the case of a mountain climber faced with a crevasse or chasm which has to be crossed; if the climber believes that he can make the leap, the belief itself will strengthen him to make it. Or, if a suitor believes he can win his lady, the belief will help. [8]

Proceeding upon his own pragmatic or empirical grounds, James made out a somewhat stronger case than this for the objective existence of God. Attempting to interpret the experiences of mystics, he held that there was contact between our minds and a "More of the same quality," which gained access to our minds through the subconscious.[9] But for James most ideas of God which would be recognizable in theology were overtones.

The clearest expression of pragmatism as applied to philosophy of religion is reached in the work of E. S. Ames. Here the older rationalistic views are confronted by the newer functional views: the function of ideas is to aid us in realizing the values of life. If an idea helps us in this way, we need expect nothing more from it. No one would expect, for example, that the idea of Uncle Sam corresponded to an objectively existent person; this idea is functional, and effectively summons up our loyalties without involving any existent counterpart. The same may be said of Alma Mater. The idea of God is in this respect like these other ideas; it aids us in assembling or maintaining our highest social values, and we need not raise the old rationalistic, dualistic question as to whether a God corresponding to our ideas exists or not.[10]

In his later book, *Religion*, Ames exhibits some shift of emphasis in the direction of evolutionistic, realistic and naturalistic views. He still insists on the originality and reality of personal and social points of view. But God, instead of being a mere functional idea, is now at least a pictorial representation of the life process, or the group spirit, and is as real as the life of a city, or of humanity. Since such social processes are interwoven with the objective world, we can say that God is not merely the life process, but the world and life taken in certain aspects—those which are consonant with order, beauty, and expansion. Just as Alma Mater, after all, is not a myth or mere idea, but the reality of an organization of things and people, so God is a reality in the universe of nature and history; thus reality comes to be regarded as loving and lovable, known and knowing, orderly and ordering.[11]

The most influential pragmatist has been, of course, John Dewey. His treatment of problems of religion differs so much from that of James that the two afford one of the best examples of the divergences which pragmatism engenders. Reared in an early systematic Hegelianism which at first intrigued him, Dewey began to distrust its global generalities and acutely to feel that it was out of touch with practical social questions.[12] Religious groups, too, were either out of touch with such questions or were dealing with them in vague or insincere ways. So Dewey forsook Hegelianism and for decades practically avoided problems of religion, while he developed the vigorous social and ethical theories which have become associated with his name.

With stringent criticisms of past philosophies as abstract, academic, artificial, and aristocratic, Dewey insists that the path of recovery must be marked by the creative use of intelligence.[13] In our given situations we must attempt to locate and define the difficulties, develop the suggestions which present themselves, and test them by their consequences, until by our inquiries and the operations which we perform the situations are progressively made more and more unified, coherent, and subject to our control. Thinking is thus not an end in itself but is distinctly a means to ends which lie beyond it.[14] The ends are controls of man's precarious environment so as to obtain the fullest possible measure of shared experience for every one. Moreover, the ends are not fixed, but are growing and developing so that we must continually be looking to future issues rather than to past achievements. And the ends are neither unified nor hierarchized; they develop more or less independently of one another.[15]

Thus we get an ethics with much consideration of economics, politics, and education, in a world where man should be working out his destiny by the exercise of his intelligence. The process goes on in man's natural environment and at its best leads to the transformation of that environment until it is better suited to human needs and aims. Intelligence is not merely interpretive, it is creative. The emphasis is upon man, but Dewey is enough of an idealist to say that the qualities of man's experience belong to nature as well as to man.[16]

Religion, for Dewey, has traditionally been too much concerned with supernaturalism, which has a distorted view of man and is not verifiable. Worse still, supernaturalism furnishes an escape mechanism and virtually encourages an evasion of man's serious human responsibilities. We can be stronger personalities, with more robust reactions and more effective control over the means of happiness, if we stop relying on the supernatural and begin to rely on ourselves. This, as we said, is Dewey's answer to the moral argument for the existence of God.

Without supernaturalism there is still a place and function for religious experience, though we must beware of "religion" as an abstraction which leads us back into the old associations. Dewey's description of experiences to which the term "religious" properly applies varies somewhat in different books. The term may indicate a consciousness of the whole, and of the infinite or universal connections and consequences of our actions.[17] Again, the term may be applied, under some conditions, to an intense experience of completeness of the object enjoyed.[18] In his later work, Dewey is closer to realistic views concerning the object of religion, but he still places marked emphasis upon the human factors involved. There are, he says, forces in nature and in society which generate and support our ideals. Since our successes depend upon our cooperation with nature, the sense of the dignity of human nature as a cooperating part of a larger whole is religious. If any one wishes, he may apply the name "God" to the active relation which connects the actual and the ideal.[19] In a later discussion, Dewey emphasizes the human factor, stating that the union of ideals and some natural forces which generate and sustain them, accomplished in human imagination and realized through human choice and action, is that to which the name God may be applied.[20] This emphasis on what takes place in human experience rather than in the cosmos, so characteristic of Dewey, accords with his general philosophy of pragmatism and his religious interest in humanism.

E. W. Lyman shows important influences of both pragmatic and idealistic thought. He says that moral faithfulness brings into existence that quality of being which it is of the very essence of religion to discover, possess, and create. Actual participation in a spiritual order is experienced by man as he lays hold on values which are intrinsic and ultimate and embodies them in the social and physical orders. He has then a relation of co-working with the Cosmic Creative Spirit, a cooperative divine energy, an eternal creative good will. This receives confirmation when our moral and religious experiences are integrated with our experiences of nature and history. Thus Lyman concludes that God is personal, that ethical values are supreme, and that human personality is of unique worth and eternal destiny; the theory of physical nature is definitely subordinated to these teachings. God is creative love and in his own nature transcends the world process, while resisting the world's evil.[21]

CRITICISMS OF PRAGMATISM

In approaching the criticisms of pragmatism let us note first some of the strictures passed upon its affiliates, the idealistic philosophies of values. In general, these philosophies share the defects of idealism. For example, they have tended to be introverted and tender-minded, and they have arrogated to our minds (in their valuational capacities) an importance which has all but dwarfed the order of nature. They have warped or disregarded many hard facts of the world and its evils in order to suit their comfortable interpretations, and in their interpretations they have made free use of absolutes and ultimates. In particular, the value philosophies have made a mystery out of the normal psychological process of valuation, which is no more to be wondered at than is the process of perception. Valuation is more inclusive and complex, with more emotional components and more reference to remote objects represented in conditionings and abstractions. Just as we distinguish between perceiving, perception, perceived objects, and perceivable objects, so we ought to distinguish between valuing, valuation, valued objects, and valuable objects, and not lump all these together in the term "value." The term "value" should be kept to indicate the intrinsic quality of the psychological process of valuation—the quality which just because it is intrinsic makes a valuation, especially in its future reference, different from a perception.

"Value" should not be reified into an entity, nor in this way made into a foundation for ethics or metaphysics. We should not say that a value is any object of interest: this confuses a value with a valued object. If we say that a value is a relational quality where the terms of the relation are consciousness and its object, we must remember that the relation between subject and object is involved in valuation anyway. The process does not take place in a subjective vacuum; all that we need to say is that value is a quality of a valuation, which of course is a valuation of some object. Moreover, a valuation can be as immediate and intrinsic, or as mediate and instrumental, as a value is ever said to be. In short, value taken by itself is an abstraction, and attempts to make values independent and eternal are overworked abstractions.

The whole structure and process of valuations ought to be naturalized among the cosmic structures and processes. We should see that the strength of our valuations is not in their demands upon a plastic or unfriendly universe, and not in an intrinsic quality which affords us entry into an Absolute Mind, but rather in the conforming of the structures and processes of our valuations to the principles of structures and processes in the cosmos which has produced them. The philosophies of values are right in hoping that our valuations have some cosmic status, but they should look to the cosmos first, then to the valuations.

On its own account, pragmatism has been open to some peculiarly incisive criticisms.

(1) First we may take its vagueness and lack of precision. Its shift of emphasis has been away from abstractness, but it has also been away from sensations, perceptions and ideas. This means that pragmatism reduces to secondary importance the processes which afford us whatever clearness and precision we have in our interpretations of the world; on the other hand, it gives prominence to emotional and valuational factors which may operate more than anything else to warp our judgments. Emotions are characteristically diffuse, and satisfactions are typically ill defined. These are some of the reasons why it is so difficult to define pragmatism; we can not be very precise in dealing with a movement which so casts in its lot with portions of experience which lack precision. This explains also why it was possible for Lovejoy to distinguish his "thirteen pragmatisms," [22] each with a different theory of truth.

(2) Again, this emphasis of pragmatism means that it has typically aligned itself with anti-intellectualist movements. It has not shared all the vagaries of all of them, but it has gone so far that any man who has not

liked the results of any intellectual analysis of our time could call it "logic-chopping" or "snarling logicality" with good chance of winning approval from an enthusiastic group. The history of the past few decades seems to show, however, that such enthusiasm is hard to sustain and is likely gradually to exaporate. Unkind critics might add that pragmatism's "new intellectual climate" has been one characterized largely by wind!

(3) Pragmatism shares a chief defect of its parent, idealism, and continues in new ways to exaggerate the status of our minds. Never far from idealistic philosophies of values, pragmatism has flirted with the prospect of letting our emotions and valuations have free rein and dictate what the world shall be, with little or no regard for what the world is. But our emotions and valuations, after all, must be tempered by their cosmic settings, and developed and enjoyed where they occur, in our bodies and our universe.

To employ pragmatism as a method does not necessarily prevent acceptance of realism as part of the content of one's philosophy; some philosophers can derive more genuine satisfaction from a world which is independent of their minds than from one which their minds construct or reconstruct. So a pragmatist may be a realist; but a realist can hardly return the compliment. A realist maintains that any given belief is not true because it works, but works because it is true, that is, because it corresponds to conditions in the world independent of us. Pragmatism confuses utility, which is often an agreeable accompaniment of truth, with that matter-of-fact correspondence between our ideas and the objective universe which the realist regards as the indispensable condition and characteristic of truth. Or, if the pragmatism is more active, it confuses our search for truth with the object of the search.

There are cases where the truth is uncertain, and no one knows what ultimately does work. In these cases it is no great help for pragmatism to set up a psychological substitute, satisfaction; this may be the very thing which will distract our attention, or lull our senses, and hinder the search. Again, there may be cases in which an illusion, frankly understood to be an illusion, has more value than the hard fact it offsets; in such a case, whether truth is ascribed to the illusion or to the fact, the pragmatic theory of truth is hard to maintain.

(4) Where pragmatism, as with James, has dared to emphasize the part of our wills in making up our beliefs, critics have been quick to urge that the world is not plastic, and that even mind in all its glory can not, in any primary or fundamental way, remold the scheme of things nearer to the heart's desire. James indeed saw that his principle did not apply to objective nature, but only to certain problems in human experience where intellect could not furnish the answer.[23] But even this restriction did not satisfy the critics. There are, first of all, considerations from the problem of freedom, but granting that we have some "options" in these matters, it will hardly do to call our option about God forced; many a man feels no such urgency about it. We ought not to get the impression, either, that the odds between affirmation and denial are necessarily even. A negative is always in some respect indeterminate, and may have reference to untold probabilities which the syntax of an alternative or a balanced sentence conceals.

James' contention that if a man believes he can jump the chasm his belief will help him must be checked, for pragmatic consequences, against the mute testimony of the men who have believed that they could, and have jumped and fallen in—or by asking the suitors who believed they would win, but whose presumption made them so disagreeable that they lost. Finally, even if the legitimacy of such supposed reinforcement from psychology be granted, there is the further question whether this reinforcement amounts to belief, or merely to a confused proceeding in the absence of belief. Such procedure of course may be only temporary. It may stimulate increased devotion to the work in hand. It may aid a man to formulate or hold tentative assumptions. It may lead eventually to belief, as well as to satisfactory results; but it may also lead the other way and run up against bewildering realities for which it is not adequately prepared. Mountain climbers, suitors, and men who seek God ought always to hope for the best and on occasions let their hopes sustain them, but not to think that just because they hope and seek and strive, they therefore believe. James himself later said that the title of his essay might well have been "The Right to Believe," but it is doubtful if such a change would save him from fundamental confusions.

(5) Many absolutists have criticized pragmatism for its relativism, and have insisted either that the pragmatic theory concealed an absolute or could not hope to endure without one. A formula such as is reached in the term "practical absolute" might be expected to satisfy both parties, but has the weakness of a verbal compromise, if not an adjectival contradiction.

(6) Most critics think that pragmatism has exaggerated the importance of change, flux, and dynamism, and that it has been in too great haste to see old landmarks and standards carried away. Pragmatism has sometimes merited description as the philosophy of impatience, and even of barbarism as regards historic achievements. Even where it is recognized that standards and opinions do inevitably change, it has to be granted that they do not all change at the same rate and that the more slowly moving, provided they are not retarded by mere laziness, stupidity or prejudice, are entitled to rank as relatively permanent. This differential rate of change is probably what gives us the world structure, but the pragmatists often seem to be blind to structure and its importance.

(7) Closely allied to its emphasis on change is pragmatism's flair for the future. Dewey has emphasized the prospicient attitude so much that he sometimes seems to urge an utterly impossible procedure with regard to our accumulated and accumulating past. This pitch toward the future has been urged for problems of religion in some of the later writings of Wieman, who continually voices enthusiasm for new and unexplored values.

(8) From the first, the critics of pragmatism have objected to its drift toward pluralism. Just as one man's meat is another man's poison, so one pragmatist's truth is another pragmatist's error. What is to be the norm when the satisfactions of different persons, or of the same person at different times, show such variations and discrepancies? The pragmatists might reply that as time goes on, and men compare their experiences, they will come at least to a broad general agreement; but the more characteristically pragmatic answer, both in James and Dewey, amounts to pluralism. And pluralism, here as always, raises more problems than it answers.

(9) With all its emphasis on practice and practical tests, pragmatism, when judged by its own fruits, has little to show. At its best it has been a theory about practice rather than a practice, and a ferment rather than a program. At its worst it advocates what is virtually a mere opportunism, a changing of the course at each new turn, with all the attendant dangers of temporizing and following the lines of least resistance. In matters of religion, pragmatism has certainly not been an unmixed blessing. As seen by its more extreme critics, it served only to delay the collapse of an outworn supernaturalism and a fantastic idealism; but with supernaturalism and idealism headed into a decline, the pragmatic appeal to our satisfactions was futile and after a while could not deliver the satisfaction to which it referred.

BRIEF ESTIMATE OF PRAGMATISM

It is true that pragmatism is vague, but only an artificial ideology can appear without its penumbra. Pragmatism is, on the whole, anti-intellectual, but its charge that our choice of theories and beliefs is linked with our satisfactions is hard to refute. The best way to meet the charge is to admit it, with the proviso that we shall be satisfied only by trying to know the facts of the world as they are, however hard and cold they may be.

The criticism that the pragmatists, while urging the relativity of our judgments, conceal a latent absolutism in the very finality with which they hold their own doctrine is not very serious; the absolutism can be said to be in the form of their statement rather than in the content. Again distinguishing between the "that" and the "what," we may legitimately assert that the truth about the world is absolute, while leaving quite relative the question as to what the truth is.

While the dynamism, futurism, and pluralism associated with pragmatism have the defects of their several qualities, the freshness and vigor which they bring into philosophy might be envied by any system. Pragmatism ought to study liquid crystals and from them learn that flux and structure are quite compatible.

The great defect of pragmatism, as with most of philosophies of values, seems to be its failure adequately to observe the structure and nature of the universe, and to govern its claims accordingly. Granting that there is some place for it, and that our efforts in the world are of some significance, pragmatism has not clearly enough recognized the fact that where it operates at all it operates on a sliding scale. It is more effective in the environments where it originated, on university campuses, where there is some measure of quick control and transforming activity, than it is when applied to conditions further afield. Its effectiveness begins to decrease as soon as it is applied, off campus, to situations in economics and politics, and it is still less applicable to psychology, to biology, to the physical sciences. And it is ludicrous when applied to astronomy.[24] Certainly there is a difference in procedure as one passes from education to astronomy, from campus to Canopus. As far as astronomy is concerned, pragmatism, instead of being a cosmic philosophy, is only a cosmetic philosophy, busied with a little make-up on the surface, a little civilized rouge and powder on the face of nature.

SUMMARY AND ESTIMATE OF FOUR PHILOSOPHIES

The four principal ideologies which we have studied thus far—mysticism, supernaturalism, idealism, and pragmatism—have developed in close association with one another. Except for Dewey's humanistic version of pragmatism, the four virtually agree in affirming theism, the existence of a Being with attributes markedly personal, usually the God of one or another of the religions. All the philosophies emphasize the element of mind in the world and usually understand that mind in terms of purpose. With the exception of pragmatism, all the philosophies are old, and originate in a pre-scientific age; pragmatism is admittedly a new name for older ways of thinking. All four major philosophies of religion show a common defect: they all fail to devote adequate attention and concern to the data of the sciences and to the natural universe. Frequently they encourage indifference to the empirical data and try to discount theories based upon such data. If the world had remained as it was in the days of Plotinus, or Thomas Aquinas, or Kant, or Hegel, or even of William James, the effort for a philosophy of religion might have stopped with these philosophies. But new considerations fairly force themselves into the picture, and are formulated in new ideologies.

REFERENCES

[1] On pragmatism in general, see W. James, *Pragmatism,* 1907; A. W. Moore, *Pragmatism and Its Critics,* 1910; S. Hook, *The Metaphysics of Pragmatism,* 1927.

[2] H. Lotze, *Microcosmus,* transl. E. Hamilton and E. E. C. Jones, 1888, Vol. I, p. xvi.

[3] A. Ritschl, *The Christian Doctrine of Justification and Reconciliation,* transl. H. R. Mackintosh and A. B. Macaulay, 1902, pp. 204*f.*

[4] H. Höffding, *Philosophy of Religion,* transl. B. E. Meyer, 1906, pp. 134, 223.

[5] W. R. Inge, *God and the Astronomers,* pp. 174, 180, 192, 260.

[6] R. B. Perry, *The Thought and Character of William James,* 2 vols., 1935.

[7] H. Vaihinger, *The Philosophy of As If,* transl. C. K. Ogden, 1924.

[8] W. James, *The Will to Believe and Other Essays,* 1907, pp. 1, 11, 24, 96*f.*

[9] W. James, *Varieties of Religious Experience,* pp. 511*f.*

[10] E. S. Ames, *The Psychology of Religious Experience,* 1910, esp. pp. 308*ff;* Ames, in *Journal of Religion,* 1, 1921, 463*f.*

[11] E. S. Ames, *Religion,* 1929, pp. 132*f,* 154*ff,* 178; *cf.* Shailer Mathews, *The Growth of the Idea of God,* 1931, p. 219.

[12] J. Dewey, in G. P. Adams and W. P. Montague, edd., *Contemporary American Philosophy,* 1930, Vol. II, pp. 20*ff.*

[13] J. Dewey, *Reconstruction in Philosophy,* 1920; Dewey and others, *Creative Intelligence,* 1917.

[14] J. Dewey, *How We Think,* 1933; *Logic, The Theory of Inquiry,* 1938, pp. 103, 177.

[15] J. Dewey, *Democracy and Education,* 1916; *Human Nature and Conduct,* 1922; *Experience and Nature,* 1925; *The Public and Its Problems,* 1927.

[16] J. Dewey, *Experience and Nature,* pp. 108, 267.

[17] J. Dewey, *Human Nature and Conduct,* pp. 331*f.*

[18] J. Dewey, *The Quest for Certainty,* 1929, p. 224.

[19] J. Dewey, *A Common Faith,* 1934, p. 51.

[20] J. Dewey, in *Christian Century,* 51 (2), 1934, p. 1551.

[21] E. W. Lyman, *Meaning and Truth of Religion,* 1933, pp. 125, 253, 345, 380, 455.

[22] A. O. Lovejoy, in *Journal of Philosophy . . .,* 5, 1908, pp. 5, 29.

[23] W. James, *Will to Believe,* pp. 20, 22, 24*ff.* With all his faith in the conservation of values, Höffding felt that it was impossible to find an objective foundation for it, or to give it a definite or interesting form (*Philosophy of Religion,* transl. B. E. Meyer, 1906, pp. 255*f.*)

[24] *Cf.* J. Dewey, *Quest for Certainty,* p. 82.

CHAPTER XI

EVOLUTIONISM

Foremost among the new considerations which have forced themselves in upon the older ideologies of religion must still be reckoned the data of evolution. The ideology called evolutionism, based on those data, provides an account of the world as a process in time, usually marked by the coming forth of something formerly latent or immanent, with emphasis upon inherent causes rather than upon initiating and intervening causes.[1] Evolutionism is, of course, not confined to the data on the origin of biological species, but is cosmic in its scope. It offers not altogether clear nor consistent, but still plausible accounts of the origin and development of practically everything comprised in the realms of matter, life, and mind—thus including atoms, stars, planets, geological formations, living organisms, nervous systems, minds, societies, arts, sciences, institutions, and religions. The theories of evolutionism are accepted in principle by practically all scientists and by many groups of religious persons, conservative as well as liberal.

Most of the philosophies which we are considering accommodate, if they do not welcome, evolutionism's chief points. The mystics have often declared that their experiences are to be obtained in successive stages of development, and in more recent years the philosophy of Bergson has established even more direct contact between evolutionism and mysticism. Most supernaturalists have more or less tacitly accepted some indications of evolution as descriptions of ways in which God works in nature; the Protestant Fundamentalists have made some difficulty about it, but their movement, a kind of revival of nineteenth-century controversies, seems now to be lapsing into quiescence. Hegel's Absolute developed through a series of stages or cycles, and although since Hegel absolute idealism has traditionally had small use for time or for history, and has tended to minimize the evolutionary process, the process still receives at least a kind of local recognition. If the cosmos is like an ocean, evolutionism is at least a major current, a kind of Gulf Stream, in it. Pragmatism, with its dynamism and futurism, has been thoroughly committed to evolutionism, and appears sometimes to have communicated some of its weaknesses to it. Naturalism and evolutionism together yield evolutionary naturalism, as in the work of Sellars, who also shows how these tendencies can be assimilated to humanism.

Along with all this, the evolutionists have developed their own types of ideology of religion. They have attempted to discern either through or in the scientific data of an evolving universe, the Object of religious sentiment and devotion. In an earlier discussion, John Fiske and Henry Drummond construed the data of evolution virtually in terms of supernaturalism, regarding evolution as the ongoing thrust of the will of a beneficent Deity, and as God's method of creation. Later on, Bergson interpreted the data as a "creative" process whereby the mystics at length are led to see God, and Lloyd Morgan and Alexander made current the phrase "emergent evolution."

Bergson's philosophy may be illustrated by amplifying one of his own metaphors, comparing the universe to a fountain.[2] There is first of all the intense, powerful upshoot of the central jet, in which the water rises to a considerable height—the primal "mounting upward" of the universe, the failure or refusal of the universe to remain in an undeveloped state. Bergson would not so much picture the upward thrust, as he would urge us to imagine ourselves feeling it in its urgency and drive. As the mounting column spends its energy it lapses, and as the water falls backward it is shattered into drops separated from one another. This externality of parts to one another, according to Bergson, is characteristic of matter; it has lost its primal energy and is what is left after that loss. In contrast to this, the upward thrust is unified; its "parts," if we must speak of parts, interpenetrate one another. So there is a primary thrusting or mounting upward, in contrast to which matter is a secondary lapsing or falling downward, and both are characteristic of the universe.

The cosmic fountain must be pictured in more than one tier. Above the first tier, with its primary upthrust which we have just described there is a smaller one, growing out of it, with a jet in which a part of the central stream is carried further upward in the same direction, although on a smaller scale and in somewhat restricted fashion. This small-scale continuation of the main cosmic process is the life process; in life the primal upthrust of the universe is continued, specifically now by the *élan vital*, or vital impulse. This, again, is to be imagined as if we could feel it in its urgency and drive, rather than as if we could analyze it into its structures and processes. The physical and chemical factors in the living process, as well as the more static forms of life itself, are represented, again, by the falling downward after the initial impulse has spent itself and has at length had to make terms with the non-living portions of the environment, whose forces tend all the time to check it and to splinter its unbroken column into fragments or parts external to one another. We may say that just as the water of the second tier of a fountain falls back to the first and to the ground, so the living species, as they lose their *élan*, tend to collapse into mechanism, without further evolutionary advance. And the individuals of the species, too, as life spends itself, tend to collapse into the mere physics and chemistry of death.

Diverging still more widely from Bergson's metaphor, but keeping essential features of his thought, we may say that there is a third tier to the fountain, and that the central jet is a further upthrust. This upthrust represents the processes of mind; it is contrasted now with the downward fall which represents the processes of the brain as they lapse into the physiological and the material. The mental processes are typified in memory, upon which Bergson's chief study in this connection has been directed. Pursuing this study, he finds marked differences between mind and brain, and regards brain structures as decidedly secondary, as mere "canalizations" useful for mind in its contacts with the material world, contacts which are effected by way of the brain and the body. Here again, the central thrust, which may be called pure consciousness, is likely sooner or later, in the face of the difficulties which confront it, to achieve no further heights, but to collapse into the mechanical routine of habit and the mere physiological structures and processes of brain, where the living unity and urge of consciousness loses its unique character.

Now, says Bergson, in effect, there are two ways of regarding the fountain of the universe; we might almost say, two ways of catching its drift. One way is quite external to the heart of the process, as if a man might try to reconstruct the fountain by piling one upon another the drops from its run-off, or even freezing them first into little hailstones or ice-cubes and piling up the fragments. One could, after a fashion, reconstruct the fountain out of such parts external one to another, but of course all the push and force would be lost. The only adequate way to get the force of the fountain is to keep close to its central jet. In the cosmic process the case is somewhat similar; the process may be studied externally, in terms suited to physics, chemistry, and arrangements of parts in space. This is precisely what Herbert Spencer has done, and the Spencerian way of thinking of the process of evolution is fragmentary, artificial, and misleading. According to Bergson, the way to get at the heart of the cosmic process is not by such an external approach as thinking affords; thinking is done essentially in spatial terms, in concepts external to each other. We get at the heart of the process not by intellect, but by intuition which is more like animal instinct; not by thinking in spatial terms, but by living in the reality of time. We must, so to speak, get in touch with, or even feel ourselves immersed in the central jet in its upward flow; we must cultivate our own intimate sense of the ongoing of time, and of our own endurance or perdurance, our growing older, in it. We must live forward, strive forward with it, in the upthrust of free acts which refuse to be bound by the limitations and obstructions of matter. Then we get the force and sense of evolution, when we catch its inner drift, feel ourselves carried in its power and capable of furthering it. We must not try to indicate, and least of all in terms of matter, where the central jet of the fountain will take us, or to what height it may rise; the future must be pictured as wide open, and life and personality must be experienced as essentially free.

Bergson's philosophy of religion may also be pictured in accordance with the metaphor of the fountain, by supposing first that the central jet increases its pressure in order to counteract the tendency to disintegration and falling backward. This will indicate roughly what he means by "static religion," where the *élan vital*, in order to prevent man in his early stages from making fatal mistakes when he depends on intelligence rather than instinct or intuition, supplies him with the "myth-making function" and keeps him steady by the mythical beings and prospects which it puts before his eyes. But this is after all a makeshift. The highest religion does not come until now and then, as in the fountain by a great spurt of the central jet a little of the water is shot upward to an unprecedented height beyond anything ordinarily achieved, so in human history the primal thrust of the cosmos sometimes produces a new kind of man. The human mind is then lifted to a new level, as in the Hebrew prophets and Jesus; these are the great mystics, almost a species by themselves. The great mystics show what the cosmic process is at its highest reach; they know that God is love.[3]

According to Lloyd Morgan's evolutionism, new levels appear in the universe in a process called "emergence," marked by "new types of relatedness." The principal levels in the universe are those of matter, life, and mind, but within these there are uncounted instances of emergence of new qualities. This emergence does not mean that the new qualities were once submerged in or among the entities of former levels, in latent or implicit fashion; it refers rather to the simple and otherwise inexplicable fact that something new has occurred, in discontinuous fashion. So far as former units are concerned, the first units of a new level are unpredictable. If ever we are able to predict what is about to occur, the concept of emergence will no longer be useful, and we shall have merely the "consequent" operation of causes and effects.

Emergent evolutionism as developed by Lloyd Morgan keeps close to the data of the sciences, and treats the problem of religion initially from a standpoint familiar in the idealistic philosophies. Accepting a number of traditional views "under acknowledgment," he regards the three levels of matter, life, and mind as related by what he calls involution and dependence. It will be clearest if by his word "involves" we understand "can not exist without," and by his "depends upon" we understand "is thereafter modified by." We may say, in Lloyd Morgan's terminology, that mind involves life and the living organism depends upon mind; we are immediately aware that mind in the ordinary sense can not exist without the organism, and that the organism after mind develops is modified by it. Now we may, in deference and courtesy to the realistic sciences, extend the principle of involution downward along the levels and admit that living organisms involve, or can not exist without matter; it is plain enough also that matter depends upon, or is increasingly modified by, the living organisms. But if we, out of courtesy to the sciences, extend the principle of involution *downward* from mind to matter, they ought in turn to allow us to extend the principle of dependence *upward* from mind, so that we can say that mind depends upon God—or, taking all the cosmic levels together, that matter, life, and mind depend in a unified way upon God and are modified by God's action upon them. Lloyd Morgan's philosophy of religion is avowedly a move in the direction of Spinoza.[4]

More imposing and original than the emergent evolutionism of Lloyd Morgan is the related system of Samuel Alexander; Lloyd Morgan inclines to idealistic views, but Alexander develops a whole system of metaphysics from the standpoint of realism, affording, almost for the first time in recent thought, a philosophy of religion worthy to be measured against that sponsored by the idealists. Alexander regards epistemology as a chapter within metaphysics, not its indispensable foundation. This foundation or fundamental level of the universe, Alexander finds in Space-Time, the matrix of the metaphysical categories and of all later cosmic developments. His list of levels is more elaborate than that of Lloyd Morgan. After the initial Space-Time come primary qualities, then matter, life, secondary qualities, and mind. Each of these levels has already emerged from the one preceding it, and there are some indications of a future level, not yet actual, which Alexander calls deity. In ourselves we are most intimately aware of the difference of level between mind and body —the emergence in us, that is, of the quality of consciousness, from a lower level of complexity which is vital. This is our criterion for differences of level anywhere—not that at other levels we find the qualities of mind, but that throughout the universe we find other differences of quality comparable in range and abruptness to the familiar difference of mind and body. The word "mind" is used in what may be a different meaning in the statement that "time is the mind of space"; it indicates a mobility or process, and the difference between time and space may be compared to that between mind and brain. The universe evolves from level to level always with a "Nisus," or urge to something higher; it marks a trend in the whole cosmos, not merely in the living organisms. The Nisus is the urge in the process up to date, but it tends to push further, toward the unrealized level of deity.[5]

Alexander's statements about deity are quite novel. It is not necessarily a human mind nor an aggregation of such minds, but it is of the mental order, and is borne by a complex and subtle portion of the mental structure. We can not yet know what it is, and can neither enjoy it nor contemplate it. It is not spirit, but a complexity and refinement of spirit. It is not God, for God is the Nisus of the universe toward it. It is to be conceived by the aid of the concept of mind in its difference from body, and the concept of infinity. Deity will be as far beyond mind as mind is now beyond body. But it may be identified, at least pictorially, with the finite gods of religion and mythology.[6]

Alexander argues for an adjustment of our values, sentiments, and emotions to the Nisus of the universe. Religion, he says, is an emotion incident to an adequate understanding of things. As a sentiment, religion is the sense of outgoing to the whole universe in its process towards the quality of deity.[7]

CRITICISMS OF EVOLUTIONISM

In spite of its wide acceptance, there are notable criticisms of evolutionism which ought not to be ignored.

(1) The argument for evolution depends primarily upon serial arrangements of data and either observation or inference regarding inherent causes operative between members of the series. When the criteria of belief and proof are applied to evolutionism, there are many gaps in the data, or, if the data are regarded as evidence, gaps in the evidence. The loopholes are occasionally large enough for a critic to insert the finger of scorn.

Details on these points are available in books dealing with evolutionism in general, as well as with the special sciences. For instance, in the most widely familiar problem, that of the origin of species, there are gaps in the fossil series, and even though with fresh discoveries the gaps are becoming smaller, alternative arrangements raise questions at many minor points. The newer work on mutations—particularly the experiments which, following Muller, show that the rate of mutations in the fruit fly increases 150 times when the germ cells are exposed to the action of X-rays [8]—makes a strong argument for the origin of species from disturbances of the chromosomes by radiations, but the inference involves so many suppositions about radiations available in previous ages, and so many questions of definition as to just what is a species and just what constitutes a change of species, that broad generalizations are still uncertain.

In the meantime, along other lines of evolutionist argument than that concerned with the origin of species, controversies between mechanists and vitalists keep some of the evolutionists fighting among themselves about the origin and nature of life. In the physical sciences, the bewildering data on the interlocking relationships of radioactive atoms make any detailed theories of the evolution of the chemical elements hard to set up and easy to knock down. A few years ago there were clear accounts of the supposed sequences of stages in the evolution of stars, but new discoveries at least have greatly complicated the problem. Theories of mental and social evolution are beset by corresponding difficulties, particularly when the pure line of evolutionist theories is so often crossed with theories of progress.

In the face of these difficulties, any evolutionism which is held must be held with the understanding that it has not been proved, and that questions can be raised as to whether the data at hand really amount to evidence or not. Evolutionism stands for a group of inferences hard to define, and sometimes hard to defend, for a body of generalizations not altogether harmonious, for a theory or group of theories which, instead of marching evenly along, sometimes gives the impression of sprawling or scrambling, and having hard work to cover all the questions and difficulties involved. Evolutionism is not necessarily a simpler interpretation of the available data than is supernaturalist creationism, nor a more economical interpretation; assertions that it is such depend upon what is regarded as simple or economical, and even when these meanings are agreed upon, there is no demonstration that the cosmos must be run either simply or economically.

(2) Even more fundamental than criticisms of the alleged evidences of evolutionism are those directed against some of its presuppositions. Evolutionism, with its emphasis upon inherent causes, presupposes causes operative in time, but in the general overhauling which marks contemporary metaphysics, both causality and time have been subjected to criticism which may be important. In accordance with the Heisenberg principle of indeterminacy, it now appears that our actual account of fine-structure causation in the universe must be statistical.[9] On other grounds it begins to appear that there

may also be macroscopic processes of causation on a scale and of a kind as yet unknown to us. Temporal succession, also, may be only a local characteristic of the cosmos in our neighborhood, and we must be careful about affirming that its characteristics, such as its before-and-after relationship, apply to the whole universe. Interlocked with these questions is the old difficulty, which for many minds is still as strong as ever—how can anything produce something which it is not, or how can any effect be greater than its cause?

(3) Ethically, the critics of evolutionism still reiterate the famous words of T. H. Huxley, that in view of the ruthless ferocity evident in evolution, it is the part of man, if he would be moral, not to imitate the cosmic process but to combat it.[10] Later modifications of this extreme view have seen in the evolutionary process some cooperation as well as competition, and some mutual aid as well as struggle for existence. But when any attempt is made to envisage the data as a whole, there is so much waste and loss, pain and suffering, injustice and oppression, failure and death involved that no one can clear the record and make evolutionism the equivalent of progress, to say nothing of making it equivalent to goodness or to good. The good man still has to be better than what he sees in the sub-human world around him, and valuations which he tries to call eternal sometimes seem to be only ephemeral.

(4) From the side of religion there are criticisms of a different kind, although perhaps in the long run not less weighty. The creationists have always deplored evolutionism's characteristic lack of concern with beginnings, and its preoccupation with present, rather than with ultimate outcomes of the cosmic process. Some outstanding evolutionists, like Lloyd Morgan, have met this by admitting that the beginnings of the process may be ascribed to the activity of God,[11] and at the other extreme, as regards ultimate outcomes, we have Alexander

rising to prophecy in his doctrine of evolving deity. But even with such a preface and such an epilogue it must be confessed that evolutionism has often proved religiously disappointing. When once its enthusiasm has run out, there is a kind of inner poverty about it which embarrasses most attempts to make it into a theism.

(5) Besides these general criticisms, we must note some criticisms of the outstanding individual evolutionist systems of Bergson, Lloyd Morgan, and Alexander.

Bergson is open to many criticisms which are used whenever any one advocates reliance upon intuition; there is bound to be some uncertainty and more or less mystery about it, even though intuitionism can usually defend itself on its own ground. More damaging to Bergson is his virtual alliance with a vitalistic biology and with an interactionist or animistic psychology; his system, although ultimately monistic, is shot through with a proximate dualism which many regard as archaic, and as empirically on the defensive. Bergson's partiality for time at the expense of space seems quite one-sided. I am as immediately aware of taking up room as I am of enduring through time, and thinking is not to be disparaged because it follows spatial forms. His emphasis on change and spontaneity and a future which is said to be wide open, like all philosophies of flux, offers more adventure than assurance, and affords more enthusiasm than confidence. Some details of his argument, for instance the treatment of instincts and "virtual instincts," suffer from romanticism. And it is hard to see how the common man can free himself from static religion and achieve dynamic religion, unless he follows the great mystics and becomes too much like them to do his ordinary work.

Lloyd Morgan's philosophy is clear in its discernment of matter, life, and mind as major stages of evolution, but it suffers from too much entanglement with older views. Because G. H. Lewes used the term "emergence" to signify that there is an unpredictable factor,[12] Lloyd Morgan retains the word in that confusing sense; it would be better to speak of his theory as "occurrent evolution." It is hard for him to avoid the charge that he has merely given a name to ignorance, and at best put labels upon the gaps in our knowledge. At important points, too, he lacks originality; there are too many acceptances "under acknowledgment." His insistence upon associating evolution with progress requires careful and arbitrary definition. And his complicated doctrines of involution and dependence seem curious and precarious.

The work of Alexander offers a shining mark for criticisms from many sides. Those most important for us here concern his theory of Space-Time, his use of the term "mind," and his treatment of deity.

In his treatment of space and time as essentially inseparable he has the support of outstanding mathematicians and physicists, and his work represents a great pioneering effort to bring these newer views into metaphysics. In the detailed development of the doctrine he has proceeded with a kind of common sense pictorial notion of substance and its parts, rather than with a mathematical analysis, so that the result lacks precision. It involves the receptacle theory of space, whereas many mathematicians and physicists now think of space as a function of the presence of matter in a field. There are some minor confusions, too; Space-Time is said to be prior to the primary qualities, but still must involve extension, which is one of Locke's primary qualities.

In spite of his evident attempt to subordinate epistemology to metaphysics, he still shows the influence of older discussions and standpoints. Primary qualities and secondary qualities are erected into levels of cosmic development. This seems like an exaggerated realism, which might be necessary to extricate us if we were really caught with our minds insulated from the world, in the predicament in which John Locke thought we were, but which in view of the normal interaction between our minds and the world seems, as Whitehead would say, like an artificial bifurcation of nature.

Alexander is cautious in his treatment of mind, and wishes to leave no occasion for idealistic interpretations of his system. He tries explicitly to show that he does not read mind as it is in us into the other levels of the universe, or regard us as the standard or measure of things.[13] But it is certainly still less clear if we are to attempt to use the difference of mind in us, the intuited difference between mind and body, as the criterion for other differences of level throughout the universe. What is this difference in us, if it is not mental in quality, or how can any one estimate in any other terms how different mind is from body? We noted also the apparent ambiguity when it is said that time is the mind of space.

Finally, although Alexander's God has more present existence than deity, his futurism as regards deity is of doubtful religious value, and involves at best a high venture of faith. Even the doctrine of God as the Nisus of the universe toward deity is vague and hard to differentiate from a colorless pantheism.

In spite of all these criticisms, the work of Alexander stands out like a mountain upon the horizon, and for our time serves to mark out a new land in philosophy of religion. Until it appeared, with supernaturalism for many thinkers dissolving like a cloud and the idealistic systems evaporating like a mist, there seemed little besides a barren naturalism available as the philosophical home of man. But if Alexander is right even in a few of the main outlines of his work, there are other possibilities, and realists and naturalists may find God in their own ways. These possibilities need to be studied eagerly and in detail. It begins to look as if the majesty of the universe as understood in modern times and the power of religion as experienced in the past could be combined.

AN ESTIMATE OF EVOLUTIONISM

With such a possibility beginning to appear, there seems to be no point in rejecting evolutionism. The main argument for accepting it is not its so-called proofs, nor evidences, nor economy of inference, nor values, but the apparently weak point that evolutionist thinking is an outstanding fashion of our time. In thinking as in wearing clothes, not everyone is concerned with following the fashion, and there is sometimes every reason for not doing so. But in the history of thought a hundred years are as a season, and long prevailing trends become significant. After decade has spoken to decade and century to century it is not so essential that they should conserve what passed for science among the ancient Hebrews. Evolutionism can hardly be disregarded; it may be either accepted or combatted. From the point of view of religion, it seems to be more promising and more effective to accept it and see where religion comes out, than to attempt to combat it by methods allied with either agnosticism or obscurantism.

NOTE ON LIBERAL PROTESTANTISM AND RELIGIOUS REALISM

The range of philosophies which we have called mysticism, supernaturalism, idealism, pragmatism, and evolutionism marks the principal affiliations of the so-called liberal Protestantism.[14] Like all liberalisms and freedoms, this is not precisely defined, but in general the liberal Protestants agree in a theistic view of the world, which they attempt to ground in experience or in nature or in history, particularly in the critically estimated life and personality of the "historic" Jesus. Liberals have frequently used the language and many of the doctrines of supernaturalism, but the philosophical weight of nineteenth and early twentieth century liberalism has been borne by idealism and pragmatism. This liberalism has been flexible enough to admit the evolutionisms: John Fiske and Henry Drummond saw to that in their generation, and the more recent systems of Bergson and Lloyd Morgan are quite capable of interpretation in terms of theism.

Some of the leading liberal Protestants of the day, for their philosophy of religion and theology, combine elements from the philosophies we have mentioned.

D. C. Macintosh develops what he calls an empirical approach to theology, with a scientific and critical treatment of traditional theological concepts. In the course of it, he criticizes and virtually rejects the preexistence of Jesus, premillenarianism, and the existence of the devil, but manages to retain, sometimes in modified form, a large number of the other features of the traditional theology. The religious experience is grounded immediately upon an unresolved intuition, with its conviction that God exists. With our volitional element employed, a proper selection of empirical data distinguishes divine elements in the world, and we find that we can depend upon a power not ourselves making for righteousness. God's fundamental attribute is absoluteness; it is practically necessary that this absolute be personal and intuitively certain that it is so. Other attributes are discovered with distinctions which remind one of scholastic distinctions. God must be infinite, but not absolutely unconditioned or unlimited; emphasis on transcendence is a mark of religious realism. Along with "critical monism" in epistemology, there are traces of dualism in an interactionist view of mind and body, a super-mechanical theory of life, a doctrine of revelation, and the suggestion that God is to the physical universe as the human spirit is to the body. The non-Christian religions are to the Christian religion as candles to sunlight.[15]

W. M. Horton maintains that God, besides being each person's better self and all that is best in our human heritage, is a vast cosmic drift which can be empirically detected as moving in the direction of increasing organization, harmony, and concrete relationships of fellowship and mutual aid. Horton thinks there is bifurcation if we rule out secondary qualities and values from all this, and is inclined to interpret the data as a mighty thrust of intelligent will. [16]

The evolutionism of Samuel Alexander, with its Object of religious devotion the Nisus of the universe towards deity and its promise of deity in the future, approximately marks the boundary to which liberal Protestantism ordinarily goes. If Alexander's deity is disregarded or discarded because it is so problematical and vague, we are left with the Object of religious devotion somewhere in the universe as the universe is now; we are fairly enough beyond the outposts of what has been called liberal Protestantism, and are beginning to encounter the naturalisms. We shall find many liberals and many Protestants there, too, but with a new emphasis on religion as adjustment to something in the cosmos, and a debate going on as to whether such a cosmic factor should be called God or referred to with terms appropriate to theism. This new emphasis we call religious naturalism.

The term "religious realism" [17] is not distinctive enough to indicate such a position. Realism may be understood either in the epistemological sense of affirming reality independent of our minds, or in the aesthetic sense of representing a world as it is, without reading into it what we should like to have there. Any religion short of solipsism is realistic in the first sense, and realism in the second sense is a theory of evil rather than a philosophy of religion.

Under the leadership on the one hand of those who call themselves religious realists, and on the other hand of the Barthians, the liberal Protestantism of the turn of the century has been roundly criticized. It is said to be superficial and lacking in depth, confined to relatively unimportant matters like keeping up church attendance (often by recourse to cheap sensationalism), insensitive to the tragedy of the cross or the weightier matters of the law. It is said to waver between science and supernaturalism; advocates of each see in it too much of the other. Horton calls it psychologically stupid, sociologically shallow, and politically inept.[18] It is said to represent the comfortable individualistic outlook of the capitalistic or the middle classes rather than the bitter struggle of the common people against injustice and exploitation. A frequent criticism concerns its too facile optimism and its tendency to overestimate man's capabilities. It is more ready to hope and pray for the best than to suffer to achieve it. Barthians criticize it for being too rationalistic, and rationalists criticize it for being too romantic, sentimental, and relying too much on intuition. It is said to be too worldly, too passively adjusted to contemporary culture rather than to the eternal. Still more incisive is the charge of futility; critics declare that liberal Protestantism, although it has cultivated a kind of sane uprightness, has failed to show the rock-like characters and personalities characteristic of orthodoxy. It has lost the note of moral and of cosmic urgency. It is religiously vapid. It lacks cohesiveness and definiteness, and fails to sound the note of authority. Doctrinal decomposition has set in, with only verbal associations to bind its half-skeptical opinions to the great doctrines of the past. Contemporary zeal for denominational mergers and ecumenical conferences is regarded as an attempt to consolidate lines which are breaking. Philosophically, liberalism has to take criticisms levelled against idealism and pragmatism, without being able to defend itself with supernaturalism's weapons. Practically, while it preserves the shells of outworn institutions, such as those of the denominations, other institutions are taking over with more technical efficiency the social functions once exercised by the church. Many critics with an eye for history see liberal Protestantism in a period of slow decline.

Many liberals find no difficulty in replying to these criticisms in terms of either doctrine or practice, but when pressed hard on either side liberalism falls back on the statement that what it stands for is not so much a content, but a method—the method of unhampered inquiry and generous devotion. Judged again from the point of view of history, liberalism has made a gallant effort to reform under fire the lines of free religion. Liberalism is guilty of moving some of the ancient landmarks, but it has not moved them all at the same time. It has kept religion respectable in the eyes of many students of history, philosophy, and the natural and social sciences, whom otherwise some new Schleiermacher might have found among religion's "cultured despisers." It must not be forgotten, either, that the middle class needs salvation as much as those below it or above it—religion must click in the middle registers, too!

It seems to be generally agreed that the net result of all these criticisms places liberal Protestantism in a serious plight. The position was perhaps never strong; the positions of seekers and pilgrims seldom are. Now it seems to be distrusted, and there are notable defections in two directions—one back to supernaturalism, now revised in the Barthian manner, and the other to the more radical ideologies which we shall call naturalism, humanism, and economic nationalism.

EVOLUTIONISM

REFERENCES

[1] See G. P. Conger, *New Views of Evolution,* 1929.

[2] See H. Bergson, *Creative Evolution,* transl. Mitchell, 1913, p. 247.

[3] H. Bergson, *Two Sources of Morals and Religion,* transl. Audra and Brereton, p. 240.

[4] C. L. Morgan, *Emergent Evolution,* pp. 15*ff.,* 33.

[5] S. Alexander, *Space, Time, and Deity,* esp. Vol. I, p. 7; Vol. II, pp. 38, 75.

[6] *Ibid.,* Vol. II, pp. 353-61, 366, 392*ff.*

[7] *Ibid.,* Vol. II, pp. 373-6, 402; Alexander, in *Chronici Spinozani,* 5, 1927, p. 27.

[8] See R. J. Muller and T. S. Painter, in *American Naturalist,* 63, 1929, pp. 193*ff.*

[9] See A. S. Eddington, *Nature of the Physical World,* p. 220.

[10] T. H. Huxley, *Evolution and Ethics,* 1893, p. 34.

[11] C. L. Morgan, *Emergent Evolution,* p. 2.

[12] *Ibid.,* p. 3.

[13] S. Alexander, *op. cit.,* Vol. II, p. 39.

[14] On liberal Protestantism, besides the works cited in this and other chapters, see A. Sabatier, *Religions of Authority and the Religion of the Spirit,* transl. L. S. Houghton, 1904: W. A. Brown, *Beliefs that Matter,* 1928: R. L. Calhoun, *God and the Common Life,* 1935: H. E. Fosdick, *Adventurous Religion,* 1931; *As I See Religion,* 1932: H. P. Van Dusen, *The Plain Man Seeks for God,* 1933: J. S. Bixler and R. L. Calhoun, eds., *The Nature of Religious Experience,* 1937: Bixler, *Religion for Free Minds,* 1939.

[15] D. C. Macintosh, *Theology as an Empirical Science,* 1927, pp. 17, 31, 91, 96, 103, 109, n, 122, 135, 140-2, 162*f,* 172, 178*ff,* 188*ff,* 213, 227, 240*f,* 251*f.*

[16] W. M. Horton, *Theism and the Modern Mood,* 1930, pp. 117-122.

[17] See D. C. Macintosh, ed., *Religious Realism,* 1931.

[18] W. M. Horton, *Realistic Theology,* 1933, p. 39.

CHAPTER XII

NATURALISM

In the history of philosophy, materialism, mechanism, and naturalism are closely associated. Materialism is a theory of what the world is made of, and is the opposite of idealism or spiritualism. Mechanism is a theory of how the world runs, and is, as we saw in Chapter V, virtually the opposite of teleology. Naturalism is, strictly speaking, the opposite of supernaturalism; its various meanings we shall now examine in detail.

As a starting point, let us say that according to naturalism the world is what the physical sciences, with the aid of mathematics, find it to be. The older materialism, from the days of Democritus, Lucretius, and the Indian Çarvakas, declared that the universe could be analyzed into units somewhat like those now studied in physics and chemistry. In the eighteenth century the French Encyclopaedists made materialism popular and somewhat threatening. In the nineteenth century Karl Marx, as a left wing Hegelian, applied a few of its principles to social and economic processes. Later under the leadership of Wilhelm Ostwald it was maintained that matter itself could be at least theoretically resolved into energies, and materialism began to lose its ancient content and prestige. Presently there were fresh losses due to the more empirically grounded discoveries concerning electrons and radiations and their part in the constitution of matter. Many writers on philosophy of religion hastily assumed that since this older materialism had been exploded, the universe of energies or electric charges or aether must be spiritual; but more competent and critical writers saw that the discovery of finer structure in matter did not necessarily mean any moral refinement in its nature and that in fact the way was now clear for a mechanism which would be more difficult to refute because its data were more remote.

In the meantime the steady advances of the analytical sciences made it easy to accept reductive theories. A reductive theory maintains that the statement "*x* is composed of parts *a, b, c, . . . n.*" is equivalent to the statement "*x* can be fully explained in terms of properties of *a, b, c, . . . n.*" For example, the living organism, composed of chemical compounds, can be explained in terms of chemistry. In general, any integrated whole can be explained in terms of its parts. Such a reductive naturalism or mechanism is especially attractive when some of the opposed teleological views are invested with extravagant mystery imported from realms outside the range of science; but if any one distrusts or dreads it, it can be avoided without reverting to the philosophies we have considered, by adopting another type of naturalism.

In place of the old reductive naturalism, Sellars makes the newer naturalism distinguish various levels of causality, especially those of matter, life, mind, and society.[1] This "evolutionary naturalism" attempts to be constructive without pulverizing its universe; it retains more of the content and spirit of evolutionism than does the extreme reductive naturalism, which is so concerned with the elements in the process that it virtually disregards the fact that the process takes place.

Such newer naturalism holds that the universe exhibits the combination and fusion, in one evolutionary process, of "genetic continuity and generic discontinuity." The word "genetic" refers to origins and derivations; if there is any question about the origin or derivation of later stages or levels in the universe, the answer is that they come from earlier stages continuously, by inherent causation rather than primarily by intervening causation. But the word "generic" refers to kinds, to classifications. If the question is about the *kind* of entity resulting from the continuous process, the answer may be that it is a new kind, and belongs in a class discontinuous with the old. The combination of genetic continuity and generic discontinuity may be illustrated by a helicoid spiral in which the later turns or coils are continuous with the earlier, but are wider and are considered in the order of their widths or diameters. The spiral throughout its extent may be called continuous, but the lengths of the lines measuring the diameters of the coils are discontinuous. Similarly, the universe may be regarded as generated in a continuous process, in the course of which matter, life, and mind occur with their discontinuous qualities. The point about generic discontinuity is obscured when it is said that the new product or whole is *more* than the sum of its parts; this statement raises unnecessary difficulties. All that should be claimed is that the new product or whole is *other* than its parts taken in other orders or relationships and has qualities or properties other than theirs. The new properties at the stage or level of living organisms appear in the things which organisms do and their components do not do. At the level of mind in us, the new properties may, as Spaulding has pointed out, appear in our freedom,[2] those properties wherein our actions are different from their antecedents. Sometimes the appearance of such new properties is interpreted as "emergence," and the philosophy is called emergent evolutionism, although not quite in Lloyd Morgan's sense.

Another way of avoiding rigid mechanism has been suggested in connection with the Heisenberg principle of indeterminacy, according to which individual electrons can not be so definitely located that full details are predictable, but the more general view is that statistical interpretations of the principle and of causality leave the gross physical processes as mechanistic as ever.

At the present time naturalism is often formulated in the so-called physicalism, associated with logical positivism or logical empiricism. These views exhibit variations, but in general attempt to combine a high degree of scientific caution in confronting nature with an exhaustive critique of the processes of language, etc., which are used in interpreting what is found. It is said that every "protocol" statement or record of direct experience or experiment follows a certain syntax or logical form and is subject to translation into various "languages" appropriate to different fields of research. The language of physics consists primarily of terms denoting spatio-temporal positions, spatio-temporal regions and quantitative determinations of physical states associated with them. Physicalism asserts that every protocol statement about observed data can be translated into the language of physics.[3]

NATURALISM AND RELIGION: AESTHETIC NATURALISM

There are three principal attempts to adapt naturalism to philosophy of religion—the aesthetic naturalism of Santayana, affiliated with Platonism; the religious naturalism of a large group of writers who, as we saw, look to the physical universe to find the Object of religious devotion; and the humanism which Sellars regards as the religious expression of evolutionary naturalism. The first two we consider in this chapter, the last in the following chapter. Marxian materialism will be discussed in connection with the chapter on economic nationalism.

In what we call aesthetic naturalism, the outstanding figure for a generation has been George Santayana. The subtlety of his thought and the felicity of his phrases are among the treasures which contemporary philosophy deposits with history. As regards the existent world, he has claimed to be the only living materialist; he thinks of naturalism as almost self-evidently the only explanation of existence. In contrast to it, all supernaturalist theology is only a glorified mythology. There are natural grounds for religion, and moral values are enshrined in its historic doctrines; but where the Greeks took their religion aesthetically, the Hebrews and the Christians have throughout their history insisted that their doctrines have literal truth and moral authority. Since this is impossible for a reflective mind to believe, we now face the problem of restating the Hebraic content in the Greek way.

We should retain the Old and the New Testaments as we retain the Iliad, without raising the question of their truth or falsehood. But reflection may lead us, as it led Plato, to discern not merely the existent world, which can be illumined by imaginative poetry, but also a texture of "essence," discerned as intrinsic qualities of our immediate experience, and forming the timeless theme of all imagination and all high poetry. Essences are not existents; existence is too poor for them. They are hardly subsistents, in any usual meaning of that term —perhaps "persistents" would describe them best. They are not parts of the ordinary world; they are not outside it nor above it—they are luminous within it, whenever we are intent upon the quality of any momentary experience, or think carefully of what is involved in our science, logic, metaphysics, or religion.[4]

Santayana declares that we are all, like animals, swimming for dear life in the cosmic flux; the essences, we might say, are like a rainbow gleaming in the midst of the spray. To contemplate them is, for Santayana, enough; there is a trace of pathos and pessimism about it all, and any hint that the rainbow may turn out to be an unearthly bridge by which we can escape from the otherwise inevitable flux, if the hint appears at all, appears to be withdrawn. In any event, we ought to use religion as a means of opening treasures accessible to the imagination. The rainbow may divert our attention and beautify the otherwise dull drama of our days. Contemplation of essences is not merely aesthetic, but essentially religious. Once Santayana was moved to write, "Their presence or absence, their purity or contradiction, make up the spiritual sum of life, all that matters in it, without which no one would care to raise his head from the pillow of non-being." [5]

Aesthetic naturalism as advocated by Santayana looks through the existent world and seeks to discern essences in its events; the center of spiritual gravity is not in the existences, but in the essences. Apart from Santayana, aesthetic naturalism loses most of its glamour; it becomes a more ordinary appreciative attitude with regard to existing things, shading into what we may call ethical and religious naturalisms.

Ethical naturalism, the view that the natural universe, on the whole, supports our efforts to attain moral ideals, is sometimes distinguished and given a name, but there is little to say about it that is not said about religious naturalism.

RELIGIOUS NATURALISM

What we here call religious naturalism is the view that the Object of religious devotion is identical with the universe or some portion of the universe, some process or direction or trend in it, as studied in the sciences. The view is distinguished from pantheism, either because the quasi-personification characteristic of pantheism is not studied in the sciences, or else because in this naturalism the problem of evil is avoided by restricting the Object of devotion to a portion of the universe. Religious naturalism is of course to be distinguished from the oldfashioned "natural religion," which consisted in excursions in primitive spiritisms, and from natural theology, which consisted in attempts by the use of natural reason to demonstrate the existence and some of the attributes of the God of supernaturalism. Primitive "nature worship" is either too much affected by spiritism or supernaturalism, or else it is confined to objects too familiar and obvious, to be classed with the religious naturalism with which we are here concerned. This religious naturalism is also to be distinguished from the "Thermopylae" view of Bertrand Russell's *Free Man's Worship*,[6] where man dies hard in a universe unfriendly and overwhelming. Religious naturalism regards the universe or some major trend in it as necessary and on the whole favorable to the religious adjustment.

While largely dominated by theories and beliefs concerning a Power superior to the natural universe, Western philosophy has shown numerous signs of looking to the universe itself, or to some portion of it, for the sanction of religion. In Stoicism the view was pantheistic and was tinged with fatalism; in Spinoza and Hegel there was the suggestion of psychical qualities and mental processes. Schleiermacher, in the first edition of the famous addresses which practically inaugurated liberal Protestantism, declared that religion is perception of and feeling for the universe,[7] although later he subordinated perception to feeling and set the universe aside. Of the Harvard teachers of philosophy, James, Santayana, Whitehead, and R. B. Perry, with all their varied interests and emphases, can all be quoted to the effect that religion involves adjustment to the universe.[8] General Smuts' philosophy of "holism," the tendency in nature to produce wholes of various grades, supports the same view.[9] Among contemporary scientists, Einstein speaks of the cosmic religious sense, and Shapley of a "Drift" which he finds difficult of definition.[10]

Religious naturalism seems to have been developed

more extensively and consistently at the University of Chicago than anywhere else. Its chief proponents in America have been G. B. Smith and H. N. Wieman; three other Chicago teachers, E. S. Ames, Shailer Mathews, and A. E. Haydon have much in common with them. A younger man, B. E. Meland, is also numbered in the group.[11]

G. B. Smith, finding supernaturalist theism vulnerable, especially because it was too definite and clear cut to suit our advancing knowledge, saw man as one of the products of the cosmic process, and God as a reality in the process to which man's religious adjustment may be made. Just what conception of God would ultimately emerge from all this he could not tell, but he thought that religion would be interpreted in terms of "more readily identifiable stimuli" and that God would be thought of as a cosmic support of human values, a quality in the cosmic process akin to the quality of our own spiritual life.[12]

The most outstanding of these religious naturalists has been H. N. Wieman. In his earlier work he follows Whitehead's organicism. He takes Whitehead's "Principle of Concretion" to be an integrating process, a constitutional tendency, an ultimate factor in the universe, and studies its working in some detail. This working is said to be not merely physical and chemical, but also biological, psychological, and social; the emphasis falls in the latter fields. The greatest values, the richest organic wholes spring up from nature and reveal to us this Principle of Concretion. The principle must be dealt with in valuational as well as ideational ways. As organic wholes become more intimate, with more and more mutual support and dependence among their parts, more and more value is achieved; the system of maximum value is at least approximated in human society and history, with its interconnections with physical nature.

God is this integrating, value-making process in the cosmos, yielding the maximum of security and good when man makes the right adjustment. In this sense God is the structure of the universe with determinate bearing upon some one set of interests; in another sense God is greater than this and is the undefined totality, extending into the realm of possibility, with respect to which new interests may be developed. Our method of adjusting ourselves to such a God is rough and ready, and may be compared to political adjustments under the British Constitution. We can cooperate with God in achieving the maximum of interaction and integration. Wieman may be called a naturalistic theist or theistic naturalist, although for him there are difficulties about the personality of God.[13] In some of his later writings we find a pronounced tendency to futurism.

A suggestion highly important for religious naturalism comes from H. Hartshorne, who sees along with integration a process of differentiation and emphasizes it, because it is by this that the universe offers creative opportunity to its creatures.[14] Another important point is that if the universe, as is generally supposed, is unresponsive to us, a man can have a sentiment which is at least analogous to love for that which is incapable of loving him in return.[15]

CRITICISMS OF NATURALISMS

The major criticisms of materialism, mechanism, and naturalism have come from rival philosophies in developing or consolidating positions which we have considered. Thus mysticism, supernaturalism, idealism, pragmatism, and sometimes evolutionism join forces in the attempt to show that the views centering in naturalism are inadequate, particularly in problems of origins and destiny, mind, values, novelty, freedom, and the alleged realities of religion.

Among the idealists, it is urged that naturalism is too abstract, and as applied to the whole of concrete reality is an unproved assumption, a hasty generalization. It is alleged that naturalism gives no adequate account of mind, that its identification of mental and neural processes is amateurish and absurd, and that it offers only a set of formulae in place of living experience and reality. Moreover it is destructive of so many of the higher and finer aspects of life that to accept it is to sell one's spiritual birthright in a peculiarly unsatisfactory bargain.

Outstanding after a generation of such critiques is still the work of James Ward. He maintained that naturalism, in order to be free from the metaphysics of substance and cause, espoused agnosticism. Where naturalism says the problem of theology is superfluous, agnosticism says it is insoluble. He declared that naturalism is not only abstract, with equations which are not explanations, but that it deals with approximations which do not represent finality. There is, he thought, no necessity that thermal, chemical, electric, or magnetic processes should admit of complete and simple description in purely mechanical terms. On the basis of experimental demonstration, it can only be claimed that the conservation of energy is probable, and even then it does not apply to qualitative processes. Outside all this natural science is the category and realm of ends.[16]

Logical positivism or empiricism and the physicalism associated with it can be criticized for overemphasizing language as older critical philosophies overemphasized perception; there is, after all, no very fundamental difference between a man's *seeing* and his *saying*. The new empiricism makes its veiled subjectivism a refuge rather than an instrument, and tends to set problems of method at one another instead of at the universe. In its attempt to avoid metaphysics it remains too often only a nominalism or a phenomenalism or a theory of signs and fails to measure up to the sweep of cosmic problems.

Where pragmatism magnifies a method into a metaphysics, logical positivism seeks to minify metaphysics
into a method.

Naturalism is also criticized because of the pessimism
which seems to attend it, and because of its suggestion
of the ultimate futility of man's puny efforts in such an
overwhelming universe. If it is to be adopted, it should
be only as a last resort.

The work of Santayana seems to its critics like a beau-
tiful but all but despairing attempt to salvage aesthetic
quality from the natural universe and from the traditional naturalistic doctrines concerning it. The chief
question for us is whether what he has salvaged will be
able to maintain itself as the Object of religious devotion. Perhaps God should be made of more substantial
stuff. There is much to be said for any view which sees
kinship between aesthetic experience and religious experience; these two which belong close together have
been too much sundered, particularly in Protestantism,
and in more general ways throughout Christianity and
Judaism. Santayana's work quickens a response from a
paganism which is latent in the heritage of over-person-
alized and over-doctrinated faiths. But aesthetic tem-
perament as finely textured as Santayana's is not very
widespread or common, and opportunity to cultivate it
is perhaps only beginning. Even if it is true that religion is poetry at its best and theology is mythology at
its highest reaches, it will be hard for most persons to
see it. And when they see it, there will be serious questions as to whether such aesthetic insight and experience
will be vigorous enough to carry the load or do the work
of religion. No doubt the epic and dramatic elements
in theology need to be discerned, and even refined off
for undistracted enjoyment; the question will be
whether such aesthetic experiences can be an effective
substitute for a religion which men have long supposed
was more firmly grounded. If the discernment of es-

sences is the condition of all this, the poor human faculties of most of us will need an appalling degree of refinement before we are sensitized to that exotic world in the moonlight.

Platonic realism from the days of Plato until now, seems to be an exaggeration of abstractions. Some of our ideas, in their abstractness and generality, have objects of reference which seem to be detached, like white from paper, being from existences, goodness from goods, value from valuations, or meaning from meanings. All these abstractions work themselves loose, and Platonism wafts them away to adorn a world more glorious than its own original rose-hued and violet-crowned city.

Turning to current criticisms of religious naturalism we find first (1) the assertion that we do not yet know enough about the universe to hold the position with confidence. To frame a theory of the universe as a whole requires such drafts upon the imagination that Dewey, although friendly to the possibilities of religious naturalism, prefers his more cautious pragmatism of the environment.[17]

(2) If the attempt is made to distinguish within the imperfectly known universe a process or trend which can serve as an Object of religious devotion, the difficulties appear to be increased. Some critics have declared that no such process is discernible—unless indeed it be the "running down" or "shuffling" of the universe, the trend toward heat-death, the increase of entropy predicted in accordance with the second law of thermodynamics. This to most physicists appears to be eventually very probable, although there may be some cosmic upswing to offset it.[18] At any rate, it is in the remote future and does not prevent belief in an Object of religious devotion in the universe, but at most only in such an Object as eternal. Apart from considerations about entropy, most critics see the universe as an "aimless weather," [19] or perhaps as an ocean surging up and

down, with a few currents flowing here or there. It is declared that in such a play of chance any religious interpretation is arbitrary, and often a case of special pleading. All the young Leibnitzes will find the cosmos tending toward good, although Leibnitz put it more strongly than that, and all the young Schopenhauers will find it tending toward evil, although the master pessimist himself did not stop there. To some, nature is "Mother Nature"; to others, the universe is red with the struggle of tooth and claw and artillery.

(3) Other critics find it pointless to say that we should adjust ourselves to the universe or any major trend in it. All the young Margaret Fullers and Thomas Carlyles have to accept the universe anyway. If they flee from one law they merely exemplify another. Why should this inevitable condition of natural life be dignified with any of the attributes of God?

(4) In this connection we must recall that religious naturalism, as might be expected, is opposed by other types of naturalism, in which the universe and its relationships with man are carefully studied, either without bringing in the attitudes of religion, or by evoking them, for instance, as the humanists do. Bertrand Russell counsels us to be heroically religious, but without relying upon either God or the universe. We should tend the futile altar that our hands have built until we are borne down by "the trampling march of unconscious power." [20]

Most often, religious naturalism is questioned and rejected because critics fail to find in it any deep religious value.

(5) Despite some indications to the contrary, there is no great support for it in the traditions of the historic religions. Primitive nature worship passes, by way of its mythologies, into spiritisms and polytheisms; the tribes will not long worship the sun when they can imagine a sun god. In the Rig Veda, *"rita"* represents

both the cosmic and the moral order, but is only a minor figure. In the Upanishads, we find correspondences and adjustments between man and the universe, but Brahman, though cosmic in scope, is spiritual in quality. The affiliations of philosophical Hinduism are with idealism; *"dharma"* suggests conformity to cosmic law, but it is overlaid with both spiritualism and mythology. The attempt to adjust the worshipper to the universe appears most clearly in Taoism; the practical mind of China preferred nature to spirit and talked of Heaven with a minimum of personalization. And of all the world religions, Taoism has been probably the most impotent and has shown the strangest association of high philosophy and low superstitions! Confucianism can hardly be cosmic without more emphasis on metaphysics. When the Buddhist doctrine of karma, or causation, is interpreted as a cosmic process or function, we have a rudiment of religious naturalism, but in primitive Buddhism the adjustment of the individual is too subjective and too negative, and in later Buddhism there is too much polytheism. In the Semitic religions there is on the whole less feeling for the cosmos than in the religions farther to the East. Judaism, Christianity, and Islam are historically committed to supernaturalist theism. Christianity, in particular, missed its great chance to look to the cosmos for the Object of religious devotion when it failed to develop the magnificent doctrine of the Logos, the Word, the Reasonableness of things, as anything more than a minor adjunct of its more picturesque heritage from Judaism. Among the philosophies, Stoicism, with its "life according to nature" is, like Spinozism, pantheistic.

(6) With so much testimony from history, the critics can combine the witness of their own experience to say that the emotions with which men react to the cosmos are not religious emotions, and that it is impossible to find God there. Some critics, perhaps by a survival of

old-fashioned views about matter, rely so entirely upon God that they think they can despise the universe. Others find the universe vast, powerful, and perhaps even sustaining and strengthening, but they declare that this is not God: God must be something else.

This has furnished the chief criticism of Wieman's views. Several of his main teachings—emphasis on creative synthesis or integration, (by which wholes, if not more than the sum of their parts, are at least different from their parts when the latter are ordered in other ways), his organicism, his realistic theory of the production of values, his doctrine of insights into the deeper meaning of things, and his view that values require treatment in terms other than those of ideas—are amply enough defended and shared by others. His frequently expressed view that all ideas are tentative and open to correction encourages criticism of those ideas which express his views thus far. In his central doctrine concerning God, even with evolutionism and integration to point the way, it is difficult to distinguish between what he means to say is the Object of religious devotion and what is not; and if the distinction is made, hard for many to follow him in calling the Object God or the view theistic. He says that God is the growth of connections, creative syntheses (with no attempt to discuss the status of connections), but also says that this growth may be the work of God rather than God. Again, he thinks that a being able to satisfy the needs of diverse personalities could not be personal—forgetting that even an apostle could be "all things to all men."

Wieman's theories of maximum value in growth of mutually sustaining connections is indefinite, and may be quite arbitrary: a system may be very comprehensive, or be exceedingly intricate in its operations, and for that very reason lack high value. The determination of highest value or of the "best" in every situation must be more concrete, in closer detailed reference to the facts of nature and past history. One suspects that Wieman's attention is turned away from this fact by the operationalism and futurism of Dewey. Granting that there must be in nature and in history, a growing point, an edge of freedom, we should not be expected always to tilt upon that edge. Of course ideas and beliefs change, but Wieman forgets that they do not all change at the same rate and that in this way, some achieve relative permanence. His appeal to possibilities is open to criticism based on points which we shall develop in Chapter XV, concerning procedures which run the logical ball out of bounds, where any descriptive statements may be advanced or withdrawn, but where no descriptive statement should count one way or the other.[21]

SOME QUESTIONS RAISED BY NATURALISM

In view of the defects of the other ideologies of religion, it appears that any fresh thinking in the great field must turn with anxiety and hope to religious naturalism. Again let us say that this is not because the other philosophies are disproved; it is because, in view of the weaknesses which under analysis they all exhibit, they are bound as time goes on to be more and more widely disapproved.

When we turn to religious naturalism, we have to say that thus far it is disappointing. It leaves us with further work to be done on at least eight major questions. Is the Object of religious devotion definite or indefinite? Is it finite or infinite? Is it one or many? Is it changing or changeless? Is it matter (or perhaps energy, but at all events physical) or is it "spiritual"? Is it personal or impersonal? Is it purposive or mechanistic? And if we grant that it is making goodness, how shall we recognize it?

To answer these questions, religious naturalism will have to go again to its sources in nature. It will need a more thorough examination of the data of the sciences, particularly with a search for undiscovered or disregarded relationships between the natural and the social sciences and for new facts and theories bearing upon these questions concerning the Object of religious devotion. If something of this sort is not done, it is doubtful whether the outstanding attempt of Wieman and his friends to remedy the weaknesses of liberal theology will be able to hold out against humanism on the one hand and obscurantism or dogmatism on the other. After consideration of humanism and communism we shall return to these questions, taking them up one by one in our concluding chapter.

REFERENCES

[1] R. W. Sellars, *Principles and Problems of Philosophy*, 1926, Chap. XXIII; *Evolutionary Naturalism*, 1922, Chap. I; *The Philosophy of Physical Realism*, 1932.

[2] E. G. Spaulding, *The New Rationalism*, 1918, pp. 449f; Spaulding, in *Philosophical Review*, 42, 1933, pp. 156ff; *A World of Chance*, 1936, p. 231.

[3] See R. Carnap, *The Unity of Science*, transl. M. Black, 1934, pp. 42ff, 67ff; E. Nagel, in *Journal of Philosophy*, 33, 1936, pp. 30ff. The view is prominent in the currently appearing *Encyclopaedia of Unified Science*.

[4] G. Santayana, *Interpretations of Poetry and Religion*, 1900; *Reason in Religion*, 1905, esp. pp. 10, 65ff; *Scepticism and Animal Faith*, 1923, esp. pp. 77, 179; *The Realm of Essence*, 1927; *The Realm of Matter*, 1930; Santayana, in *Contemporary American Philosophy*, Vol. II, p. 245; *The Realm of Spirit*, 1940.

[5] G. Santayana, *Platonism and the Spiritual Life*, 1927, p. 13.

[6] B. Russell, *Mysticism and Logic*, 1918, p. 46.

[7] G. Wobbermin, *The Nature of Religion*, transl. T. Menzel and D. S. Robinson, 1933, p. 26.

[8] W. James, *Varieties*, p. 516; *A Pluralistic Universe*, 1909, p. 83; G. Santayana, *Reason in Religion*, p. 191; *Reason in Society*, p. 192; A. N. Whitehead, *Religion in the Making*, 1926, pp. 60, 143; R. B. Perry, *The Approach to Philosophy*, 1905, p. 66.

[9] J. C. Smuts, *Holism and Evolution*, 1926, esp. p. 343.

[10] A. Einstein, *The World As I See It*, transl. A. Harris, 1934, pp. 264ff; H. Shapley, *New York Times*, Aug. 11, 1929, p. 2.

[11] E. S. Ames, *Religion,* pp. 168, 217; S. Mathews, *Growth of the Idea of God,* pp. 214, 223; A. E. Haydon, *The Quest of the Ages,* 1929, pp. 110ff; B. E. Meland, *Modern Man's Worship,* 1935, pp. 153, 173-80, 236.

[12] G. B. Smith, *Current Christian Thinking,* 1928, pp. 143, 155, 165ff.

[13] H. N. Wieman, *The Wrestle of Religion with Truth,* 1927, pp. vi, 59, 135, 171f, 180, 239ff; Wieman, in *Religious Education,* 23, 1928, pp. 963ff; in D. C. Macintosh, ed., *Religious Realism,* pp. 155ff; Wieman and R. Westcott-Wieman, *Normative Psychology of Religion,* 1935, pp. 46ff; Wieman and B. E. Meland, *American Philosophies of Religion,* p. 272; W. M. Horton and Wieman, *The Growth of Religion,* 1938, pp. 258, 296, 325, 360ff.

[14] H. Hartshorne, in D. C. Macintosh, ed., *op. cit.,* p. 138.

[15] *Cf.* C. D. Broad, in *Hibbert Journal,* 24, 1925, pp. 35f.

[16] J. Ward, *Naturalism and Agnosticism,* Vol. I, pp. viii, 82ff, 170ff, 187; *The Realm of Ends,* 1911.

[17] See J. Dewey, *A Common Faith,* pp. 18ff; *Human Nature and Conduct,* pp. 330ff.

[18] See G. N. Lewis, *The Anatomy of Science,* 1926, pp. 141ff.

[19] *Cf.* W. James, *Varieties,* pp. 491ff.

[20] B. Russell, *op. cit.,* p. 57.

[21] Wieman, in Horton and Wieman, *op. cit.,* pp. 296, 325, 353, 360ff.

CHAPTER XIII

HUMANISM

Humanism, in general, means emphasis upon man in nature.

Several meanings, religious and non-religious, are more or less closely associated with the word. In the Italian Renaissance, it meant a revival of interest in human achievements, as illustrated by the cultures of Greece and Rome, over against mediaeval interests in the Bible and supernaturalism, which were supposedly of divine or semi-divine origin. Later, in the work of Auguste Comte, the religion of humanity, humanitarianism, marked the culmination of the famous three stages in the development of human thought, when positivism finally supplanted theology and metaphysics. It featured a bizarre worship of humanity as the object of a religion which reflected the older supernaturalism. The movement appeared in England in the work of Frederic Harrison,[1] who held that the science of nature and of man, duly concentrated on the development of human life on earth, forms a living religion, spiritual and scientific.

Again, the English version of pragmatism, centering in the work of F. C. S. Schiller, and English personal idealism, because of its emphasis on man's problems, resources, and successes, have sometimes been called humanism. In another connection, two American literary critics, Irving Babbitt and Paul Elmer More, have been called humanists because of their emphasis on man's inner life, and on an intuitive discipline appealing to a sifted tradition, largely from Greece and India, with some distrust of science and hostility to romance. This and the next type of humanism have in common the defense of man, or of the human in man, against its enemies.[2]

Religious humanism, as the term is currently employed, means the attempt to invest with religious significance our knowledge about man in nature and our service to man in constructive efforts toward a better civilization.[3]

Of all the similarities of humanism with the great religions, those with Confucianism are most marked. Confucianism reflects the Chinese interest in mundane affairs and the anxiety to improve political and social institutions, without giving much attention to speculations about the universe or superstitions about the gods. The oft-quoted saying of Confucius might be attributed with slight changes of wording to modern Western humanists—"Reverence the spirits, but keep aloof from them," [4] or, "keep them at a distance."

As an offshoot from Christianity, religious humanism marks a protest against all the ideologies of religion we have considered; in the opinion of some critics of those ideologies, their weaknesses are such as to lead logically straight to the humanist interpretation of the world. As a matter of organization, the movement has been more or less allied with some of the Unitarian churches in America, but it represents a much less personalistic and theistic view of the world than is familiar in the older New England Unitarianism. Anticipated, for instance, in the work of Feuerbach, it finds notable expressions in the works of a number of contemporary philosophers, including R. W. Sellars, M. C. Otto, John Dewey, A. E. Haydon, and O. L. Reiser. J. H. Leuba, Julian Huxley, H. E. Barnes, and Walter Lippmann have also made notable contributions to the literature.[5]

Much of the work of the humanists has consisted in criticisms of older systems, such as are found in our preceding chapters. Its positive constructive content may be stated quite briefly, and summed up in the statement that we should know all we can about the universe and do all we can for man. This involves emphasis upon (1) knowledge, (2) nature, (3) man, and (4) social reconstruction.

(1) Although properly cautious about the achievements and possibilities of human reason, religious humanism relies on it and emphasizes it. Humanism is matter-of-fact, and often tries to confine itself to things which can be made intellectually clear and convincing. The conclusions are typically agnostic as regards the existence of God, and sometimes as regards any comprehensive theory of the universe. In accordance with the traditions of positivism, stress is laid upon carefully validated empirical results; these tend to be accepted in place of the dogmas and faith of older systems. Lippmann urges that in this time our desires should be tempered and with Stoic firmness trained to become mature.

(2) Humanism emphasizes nature rather than supernature, and relies upon science rather than on less realistic interpretations of the world. It regards traditional religious beliefs as primitive anthropomorphisms or civilized wishful thinking, and usually holds that psychology and the social sciences can account for what are called religious experiences. Often we find the statement that man can be more at home in a universe of natural law than in one governed by a God of the traditional sort. Some of the humanists pay increasing regard to nature and share many of the views of the religious naturalists, but others in their emphasis on nature see only darkness and negation. Several lay stress upon the necessity, in face of this cosmic isolation, that men shall draw nearer together in mutual support.

(3) Humanism lays its most characteristic emphasis upon man and human potentialities. Its interpretation of the world is not anthropomorphic, but anthropocentric. It emphasizes the sacredness and supreme worth of human life, lived in accordance with the laws of na-

ture. Everything that man discovers out of the past or achieves in the present, every notable development in the natural sciences, the arts, economics, politics, or any field of human interest is joyfully acclaimed. Man is ascribed vast worth, but not worship.

(4) From this point, humanism seeks to become more specific; it relies upon the quickening of human intelligence and effort in like-minded groups under stimulating leadership. There is no definite concerted program for humanism as a whole, but individual humanists or local groups join in various social, economic, and political movements, usually liberal, as ways of securing more happiness and justice and enriching human life to the full measure of its capacities. It is agreed that older orthodoxies, by holding up pictures of salvation in a future world, have distracted men's attention from urgent ethical issues in the present world.

CRITICISMS OF HUMANISM

Some criticisms of humanism amount merely to criticisms of sciences or philosophies which humanism uses, and are considered at appropriate points elsewhere. We follow the lines of humanistic emphasis.

(1) Humanism is criticized as being too rationalistic, positivistic, and withal destructive. Philosophies which, to their own satisfaction have managed to make more out of the reasoning process look upon humanism as crude and superficial. Some of the humanist teachings seem brusque, lacking in imagination and fine sensitiveness for aesthetic values. Sometimes there is an air of cocksureness, as if the loudly heralded results of the sciences were more fundamental and final than many of the critics of science and many of the scientists themselves take them to be. Again, the humanist view is said to understate our actual experience of the world, and to be unnecessarily narrow and chilling.

(2) Many critics of humanism have assailed its interpretation of nature. Sometimes in humanism, as in pragmatism, the realities of nature have been almost disregarded, as if man lived and wrought in a vacuum. When this neglect begins to be corrected, nature is ascribed more importance, but it is hard for humanism to unite nature and man in any organic or imposing way. Several acute criticisms here may be summed up by saying that humanism virtually severs man from nature, fails adequately to combine them, and oscillates, now emphasizing one and now the other. It has, says Horton, a crude realism with regard to ultimate reality, but a wistful idealism with regard to man.[6]

(3) The humanist emphasis on man and his affairs is declared to be presumptuous, the old Greek tragedians' sin of *hubris* in a new version. Deification or worship of humanity is out of the question; by the very sciences which humanism espouses, man is a tiny stirring in the dust of a minor planet, not yet sucked into one of the dwarf stars. But humanism in its newer forms affirms the worth of human existence to such an extent that it strains credulity almost as much as do some of the older faiths which it rejects as superstitions.

(4) Humanism has no monopoly on social enthusiasm or ethical consecration; most of the great religions had this before humanism was born. Sometimes the movement is criticized as not socially enthusiastic enough, or if so, not socially effective. Humanists often differ among themselves as to how to apply consecrated intelligence to urgent human problems, and sometimes they oppose one another's efforts.

(5) From the point of view of religious interests and philosophies, it is often said that humanism lacks religious power, that its strictures on older religions sometimes show little understanding, either of traditional or of modernized systems, and that its attempt to invest itself with religious values must be short-lived, having

the form of religion without the content or the power thereof. Critics declare that the humanists, like the liberals, are living religiously on the stored-up heritage of past faiths and that when the ancient patrimony is exhausted the modern movements must go spiritually bankrupt. Neither ethics nor religion, the critics think, can be sustained by human effort and intelligence alone.

AN ESTIMATE OF HUMANISM

From humanism one would surely wish to retain the healthy emphasis upon man's achievements, powers, and possibilities. It may be doubted, however, whether all this can be self-sustaining or can yield increase. The weak point of humanism seems to be its failure to link man and the universe in any other ways than those afforded by contemporary evolutionism and naturalism. It is not enough to know all we can about the universe and do all we can for man, unless we see that these two interests or aims are not divergent. Humanism itself can think more of man, and perhaps do more for man, when it learns to appreciate man's status in the cosmos.

REFERENCES

[1] F. Harrison, *The Positive Evolution of Religion*, 1913, Chaps. XIII and XIV.

[2] O. W. Firkins, in *The New Humanist*, 4, 1933, pp. 1-4.

[3] On religious humanism, see J. A. C. F. Auer, *Humanism States its Case*, 1933; C. F. Potter, *Humanism, A New Religion*, 1930; C. H. Grattan, *The Critique of Humanism*, 1930.

[4] *Analects* VI, xx.

[5] See M. C. Otto, *Things and Ideals*, 1924; *The Human Enterprise*, 1940: J. H. Leuba, *God or Man*, 1933; J. Huxley, *Religion Without Revelation*, 1927; H. E. Barnes, *The Twilight of Christianity*, 1929; W. Lippmann, *A Preface to Morals*, 1929.

[6] W. M. Horton, *Realistic Theology*, p. 38.

CHAPTER XIV

ECONOMIC NATIONALISM

We indicated at the outset that the spectrum of religious ideologies ran all the way from one extreme, "infra-red" occultism, to the other, "ultra-violet" economic nationalism—the latter including communism in Russia and Nazism in Germany in so far as these have shown religious or quasi-religious features. Italian fascism has not developed in this way, doubtless because of the strength of the Roman Catholic Church in Italy.

A few words concerning communism will be sufficient to indicate its bearing here. The materials concerning its antecedents, as in Plato, its theoretical formulations in the work of Karl Marx, Friedrich Engels, and Nikolai Lenin, its economic doctrines, its huge outworkings in Soviet Russia, and its eventual success or failure, belong for the most part to economics and politics. The question of precise definition need not concern us here; every one agrees that the Russian system now is not communism in the extreme sense, but rather a huge state socialism, with some concessions to individual capitalism. Whatever it be called, we should point out some of its major features and the opinions of critics concerning them.

(1) According to communism, the key to human history is in economic forces which appear in the class struggle of the workmen and the owners, the "proletariat" and the "bourgeoisie." In this "economic materialism" (so-called to distinguish the view of Marx from Hegel's idealism), events are practically determined by the prevailing mode of economic production and exchange. The ideologies of opposing schools are only rationalizations, or attempts to find specious reasons for

actions really motivated by economic interests. The determinism is not quite absolute, but the whole system tends all the time to drop back into mechanism, where actions are blind or automatic.[1]

(2) Traditional religion is declared to be an obstructing agency, an "opium of the people," tending to keep the working class submissive and contented, while they are deluded by dreams of future salvation in some other world. Julius Hecker pictures the communists as against every religion, orthodox, humanitarian, or philosophical. They reject idealistic philosophies and forms of religion or philosophy which try to induce awe in men. The feeling of awe, they maintain, paralyzes human thought and results in a submissive rather than a critical attitude, and is too much allied with periods and experiences of exploitation.[2]

(3) Another great principle of communism is the dialectic nature of social development. Marx was after all a Hegelian; we might accordingly expect to find him emphasizing internal contradiction and conflict, especially in human society. For Hegel, history proceeds in Hegelian triads. For Marx, the great "thesis" is that capitalistic society becomes increasingly monopolistic, whereupon the decline of purchasing power drives capitalistic governments into imperialistic competition for foreign markets and into wars. Next, as "antithesis," the resultant chaos gives the proletariat a chance to rise, and at length attain the "synthesis," in which the dictatorship of the proletariat means a truly classless society, capitalistic in mode of production, but communistic in collective ownership and control of distribution.

(4) So we find great importance attached to active, aggressive class struggle by the proletariat. Communism intends to "do something about it." Russia shows a unity of theory with resolute practice, resulting in the virtual "liquidation" of every other element in the population except the proletariat, and with bitter factional

struggles among the communists themselves. The struggle has been carried on ruthlessly, with bitterness and cruelty, but it is held that struggle is to be expected as an essential element in the whole historic movement.

(5) The result is, at least in imperfect outline, a kind of organismic state, with zones or hierarchies of representation—local soviets in factories and villages, district soviets, etc., up to the great governing body in Moscow, with its interim representatives and steering committee, dominated during recent years by Josef Stalin. In such a state, ideally burdens are borne in common and for the common good, not for the ease and luxury of a master class, and every element in the whole is responsive to the needs and demands of every other element. The moral appeal of such an ideal is self-evident. The development is supposed to be under expert guidance, with technical advice and long-time planning on a great scale.

(6) It is not quite so ironical as it seems, that communism should present itself with so many of the marks of a religion. The history of Confucianism, Buddhism, and the Roman Empire, as well as some tendencies in Nazi Germany are enough to show that more than one great mass movement in secular history has done much the same thing.

Communism is an anti-religious religion, a religion in spite of itself, both in theory and in practice. In theory it is not so strange when one remembers that Marx and Engels were made-over Hegelians. It has been noted by Eddy that Soviet philosophy is a theology; it has its revelation, its holy books, its ecclesiastical authority, its official teachers. It supposes one orthodoxy and innumerable heresies. And it attaches itself with assurance to a great cosmic process, its dialectic of history.[3] In practice, the flaming devotion of many communists to their cause, their social enthusiasm and readiness to sacrifice for vast objects beyond themselves, often far away in the future beyond us all, have a religious quality and often set a good example to the recognized religions. Materialism or no materialism, and suffering or no suffering, if the light which one sees in the eyes of many of Russia's youth is not a spiritual light, then spirituality must indeed belong to some other world than this.

In fascist countries where the traditional churches have been stronger than in Russia, economic nationalisms have not acquired so many of the characteristics of a religion. Italian fascism has even closed a long-standing controversy with the Catholic Church and remains under its influence. In Germany, with its emphasis upon the unity and destiny of the "folk," there have been two or three projects as if to make Nazism a religion[4] —sometimes with a neo-pagan, more or less poetic revival of allegiance to mythical Teutonic deities (as more expressive of the German racial spirit than a Semitic Deity could be), sometimes with quasi-Messianic honors accorded to Adolf Hitler—but these movements or tendencies have as yet been either not very definite or not very widespread. The influence of the older Churches has been too strong.

POINTS AGAINST ECONOMIC NATIONALISM

The major criticisms of communism follow its chief principles step by step. (1) Thus, it is urged that economic materialism offers only a partial account of the forces which have shaped history. There need be no question that the theory of economic materialism is partly true and no question that it has been sadly disregarded by many writers on history, but the statement that history has been determined solely by economic factors and class struggle is at least open to qualification. One can not so lightly leave out, for example, the personal influence of great men and women. Sometimes, as the Nazis would agree, the determining factor seems to have been leadership which was enlisted on one side or another of current economic controversies. According to other ideologies history must be interpreted in the light of cosmic processes or super-cosmic powers which make the class struggle look puny. The arguments about rationalism cut both ways; if the opponents of communism have rationalized their good fortune, the communists have probably rationalized the misfortunes of the working class.

(2) Against the communist attack on traditional religions, it is urged that the attack sees only the corruptions and abuses, and fails to allow for the good and healthful features of religion. To any one who knew the old Russian Orthodox Church and some of its teachings and economic connections, there can be small wonder that a modern radical movement in Russia is uncompromising in its hostility.

(3) The Hegelian dialectic, although exemplified well enough by many processes observable in nature, was dogmatic and defective when made the sole index to the world process, to say nothing of the logical process. There was enough truth in it so that it was pressed into the service of philosophy of religion, as well as of the Marxian materialism. In the one case, as in the other, the dialectic is overworked; it is not so surprising to find dogmatism in philosophy of religion, but to find so much of it among the Marxian radicals is astonishing. In the eyes of some critics, this insistence upon the letter of the dialectic process reveals a deep need of anchorage and a fear to relinquish even this supposed hold on the cosmic process.

(4) Against communism's violent class struggle, its intolerance and oppression of minorities, more pacific methods are urged, with less cruelty, and more of the milk of human kindness. One finds also the important point, well borne out by events in Russia, that all the so-called classes, at least as represented by their best

examples, are needed in any economic or political order and that attempts to eliminate one or another of them simply will not work. It may also be urged that alongside the capitalist and the laborer there is the wider public and the public interest, and sometimes it is suggested that the ideal solution would not be struggle but amalgamation—a redistribution and realignment of possessions and of functions, so that every capitalist would be in some things a laborer and every laborer to some degree a capitalist.

(5) In the light of the points last mentioned, it is a fair question whether the communist state is organismic or is truncated. The Nazi state, with all its despotism, appears to be better rounded out. In any modern state there is so much economic and cultural interdependence of the various elements that something like organismic relationships can hardly be avoided. The question is not whether there shall be an organismic state, but what types of interdependence and interpenetration shall be recognized and promoted.

(6) Regarding the religious value of communism, its critics maintain that economic materialism is too crude for men to live by. Even if communism is right in rejecting an impossible theology, it is not right in substituting for it a fragment of sociology. Where communism and Nazism make patriotism a near-religion, their opponents charge them with disregard of international ethics.

ESTIMATE OF ECONOMIC NATIONALISMS

Apart from the political, economic, and ethical problems involved, it is clear that the economic nationalisms have kindled powerful loyalties by their emphasis upon class and folk solidarity. But along with their sense for societal structures, they need more thorough orientation within the cosmic structures. In such an orientation the dialectical process at most will be only one factor among others, and each nation in all its glory will be one among the others.

REFERENCES

[1] See S. Hook, *From Hegel to Marx*, 1936, p. 19; T. Brameld, *A Philosophical Approach to Communism*, 1933.

[2] J. Hecker, *Religion and Communism*, 1933.

[3] S. Eddy, in S. Hook and Others, *The Meaning of Marx*, 1934, p. 22.

[4] See P. F. Douglass, *God Among the Germans*, 1935, Chaps. III and IV.

CHAPTER XV

THE SOURCE AND OBJECT OF RELIGION

The spectrum of religious ideologies which has been spread out in our analysis exhibits a mixture of strong and weak lines. In each region, along with many ideas which are blurred and confused, there are some which stand out clearly and which represent something genuine, something worth retaining in our world-picture.

We should, for example, retain the openness and range of occultism, with its readiness to explore new horizons. With mysticism we should wish to share the sense of immediacy and totality of experience, as well as the confident facing of the universe. Supernaturalism, even though most of its claims turn out to be illusory, may yield the strengthening sense of moral contrast and may remind us that if the personal quality disappears altogether from our doctrines of the Object of religious devotion, the survival of religion will be difficult and perhaps impossible. The idealisms, freed from their exaggerated emphasis upon epistemology, may still indicate that there are significant relationships between mind and world, between personality and the universe. Although we should not, with pragmatism, magnify a method into a metaphysics, in practice we are all pragmatic; we ought to seek high satisfactions and be eager to know from experience what is the best way of doing things under given cosmic conditions.

We need the evolutionists' sense of process to save us from stagnation, and the discernment of levels to save us from thinking too meanly or narrowly of naturalism. From the naturalists we might learn that nothing is greater or more wonderful than the universe, and with them try to find in the universe around us not only happiness and beauty, but also the Source and Object of religion. We should share the humanists' impatience with superstition, their devotion to human welfare, and their zeal for knowledge of the universe. In the ideals of communism and other intense forms of nationalism we may see outstanding, even if circumscribed, examples of structural ethics.

Some lines like these, we should say, are clear, but they seem to be picked at random; we should seek some readjustment which will bring them into more definite and stable relationships. It ought to be obvious that the way to readjustment and new understanding will be by examination not of the earlier, but of the more recent philosophies. Unnumbered studies of philosophy of religion in terms of occultisms, mysticism, supernaturalism, idealism, and pragmatism pour from the printing presses. All of them develop more or less personalistic views and depend to some extent either upon authority or upon theories of our experience or our minds. They state and restate the same views, as if the same old weaknesses and limitations did not exist at all. It is time that something new was seriously tried.

It must be admitted that the more recent philosophies of evolutionism, naturalism, and humanism (to say nothing of economic nationalism) have not yielded much for religion. They have been too analytical, too much occupied with details, and too crude. But the major difficulty, which we shall consider in the remaining pages of this book, is that their resources have not been adequately explored.

In this connection we shall within the present limits briefly indicate two major suggestions; the groundwork for each of them has been formulated at length elsewhere.[1] The first suggestion concerns the physical universe, while the second deals more particularly with the thinking process.

According to the first suggestion, when the sciences

are studied in detail there are, within the data of evolutionism and naturalism, important relationships which those philosophies for the most part disregard. The universe evolves through many different "levels"; among them are atoms, astronomical bodies, unicellular organisms, multicellular organisms, societies, reflexes, endreactions, sentiments, valuations, personalities. These levels group themselves naturally in the "realms" of matter, life, and mind. At all the levels there appear to be striking resemblances of the general features of structure and process; everywhere we find relative individuation, selective interactions, repeated productions or reproductions, and rearrangements of parts in disintegrations, aggregations, integrations, and differentiations. Not only is every level similar to every other in these characteristics, but the three realms of matter, life, and mind, each composed of a number of levels, show further and more surprising resemblances. It appears that the structures and processes of the realm of matter, the physical world, are imitated in more intricate ways by those of the living organisms, and that those of the living organisms are imitated in still more intricate ways by those of the nervous systems. The upshot of all this interpretation of the data is that man is much more characteristically a product of the universe than the rather hit-or-miss evolutionisms and naturalisms have supposed. The universe not merely evolves man, but also epitomizes itself in man; in the structures and processes which are characteristic of him, man is a "little universe." This view, worked out on a basis of empirical evidence and plausible inference from the data of the sciences, we have called the "epitomization hypothesis."

This leads, in particular, to a new estimate of the charge that supernaturalism, with its anthropomorphic projections, is illusory. When supernaturalism is said to be a projection into the universe of a magnified image of man, the way to meet the charge is not to deny it, but to look more closely at the metaphor of projection. It is only a metaphor, but it works as well for one side of the argument as for the other. The charge, as we have it from social psychology, anthropology, and history, is to the effect that man, like a lens, projects upon the screen of the universe a magnified image of himself and calls the image God. But surely it must be noted that the sciences just mentioned, important as they are, are not the only sciences, and philosophy of religion must not confine itself merely to them. An adequate philosophy must consider the other sciences, too, and include, rather than exclude, physics, chemistry, astronomy, geology, biology, and much of psychology. The metaphor favored by the former group of sciences starts with the lens, but lenses do not project light all by themselves, without first having focused the light which they receive from a source. The projection theory of supernaturalism starts with man and takes man for granted, but man does not all by himself project the gods into the universe in his own image, without first having in himself or being himself the focus where the light has gathered.

Man does not appear in a vacuum, nor spring *de novo* out of nothing; we must study the natural processes which develop him. The fundamental defect of the projection theory is its failure to see the connection between the processes of focusing in man as the lens—that is, the course of evolution leading up to man and his mind— and the resulting picture, the idea of God on the cosmic screen, with all those differences of refraction which gives us the spectrum of ideologies. It is like the relationship between the actual scene "shot" by the moving picture camera and the play of light and shade when the picture is projected on the screen in the theater. A picture is not a presentation of its scene; it is a *representation* of it. The question is not whether it is a presentation or a representation, but only whether it is an adequate representation of the scene originally presented

234

and focused in the camera. So with supernaturalism and theism. There should be no question that theism in its historical developments is pictorial and mythical. Theism is representative. The Jehovah of the mighty arm and the unsleeping eye is of course a picture, like our childhood's "Big Man up in the sky." Perhaps the same must be said of the Christian's loving Father watching over his children. In the development of most Christians, early beliefs about the Big Man up in the sky gradually give place to beliefs concerning a Great Mind behind or in the universe; but if our studies of the cosmological and teleological arguments and of idealism are sound, the indications are that such doctrines will grow weaker as time goes on, and the Great Mind may even follow the Big Man into oblivion.

Suppose, for the sake of argument, that all this is the case. Let us admit that all the traditional beliefs and doctrines about God are anthropomorphic projections, a play of man's hopes and fears over the screen of nature, a patchwork of countless little bits of human experience, some played up, some played down, some sublimated, some over-compensated, some repressed. There is of course a correlation between social institutions and ideas of God dominant at any given period. Warriors worship a war god, monarchists a sovereign god, and so on. The question, again, is not whether those ideas of God are pictures, symbols, representations; the question is whether they are good pictures, symbols, representations of the material that was focused. The great point at issue is not whether theism is a projection or whether it is anthropomorphic. The great point is whether man is a focus of the universe, so that the universe, focused in the mind of man, naturally yields the projection which we see as theism and interpret in the philosophy of supernaturalism. This is the point, and here is the application of the epitomization hypothesis. In proportion as the hypothesis becomes established, new ground is available in realism, evolutionism, and naturalism for at least some of the important doctrines and values of philosophy of religion, which at present have to depend upon the questionable foundations of supernaturalism and the idealisms, if not upon the flux of pragmatism. The long discussion of the evidence already in print, as well as studies in preparation seem to indicate that the hypothesis is basically sound.[2]

In this connection we may go on to consider others of the strong and weak points of supernaturalism as outlined in Chapters IV and VI. It has been maintained that, for better or for worse, supernaturalism is simple; but an interpretation of the evolution of nature and of man as the factors which have produced theism takes us far enough into the data of the sciences and the religions so that it can hardly suffer from this reproach. The relationships here recall the moving picture projection. The apparatus for taking and projecting pictures is enormously complicated, requiring armies of experts, but the resulting picture is simple enough for a child to understand. This is the way to interpret a situation in contemporary religious life which is becoming serious, and even tragic—the gulf that seems to be widening between sophisticated, enlightened, emancipated views of religion and the popular, orthodox faiths. Unless there is some way of reconciling the two, religion seems doomed to vacuity on one side and obscurantism on the other. But it is like the moving picture men and the children; they all see, directly or indirectly, the same situation, but from points of view quite different. The technicians in religion, who have to examine the facts, crude or refined, in its history and adjust the machinery of its psychology, ought to be sure that they keep man in the cosmic focus; and those who try to maintain a childlike faith ought to remember that the picture which appears on the screen requires scene and machinery and technicians to bring it there clearly.

Such a shifting of the point of view from the picture on the screen to the machinery which produces and projects it indicates also a shift in philosophy of religion as regards authority. For many contemporaries, there is no question that the older claims of literal authority for the Scriptures and the Church are destined to become weaker, if not to collapse altogether. But the newer claims concerning the authority of experience are in not much better shape; the result is that religion is losing authority, while the natural and social sciences, with their empirical procedures, are gaining it. Religious philosophy should avail itself more fully of the resources of these sciences. In terms of our comparison with the moving picture, we should shift our attention from the picture on the screen to the scene photographed and the machinery of focusing and projecting it. If we can turn from the traditional picturesque doctrines of theism to the universe of the sciences and find that man as produced in the midst of the universe forms a focus for it and then projects his theism, we shall find the authority of the sciences and the authority of man's experience, when properly understood, available in a new way for the problems of religion.

What has been said about pictures and projections will help, in the next place, to answer the criticism of the claim of supernaturalism to be empirical. We can begin to understand why different races and periods have so many versions of supernaturalism; we expect a picture on a screen to vary in clearness as the lens moves into clearer focus or out of it. Somewhere in the ups and downs of human history is the reason why the historic theisms present us with such a succession of dissolving views, with so many rainbow tints in the spectrum of ideologies. The picture on the screen is blurred if the lens is too far back or too far forward. The naturalisms make the former mistake, setting man back too close to his lowly origin, while the supernaturalisms make the latter mistake, tilting him forward too far in advance of that which has produced him. When the idealisms try to correct the errors of the other philosophies, they succeed chiefly in suffusing everything with an amiable vagueness. We need to establish the general fact of man's focal position, and then to learn to sharpen the focus.

We need not be surprised if the lens or focusing apparatus is complicated and compound, reflecting the light from one to another of its inner components; it is the prescientific view which regards man and his mind as simple. Here seems to be the proper answer for the intricate problem of suggestion in the history and psychology of religion. The truths of religion are reflected, always with some distortion, from one mind or one generation to another in the social group, or from one part to another of an individual's mind. To be free from social suggestion (with or without symbolisms and semantics) means only to be eccentric or stubborn; to be free from autosuggestion means to be shallow and without personal resource. The point is not that we are to avoid suggestions from others or from ourselves; the point is that we are to accept suggestions which the universe sanctions—that is, with all the inner complications of our minds, we are to keep ourselves in cosmic focus.

Before coming closer to the problem of man's focal status in the universe, we must consider another topic involved in supernaturalism. The effect produced by a picture depends largely upon its contrasts, and supernaturalism has been notable by reason of the contrasts which it presents.

Consideration of the problem of contrast brings in our second major suggestion, which is that a reexamination of the thinking process, showing that it always involves certain contrasts, helps to clear up many traditional difficulties concerning absolutes, infinites, beginnings and endings, and other concepts prominent in the ideologies.

We need to recognize as involved in our thinking a characteristic which is evident in perception and involved in any act of attention—the characteristic of contrast, or *selection and correlative neglect.* Any object which we perceive is perceived against or in the midst of a background; the object is selected, while the background, although it may be more or less vaguely perceived and the boundary between object and background may be vague, is for the moment comparatively neglected. If we call any selected object *A*, we may refer to the background as *non-A*. If at a later moment we shift our attention to the background, we merely select it in the midst of some other background which is now at the new moment neglected. The great point is that at any given moment we can not treat the selected object and the neglected background in altogether the same way; there is a very important difference in our procedure. An object which is selected may be analyzed and described in its relationships with other objects which are selected with it or which come to be included in the field of selection; but any analysis or description always carries with it a correlative neglect for whatever at the moment happens to serve as background. Concerning the content of the background at the moment we do not make affirmations or denials; we merely leave it open, unexplored. Whatever is selected and neglected may shift very rapidly, but not so rapidly as to overcome the characteristic of selection and correlative neglect. Moreover, since no perception and no analysis of a selected object need be regarded as complete, we may say that some features of the object itself are neglected along with the background. All this, we hold, applies not merely to perception but also to thinking. Any perceived or conceived *A* is perceived or conceived relatively to a neglected *non-A;* the characteristic appears with the great objects and concepts as well as the small; and applies not merely between any selected *A* and its correlative *non-A*, but also between properties or attributes of *A* which are selected in contrast to others which are neglected.[8]

Let us refer to these characteristics of selection and neglect in our perception and our thinking as the "horizon principles," and trace some of their applications in the ideologies of religion. We find, for example, that any so-called "identity" is relative to differences which are neglected, and that any individuation, as we saw in connection with the epitomization hypothesis, is relative to an undescribed milieu or background. Any so-called finite is selected with reference to a non-finite, which ought to be left open and unexplored, but which is usually mistakenly given some description as a supposed "infinite." The term "infinite," if used at all, should be used non-committally, with no attempt to describe its content. Anything definite is selected in contrast to what we ought to call non-definite, and the boundary between the two can not always be discerned with precision.

Further applications are useful in problems of beginnings and endings, particularly when beginnings and endings are sought for the whole universe. Such theories do not settle any logical question, but at best neglect what they can not describe; if some one says that God began the universe, some one else may ask, logically if not theologically, "What began God?" Somewhere the question of beginnings has to be left open, without affirmation or denial; affirmation and denial are equally pointless, as Kant's antinomies showed. Proceeding to other illustrations, we find the reason why some philosophers say that it is easier to say *that* God is than *what* he is; it is because the word "that" signifies a mere indication, whereas "what" connotes a description. If we tell what a thing is, we treat it as a selected object, but a mere indication that something is may refer either to an undescribed object or to an open or vague background of an object or a world. We find, further, that any so-called "absolute" is properly relative to a "non-absolute" which should be left undescribed, with neither affirmations nor denials concerning it. The same limitation should prevent confident descriptions of the "Unconditioned," particularly descriptions of it which merely reaffirm supernaturalism, idealism or theism. Anything said to be conditioned may be held to involve a "non-conditioned," but any descriptions of a non-conditioned are arbitrary and any references to an unconditioned are properly only negative and non-committal.

Similarly, any so-called unity involves some non-unity, any continuity or "continuum" some lurking non-continuity, anything said to be perfect some non-perfection, anything said to be complete some non-completion, and anything described as a whole, or "the whole" some aspect of a non-whole. Anything eulogized as "Being" trails with it some non-being, even though "being" has a growing edge of "becoming." Any universe, physical or logical, involves the neglect of a non-universe; if we call the latter "nothing," this term merely gives the neglected a name, while properly forbearing to give it a description. Our world of thought is like an island, surrounded by an open ocean and still containing within its boundaries some lingering lakes and marshes from which the water of uncertainty has not yet evaporated. But the island of our knowledge is not a speck like Guam; it is by this time a continent like North America, with enough that is solid and dependable so that there is room for construction as well as exploration, and though we are properly confined to it, we are not cramped.[4]

A very complicated case of horizons appears when we try to think accurately of actuality and potentiality, necessity and possibility; subtle instances of all these are involved in the very process and conditions of thinking. Let us say briefly here that anything regarded as actual involves the non-actual; the latter includes what is *not* actual, and thus includes some things which are potential and possible. When we turn to the possible, we find that any selected possibility can be described, after a fashion, but that it involves a still more open "non-possible," which must be left utterly undescribed and moreover without definite boundary to distinguish it from the possible. Thus, although descriptions of anything regarded as possible may be forthcoming, no description can exhaust the possible, to say "nothing" of the non-possible. The complications and difficulties of these concepts yield to consistent applications of the horizon principles, and the principles serve as a kind of natural limitation upon the extravagances of many systems of metaphysics, without needing to appeal, as the logical empiricists do, to an arbitrary phenomenalism or nominalism, or to an elaborate and perhaps artificial analysis of language.

In the light of our two suggestions, the epitomization hypothesis and the horizon principles, some answers begin to appear for the eight questions which, as we said in Chapter XII, contemporary religious naturalism leaves without adequate treatment.

The first question was, Is the Object of religious devotion definite or indefinite? The Object, we said, is that trend or process (leaving for the moment the question as to whether we should use the singular or the plural) in nature and history which "makes good." We can see now that in such an Object indefiniteness need not be fatal. The Object can be as definite as goodness in the world; but ethics is not an exact science, and with or without the horizon principles we must expect here some margin of indefiniteness, where any assumed good is tentative and any effort to achieve good is for the time being experimental. This, in fact, provides just the growing edge which pragmatic theories with all their urge for inquiry and adventure, crave; but on the other hand this does not forget the accumulated body of established good which makes up the reserve for ethical striving and sustains the doubtful struggles at the frontier. One must not forget that ethics is not all striving; as Oriental thought should have sufficed long ago to teach us, there is an ethics of contentment as well as of conflict.

Is the Object of religious devotion finite or infinite? many paradoxes concerning the infinite God of supernaturalism and idealism receive their clearest solution when we recognize the fact that infinity is essentially to be neglected and left unexplored. As a matter of fact we can not quite manage the concept of infinity. We can not ascribe infinity to God and at the same time describe what an infinite God does. If we could, we might say that God in his infinite wisdom thinks up unsolvable puzzles, but we should have to add that in his infinite wisdom he must solve any puzzle which is thought up. Infinity does not lend itself to descriptions, but is to be left undescribed; in the example given, we use it properly if we say that we set no limits to God's wisdom. In the present connection, the restriction of the Object of religious devotion to the good in nature and history makes it at least in some respects finite; but we must remember that such an Object, even if finite, is not necessarily weak or lacking in power. Nor is our adjustment to such an Object lacking in cosmic quality. The Object, let us say, is not the whole universe, it is only the good in the universe; but none the less the living experience of the religious man is an adjustment to the whole universe. This is because any adjustment, like any perception, involves a selection and a correlative neglect. If, for example, we walk toward one thing, in so doing we walk away from other things. Similarly, the religious adjustment is in some sense positive toward whatever is good in the universe and at the same time in the opposite sense negative to whatever is evil.

Is the Object of religious devotion One or many?

Anything which is said to be "one" is a selection, with somewhere a correlative suppression or neglect. Whether the world, or God, or anything else is said to be one or many depends upon what aspects we are willing to neglect. Meland thinks that in worship we see the plurality of the world under the aspect of unity.[5] Is the Object of religious devotion changing or changeless? These terms are also relative; when either is put forward as an account of the world or of God it may be taken to imply that the other has been neglected.

Is the Object of religious devotion material or spiritual? The supposed contrast of matter and spirit has been the mainstay of supernaturalism all the way from primitive animisms to Karl Barth, and the subordination of matter to spirit has been the sum if not the very substance of the idealistic philosophies. But the weaknesses of these philosophies make it increasingly clear that God can not much longer be envisaged either as a glorified ghost or a magnified consciousness. One of the most important questions of our time is whether the valuations centering in that kind of God can be transferred to an Object frankly material. In this connection Lloyd Morgan left us a thought worthy of deep consideration when he suggested that our religion will become more spiritual in proportion as it becomes less spiritistic.[6]

Several signs of the times afford hope of a revision of the older views; this is particularly true in the newer ideas of matter. Once, for instance, matter was regarded as essentially inactive, but now any piece of ordinary matter is known to be a storehouse of energies, and the whole material world is thought to be a pattern, or pattern of patterns, in a field of energies. It should be remembered that this shift of view does not, as is sometimes held, mean that the universe is now for this reason to be regarded as mental or spiritual; nevertheless it softens the old contrast between the material and the spiritual.

Another important transition leads from the old view
that matter is coarse to the present-day measurements
which, sometimes of the order of quadrillionths of a
centimeter, establish for matter a fineness of structure
never dreamed of even for spirit. On the other hand,
the old view that matter was limited in time if not space
has given place in the new astronomy to a universe conceived on a scale which, instead of magnifying God,
tends to dwarf man and all his works and days.

One of the most common ways of contrasting matter
and spirit has long been to picture matter as evil. Sometimes for centuries asceticism, with its self-tortures and
repressions of normal functions, has dominated the great
faiths; almost everywhere it has left its mark on what
had been regarded as the religious way of life. The
boundary between the undue restraint of asceticism and
the due restraint of intelligent morality is hard to fix in
this field which can never be that of an exact science,
but the conviction grows more clear in the Western
world, if not yet altogether in the Eastern, that it is
wrong to identify asceticism and morality or to suppose
that the good life requires that matter be treated as evil.
The fact is that the good life or "spiritual" life requires
matter as much as does the bad or carnal life. The distinction between evil and good is not in the fact that
matter is present; it is in the effect which matter has, or
the use to which matter is put. There is no point, either,
in tracing disease specifically to matter, when the corresponding state of health must also be located there.

It appears that matter is not necessarily a drag even
upon the traditional beliefs in life after death. From the
Book of Revelation with its golden streets and pearly
gates to the alleged messages from Raymond to Sir
Oliver Lodge,[7] matter enters into Western man's pictures of life after death, while untold millions in the
East believe in reincarnation, at least as the way to
eventual discarnate immortality.

In the late nineteenth century some evolutionists, following Tyndall,[8] discerned in matter "the promise and the potency of life." The epitomization hypothesis finds in matter not merely the potency of life and mind, but a parallel or set of parallels of those later developments, a kind of crude cosmic rehearsal of the principles of structure and process which appear in life and mind in successively more intricate forms. The differences between matter and life are differences of levels and realm. In the cosmic sweep, matter and life and mind run parallel; as in a great symphony, the theme repeats.

All these considerations help to strengthen the tendency in contemporary religious naturalism to revalue the physical world and find in it the Object of religious devotion. Nor is this altogether destructive of older valuations; in fact it might mean an actual strengthening of religion. In proportion as we can rid ourselves of superstitions, a material God in whom we live and move and have our being may be more powerful for us than a God conceived as spiritual. God regarded as distinct from the universe may be quite remote from us; even God hidden in the heart may be stifled or silenced. But if God is as plainly before us as matter is, religion may become characteristic of common life, without staking everything upon doctrines of the supposed spiritual which are in danger of evaporating.

This does not mean that any particular thing is God; any particular thing is at best only a part of God, and may be a part at one moment and not at another. Precisely such inclusion within or exclusion from the Object of religious devotion affords a basis for a vivid reinterpretation of religious consecration and its opposite desecration. Any ordinary thing, the great earth itself and all that it inhabit, could at most be only small portions of the great Object; the nations are counted but as the small dust of the balance.

Those for whom the supernaturalistic and idealistic meanings of "spirit" point to unreality may find in a reexamination of the facts of nature a new meaning for the old term. When we contemplate the universe of matter rising into life and of life rising into mind and personality, we need some word by which to designate the upthrust of things, some word which will represent in the model of the universe what an architect's elevation line represents in a plan of a building. The universe does not stay down; it "a-mounts" to something. Spirit, let us say, is difference of level in matter; and if we ourselves do not stay down, like clods or animals or savages, spirituality is difference of level in us. Or, spirit is a kind of "high test" matter; spirituality is high test personality.

Is the Object of religious devotion personal or impersonal? In its religious importance, this question probably dwarfs all the others. In an attempt to answer it in ways other than traditional, we shall explore a number of possible views, involving the horizon principles and the epitomization hypothesis.

The answer may well begin by a study of the question. What do we mean when we ask "Is the Object of religious devotion personal?" If we ask it from a standpoint influenced at all by traditional doctrines, we probably more or less tacitly mean "Is the Object a person in and by itself, independently of other persons?" This way of understanding the question is in accord not merely with traditional theology, but also with some traditional theories of the nature of society and personality, according to which society is an aggregate of individual persons, somewhat as a stone-pile is an aggregate of individual stones. In the more recent social psychology, society is less like a stone-pile and more like a network of interlacing strands. Biological individuals are knots in a social network; individual personalities are differentiations within a social matrix. It is not in the nature of human personalities to be in isolation from one another; if we demand that God shall exist in cosmic isolation, we are demanding something which is required of no other person, and which is against the nature of personality as we know it. Miss Harkness has suggested a distinction between the question whether God is a person and the question whether God is personal,[9] but the line between the two is surely hard to fix. In either case, the most that we should ask, if we keep to personality as we know it, is that the Object of religious devotion shall be a person or personal in its relationships with other persons, in that network of mutuality in which all our personalities arise. On the other hand, we ought not to insist that the Object shall be too narrowly personal, or just like us. It may well be more unique than that, and in some sense over against us all. If it does not play a personal part, it may play an impersonal counterpart. Even if it does not respond to us, it may correspond to us. It is the mold in which our personalities are poured; we bear its image, even though the image is reversed.

Another avenue for exploration is suggested when we remember that even if the Object can not be described as personal, the way for us, as persons, to make any adequate adjustment to it is a personal way. Each individual's adjustment to the universe must be by way of the societal groups in which he belongs, and through those groups to the universe which produces him. Perhaps the cosmic process does not have to be personal, but at all events *we* have to be personal, and to work out our personalization in our cosmic locus in society.

Again, does the term "personal" as applied to the Object of religious devotion need to mean "personal exclusively in the human sense"? Ordinarily we make it anthropomorphic, as if of all the living species in the earth (to say nothing of possible living forms elsewhere) man alone has cosmic ground or sanction. Long

248

ago Xenophanes said that if the lions were called upon to describe God they would say that God is a lion. Hinduism has gone beyond the West in extending some recognition to the non-human species; the elephant-headed Ganesh and the monkey-god Hanuman seem grotesque to us, but they testify to something elusive and important in the Object of religious devotion. Do the birds, for instance, have to be content with the little which to us they seem to get out of life, or do they, in some ways utterly strange to us, which even our good St. Francis could not share, have their own access to the cosmic process which shapes and sustains us all? For us to insist that the process must be all human is as indefensible as our inhuman preying upon the defenseless animals in our heartless sports and slaughters.

Still another answer is available if we extend the meaning of the term "personal" in another way. Its meaning is already broader than we usually think. There are, of course, individual persons like you or me; but if you and I together form a business partnership then our firm or company is also a person—a legally responsible "corporate person." Each partner or member is in one sense a person, and each incorporated group of partners or members is in another sense a person; that which contains persons of one order is a person of another order. Now if the meaning of the term "person" has been extended in this way, let us say horizontally, at our level, why may it not also be extended in another way, let us say vertically, along the levels of the cosmos? Why may we not say that just as individual or individuate persons can be members of corporate persons, so individuate and corporate persons are together members of a Culminate Person, the cosmic process which, as nature and history, culminates in them?

There need in this view be no attempt to maintain that the Object of religious devotion has always been personal. The realm of matter, before the advent of life, is not personal, but it is not for that reason of no importance for religion. There is a relationship which demands recognition; a cosmic process which produces persons, which apparently epitomizes itself in persons, should not be described and approached as if it did no such thing. Personality is not found throughout its whole extent and is best not sought there. The process is hardly to be called "super-personal"; efforts to get meaning for this term are strained. Apart from man, the process appears rather to be sub-personal or prepersonal. But when the process is studied together with man who appears in the course of it, it has to be regarded as in its own way germane to the personalities in which it now culminates.

We may approach the question of personality in the Object of religious devotion in still another way by considering how any one person among us has knowledge of other persons. Perhaps such knowledge is direct, immediate, but it is at least corroborated by resemblances between the appearance and actions of other persons and one's own appearance and actions. In either case we may get a clue for our question. If knowledge of other persons is direct, and personal things must be personally discerned, perhaps we may extend their range, in accordance with the testimonies of the seers and the mystics, and seek personal depths, depths beyond words and thoughts, in the cosmic process. Or, if our knowledge of other human persons depends upon resemblances between them and ourselves, we may, in accordance with the epitomization hypothesis, point to a long line of resemblances in principles of structure and process in the universe and in man. The detailed analysis, of course, can not show that the structures and processes of the universe in their relationships to our organisms and our minds are as human or as personal as we are to one another, but it can show far more striking similarities between the cosmic and the human than are commonly supposed to exist. In the universe there is at least something which resembles man, and which indeed forms him in its image.

In all these considerations we have not yet brought in the point which is perhaps more characteristically theological than any of the others. In theology it has been a cardinal principle that God reveals himself, particularly in the lives of certain men, preeminently those men who have founded religions. In philosophy evidence for God has been sought almost everywhere else, in the earthquake, the wind, and the fire of the cosmos or in the still small voice of personal experience. Perhaps the philosophies are trying to play Hamlet with Hamlet left out—to show that God is personal, without bringing in the most completely personal data available. If this is the case, then the stir of a great religious movement in history, inspired by the life of a great founder, is a process in which we may recognize our Object of religious devotion as revealing itself. In such a historic process, the Object comes to a new personal culmination in a societal group of persons, each of whom is thereafter to win his adjustment to the Object in the personal way and make himself one of the more nearly adequate foci of the cosmos. Whatever the extent to which, under modern criticism, personal quality seems to disappear from the Object of religion, it may be recovered in another form in a heightened sense of the personal qualities of the founders and revealers, as this sense is developed in and through membership in the revealing religious groups.

We have one more suggestion regarding the personality of the Object of religious devotion; the Object, somewhat as Alexander holds, may as yet be incompletely personal. No one needs to suppose that the cosmic process, taken where it is now, is at its best; even without achieving any new level, personalities are constantly being more fully developed and enriched. In some ways the cosmos gives the impression of an imperfect and almost thwarted tendency to achieve, among other things, something like human personality. It appears as if, in the very act of developing ourselves, we contribute an increment to make the larger Object more and more highly personal. And it must not be forgotten that personality, like all higher mental functions, involves organization in time. Here, in human thought's far reaching synthesis, we have a right to reckon with the future and to count our far off ideals.

So far as we can see, any of the foregoing possibilities or all of them together may be offered as plausible alternatives for the older supernaturalism and idealisms which have been so simple and so sweeping in their assertions about the personality of the Object of religious devotion. Referring to the proposed substitutes collectively, there is no point in insisting that the newer view be called or recognized as theism. Contemporary religious naturalisms have been overly reluctant to cut loose from the word or the pretension of theism, but those naturalisms have not adequately analyzed or appreciated their own resources, nor understood that kinship of epitomization between the natural universe and human personality which makes emancipation from older personalisms much easier. Whether or not the view here presented is to be called theistic depends upon one's definition of the term "theism" and "person"; in many respects it would be clearer to avoid difficulties and controversies by coining a new word and calling the view "theitism." Incidentally, this would avoid the problem of subordinate cosmic personalities. If, in accordance with the epitomization hypothesis, we say that any cosmic tendency is more or less like a personality, we may go on to say that the Object of religious devotion is the cosmic tendency most like human personality at its best. We shall return to this point presently, in discussing the goodness of the Object.

In our interpretation of the Object the doctrine of the Fatherhood of God undeniably loses something; but at least part of what it loses is its too picturesque anthropomorphism, its "demonic" quality, its infantilism, and the suspicion of Freudian complications. It retains the sense of our having come from a source, our having occurred in accordance with some principles, and our moving onward in a powerful grip. A man's religion ought not to be marked by his reversion to childhood's irresponsibility. It ought to be that which holds him steady and, in the root sense of the word *re-ligio*, binds him back, gives him his anchorage, status, and momentum in the structures and processes of the cosmos. It is said that high in the Alps one sometimes finds channels gouged for long distances in the mountain side, and that when one follows one of these channels to the forward end, he finds a boulder which has been gripped by a glacier and used like a huge stylus to etch a path in the solid rock. So that great trend in the cosmic process which we call the Object of religious devotion grips a man, binds him in its grip, and helps him to leave upon mankind through his career the imprint of his character.

Is the Object of our religious devotion purposeful? The answer is implied in much that has been said. The cosmic significance of purposive social behavior is not, as some of the idealists have it, in the fact that it can be extended to the universe, or to a Mind behind the universe; its significance is in the fact that an end-reaction or a more complicated unit of purposive behavior is one of the universe's natural organizations, and is in its own way an epitome of the universe. In order to interpret the relationships of mind and world we do not need to say that the universe is a great Mind; but we shall never fully understand either of them until we see that the mind, the nervous system at work, is a little universe. Moreover, after our examination of the teleological argument it seems wiser to say that the cosmic process is not so clearly purposive as it is telic; there seems to be no prior conscious intention about it, and still the process does issue in much good. Supernaturalism with its foreshortened faith paints the universe too darkly and fails to bring out with adequate clearness the natural wholesomeness of things. In spite of all the evils of the world, we must not fail to recognize its goods and to trace them to their source. If to describe that source we amend the famous formula of Matthew Arnold so that it will not appear too personalistic or too purposive, we may say that there is a process in this universe, not ourselves, which makes righteousness.

This carries with it the answer to the last of our questions, as to whether the Object of religious devotion is good. The Object is not the whole universe, but it is what is good in the universe—the process which makes righteousness, which makes good in nature and history, which promotes whatsoever things are true and honest and just and pure and lovely and of good report.

This view even though logically sound is psychologically at first sight not very attractive. One of the most deeply ingrained difficulties is in the psychological fact that it is extremely distasteful for any one to reorganize a sentiment. Any man or woman who ever fell deeply in love and then fell out again knows this all too well. The more elaborate sentiments are typically hard to change, because they involve so many ingrained habits, powerful emotions, intricate associations, and cherished purposes. But sentiments, after all, are complexes, composed of elements which after a fashion can be distinguished and, like elements and compounds in chemistry, can be isolated and recombined. Sentiments can be disciplined to dispense with some emotions and ideas, and to substitute others in their places. Sentiments can be conditioned; they can be reoriented, wholly or partly, as to their ends and reorganized as to their means. It goes against the grain, but it can be done.

A sentiment which is sufficiently typical of religious experience to serve as its representative here is the sentiment of reverence, and reverence includes among its constituents two which are sufficiently typical to serve as representatives of the others. The problem of analysis and reorganization is more complicated than this, but for our present purposes let us say that reverence is composed of awe and love, and that both of these have been traditionally directed upon the supposed God of supernaturalism. It begins to look as if the present difficulty in the religious adjustment is that this sentiment of reverence needs to be reconstructed, and that we have to go through the painful process of redirecting its constituents. The natural universe appears to be more and more significant as affording our Object of religious devotion, and in the meantime all social and economic problems increase in sharpness and importance. Perhaps we must learn to direct our awe toward the universe and our love toward our fellow-men!

When we come to think of it, it is only ignorance or diversion of imagination which prevents our sense of overwhelmed awe in the presence of the stupendous universe as it is revealed to us in the data of the sciences. On the other hand the energy of our love during many generations has been burned out in "communion" or sent off to some supposed celestial Object, too often to the neglect of the poor and the oppressed, the underprivileged and the exploited. Love is like a searchlight; if directed into the skies the beam becomes more and more faint until it disappears, but if turned on the earth around us it transfigures the scene, and brings out shadows, too, which we never knew were there.

Humanism has taught some of these things, but has tended to treat the universe and man separately, as if they had little to do with one another. The epitomization hypothesis tries to see the two in their relationships, in the way in which they belong together. The universe epitomizes itself, over and over, in man, in societal groups, and in a man's ideas and sentiments. When a man adjusts his ideas and sentiments to his fellow-men in society, the process on its relatively small scale is an epitome of the larger process whereby human society adjusts itself to the universe. The ethical adjustment belongs within the cosmic or religious adjustment, not apart from it. The cosmic process which elicits our awe is at the same time the deeper sanction of the love which we bear toward our kind.

Finally, this helps to suggest how we are to find our way to the Object of religious devotion, where we are to find it, and how we may know it when we have found it. The argument can be indicated here only briefly, but its practical result can be stated without difficulty. The argument over a considerable distance follows the lines already indicated: in a universe where matter and spirit are not opposites and where nature and history are not sundered, human societal groups in their various environments are natural products, germane to the universe and repeating in themselves its own essential structures and processes. The adjustment of the sentiments and ideas of each individual within these groups to the other members of the group is a further, sharper focus, a new epitomization of the larger structures and processes around them. Each man for his personal adjustment should then seek a societal group which is best adjusted to the cosmos. Of what groups, in society or in history, may this be said? The answer requires a long view of history and a broad sweep, but nothing beyond our purview. The definitive groups in history are not merely nations, as contemporary events would sometimes seem stridently to proclaim, nor are they merely the races which spread themselves over the lands and across the seas. Important major groups identify themselves at least approximately by their religious cultures: witness Judaism, Hinduism, Islam, Christendom. So inevitable is this, in the long run, that nations or sects which set out to neutralize or destroy an established religion, if they do not end prematurely for other reasons, end by becoming new religions: witness Confucianism, Buddhism, or even Russia or Germany. The great religious groups, in spite of their abuses and mistakes, are mankind's most inclusive adjustments, humanity's most majestic efforts to work out adjustments to the universe. And the ethical adjustment of each individual within the group is an epitome of the larger religious adjustment of the group to the universe.

So the place for any individual man to look for the good in nature and history, for the process which makes righteousness, for the Object of religious devotion, for God, is in and through those major historical-social-cultural groups and movements which we know as the religions of the world. It is a mistake to construe them as altogether other-worldly; their economic and political features and aspects should be included in our thought of them, just as they really are included in our adjustments to them, or our adjustments through them to the universe around us.

Each of these great groups, in its own lands and times, is among the epitomizations of the universe. Each is of course different from the others, and sometimes sharply at variance with them in matters of doctrine and of practice. Each is shot through with errors of philosophy as well as of science, but in spite of all its defects, each is a rich treasure from the past and a great hope for the future. Something can be said for the view which makes no attempt to choose one of the great religions rather than another; in the present state of the world, it is more important to justify religion, or even the divergent religions, than it is to urge the claims of any one to superiority or supremacy. As a first approximation, all the great religions have enough in common so that any man who finds himself in one of them or can find his way to one of them, if he is true to the best in that one, is in the way appropriate to his own cultural heritage adjusted to the process which makes righteousness, the Object of religious devotion. He has caught in his own life and is bringing more or less completely into focus the light which lighteth every man that cometh into the world.

In the midst of all such catholicity, for any one of several reasons, searching questions about Christianity are bound to arise, and any book which seeks to come to grips with religious reality can not altogether disregard them. In a naturalistic interpretation of the world and the Object of religious devotion, "what is left of" the Person of Christ, and what of life after death? At first sight it seems impossible to find any content for these traditional doctrines; for ordinary naturalism Jesus is a man among other men, and since we are all dust, to dust we shall return.

But our contention all the way has been that the ordinary naturalisms are superficial. We may now add that a naturalism more adequate to the actual structures and processes of the universe, when these are studied out, provides ample basis for a specifically Christian faith. The structures and processes of the universe which are found at various levels and realms resemble one another, epitomize one another in essential features. The traditional doctrines about Jesus and about ourselves are statements about some of these structures and processes and should be interpreted in accordance with their ordered resemblances to the others.

A more complete account than is here possible analyzes these ordered resemblances in detail, but the features which are here essential can be stated much more briefly. The structures and processes particularly involved are, in history, societal groups organized with reference to leaders, and, in individual experience, sentiments, valuations, etc., organized with reference to dominating ideas, purposes, or ideals. The development of an idea within the organized sentiments, etc., of an individual experience epitomizes, or exhibits on a smaller scale and more intricate fashion, the same general principles found in the development of an individual within the organized societal groups of history, and the expression of such an idea epitomizes the death of such an individual.

Now one of these sets of epitomizing structures and processes occurs in precisely the present situation, where some one is writing or reading these words. The ideas formulated in the sentences on this page are expressed by one person and, let us say, received by another person as parts of a structure of ideas, emotions, end-reactions, sentiments, valuations, personality. And in proportion as any writer or reader, or any speaker and listener, in mutual understanding reach an agreement or approximate to the truth, the ideas of one are received by the other and, after due modification, are given new expression and continued on their way.

For a naturalism construed in terms of epitomization, the idea-patterns in the sentiments or valuations in the experience of an individual are small-scale epitomes of individual men in their societal groups in the history of the earth, and one of these may serve as a key to the understanding of the other. An idea in its passage from one of us to another is like any one of us in what we may call his cosmic pilgrimage. Ideas, let us say (agreeing to this extent with the pragmatists) are continued or discontinued in accordance with the degree to which they fit or fail to fit into the course of experience, organized as it is with reference to its dominating ideas, *i.e.*, its ends or purposes. And in the larger parallel, each of us is "continued" or "discontinued" in accordance with the degree to which he fits or fails to fit into the course of history, organized with reference to its leaders.

Whatever is to be said about Jesus, he was at least one of the great leaders in one of the great societal groups; he leads in the major structure and process which historically we call Christendom and ideally we call the Kingdom of God. Jesus was a man of the first century, who thought and spoke in its terms and lived and died in its ways. Many of his ideas about man and about God this discussion, in common with large sections of modern thought, is forced to abandon. But the first century, too, belongs among the cosmic structures and processes, and any one century may be uniquely significant for others.

As to traditional doctrines of his Person, we do not need to think that Jesus came out of the sky; in any perspective truly cosmic the sky "above" us has no advantage over the good earth beneath our feet. The great point is whether or not Jesus has cosmic significance, and the present interpretation of naturalism says that he has. Just as a dominating purpose in the experience of an individual secures further acceptance of its constituent ideas, so a dominating leader in history secures further acceptance of its constituent individuals. As a purpose dominating the sentiments of one individual implements the acceptance of his ideas throughout society, so Jesus, the leader of Christendom, implements to us our acceptance throughout the universe. He establishes us in that Process not ourselves which makes righteousness.

Thus a Christian may argue, from his natural place within the Christian societal group in history—but how about a Hindu or a Buddhist? Was Jesus unique among the great leaders and founders of religions? Is his implementation or mediation superior to that of others, or supreme among them? Pragmatic arguments which used to point to the achievements of Christianity as contrasted with those of other faiths are in these years of wars and frustrations not as strong as they were thought to be; at all events Christianity needs the corroboration of a structural argument, an argument grounded in the structure as well as the processes of the cosmos.

We can get such an argument if we go back to the situation between two persons who accept one another's ideas. Between speaker and listener there is mutual recognition of sincere intentions and some degree of common purpose. This is most marked when the purpose has been formulated and expressed between the two persons as some kind of agreement, promise, or contract. A promise, expressed in advance of its fulfilment, binds the two persons to mutual consideration and acceptance of one another's ideas. A unique or pivotal promise may bind the two for a lifetime.

Again in the larger parallel, and in accordance with everything which has been said, a pivotal promise in individual experience may be compared to Jesus as a leader in human history. As a pivotal promise, brought to expression before the fulfilment or attainment of the end of the sentiment or valuation which it represents, secures elsewhere the acceptance and further development of ideas which belong to it, so Jesus, brought to his death before the complete development of the societal group which he led, secures elsewhere the acceptance and further development of individuals who belong to it.

But was he unique, pivotal? Among the other great leaders and founders, none was so forced to his death, none died so sacrificially. There is room here to develop a new argument whereby the death of Christ regains its traditional central place in Christian teaching, becomes again the pivot of history and the way of salvation. "His visage was so marred more than any man, and his form than the sons of men . . . The chastisement of our peace was upon him, and with his stripes we are healed."

REFERENCES

[1] See G. P. Conger, *A World of Epitomizations,* 1931, and *The Horizons of Thought,* 1933 (Princeton University Press).

[2] The epitomization hypothesis has sometimes been criticized with objections which are obvious as regards many of the older fantastic theories concerning microcosms and macrocosms, but which hardly apply to the empirical evidence and plausible inference on which the new hypothesis is based. For the history of older theories in the West, see G. P. Conger, *Theories of Macrocosms and Microcosms in the History of Philosophy,* 1922 (Columbia University Press). For such theories in Indian philosophy, see Conger, in Asiatic Society of Bengal, *Journal and Proceedings* (NS), 29, 1934, pp. 255ff. The hypothesis has also been criticized because of its use of analogy, but the fallacies in the ordinary use of analogy are elementary and relatively superficial, and the analogies and parallelisms discerned in the epitomization hypothesis are so numerous, so systematic and so detailed that they can hardly fail to be deeply significant. Any supposed logical difficulty in their use can be met by considering the different parts of the universe as a series of transformations within a system-model or as systems within a system-form, with characteristics which are "continuants" or "cosmic variables."

[3] Technically we call an indication of anything which is perceived or thought about, whether it is a selected *A* or a neglected *non-A,* denotation. An analysis or description fo a selected *A* is *connotation;* this is the process which at the given moment can not properly be extended to the neglected *non-A.* As far as connotative description goes, *non-A* is left *enotative* or *innotative.* There is no precise distinction between enotation and innotation, but in general the former marks neglect of anything other than the selected object or concept, anything beyond it or excluded from it, while the latter marks neglect of any quality or attribute of the selected object or concept. The difference between innotation and enotation is like that between analytical and synthetic propositions, and like that between internal and external relations. In an analytical proposition a subject takes as its predicate an attribute or relationship hitherto left innotative; in a synthetic proposition the attribute or relationship has been left enotative. The reason why internal relations sometimes appear to be alone real is merely because external relations are left enotative.

[4] Barth's "dialectic" and Tillich's reliance upon paradox may be understood as complicated instances of partial recognition but ultimate disregard of horizon principles. What may be regarded as lying beyond our horizon, but should be left there enotative, is claimed as if it were guaranteed. With a technique of "both-and," Barth combines a bewildering array of concepts from both regions in almost haphazard fashion. Thus God is transcendent, but also in a sense immanent; sublime, but also personal; absolute personality, but also revealed in history; everywhere, but also in Jesus. In Jesus, God is both revealed and hidden; Jesus belongs to the world "never and ever." In the Bible we must discern the immediate Word of God, as well as the words of the apostles or authors. We find grace and judgment, forgiveness and penalty, the "no" of the cross and the "yes" of the resurrection. (See H. E. Brunner, *The Theology of Crisis,* p. 45; J. McConnachie, *The Significance of Karl Barth,* pp.

30, 80; W. Pauck, *Karl Barth, Prophet of a New Christianity?*, pp. 48*f*, 80, 100, 123, 156*f*, 181).

Tillich's "belief-ful realism" attempts to combine matter-of-fact regard for affairs within our horizon and retention of traditional assurance concerning "unconditioned" realities beyond it. (See Tillich, *The Religious Situation*, translated by H. R. Niebuhr, 1932, pp. x*ff*).

[5] B. E. Meland, *Modern Man's Worship*, pp. 173*f*.

[6] C. L. Morgan, *Life, Mind, and Spirit*, 1926, pp. viii-xiii.

[7] O. Lodge, *Raymond, or Life and Death*, 1916, p. 198.

[8] J. Tyndall, "Belfast address," in British Association for the Advancement of Science, *Report*, 1874, p. xcii.

[9] Georgia Harkness, in *Christendom*, Vol. 3, 1938, p. 516.

INDEX

An asterisk (*) indicates the place of principal treatment

INDEX